Bauxite, Sugar and Mud

BAUXITE, SUGAR AND MUD

memories of living in colonial Guyana
1928 - 1944

Patricia Wendy Dathan

Shoreline

© Patricia Wendy Dathan, 2006

Editing: Ryan Bergen
Production: Shanti Maharaj
Cover design and graphics: Sarah Robinson
Map of Guyana: Ragnar Muller-Wille

Printed in Canada by Lovell Litho

Published by Shoreline, 23 Ste-Anne
Ste-Anne-de-Bellevue, Quebec, Canada H9X 1L1
Phone/Fax 514-457-5733
shoreline@sympatico.ca   www.shorelinepress.ca

Dépôt legal: National Library of Canada
et la Bibliothèque Nationale du Québec

Library and Archives Canada Cataloguing in Publication

Dathan, Patricia Wendy, 1934-
Bauxite, sugar and mud : memories of living in colonial Guyana,
1928-1944 / by Patricia Wendy Dathan.

Includes bibliographical references.

ISBN 1-896754-45-7

1. Dathan, Patricia Wendy, 1934- -Childhood and youth.
2. Mackenzie (Guyana)-Biography. 3. Mackenzie (Guyana)-History-
20th century. 4. Aluminum mines and mining-Guyana-Mackenzie-History-
20th century. I. Title.

F2380.6.D38A3   2006 988.1'4   C2006-903675-6

I would like to dedicate this book to my parents, Joshua and Gladys Whalley, who endured all the frustrations and deprivations; to my sister, Margaret Lang, who was too young to remember; to my sons, Anthony and John Dathan, my nephew Angus Lang and nieces, Kirstie O'Connor and Tamaryn Lang, who missed knowing a wonderful grandfather; to my grand-daughter Michèle Dathan, who, when she was a little girl, patted her great-grandmother ever so gently on the knee; and to all those 'bauxite babies' who may remember as I do a world that has gone forever.

Contents

8

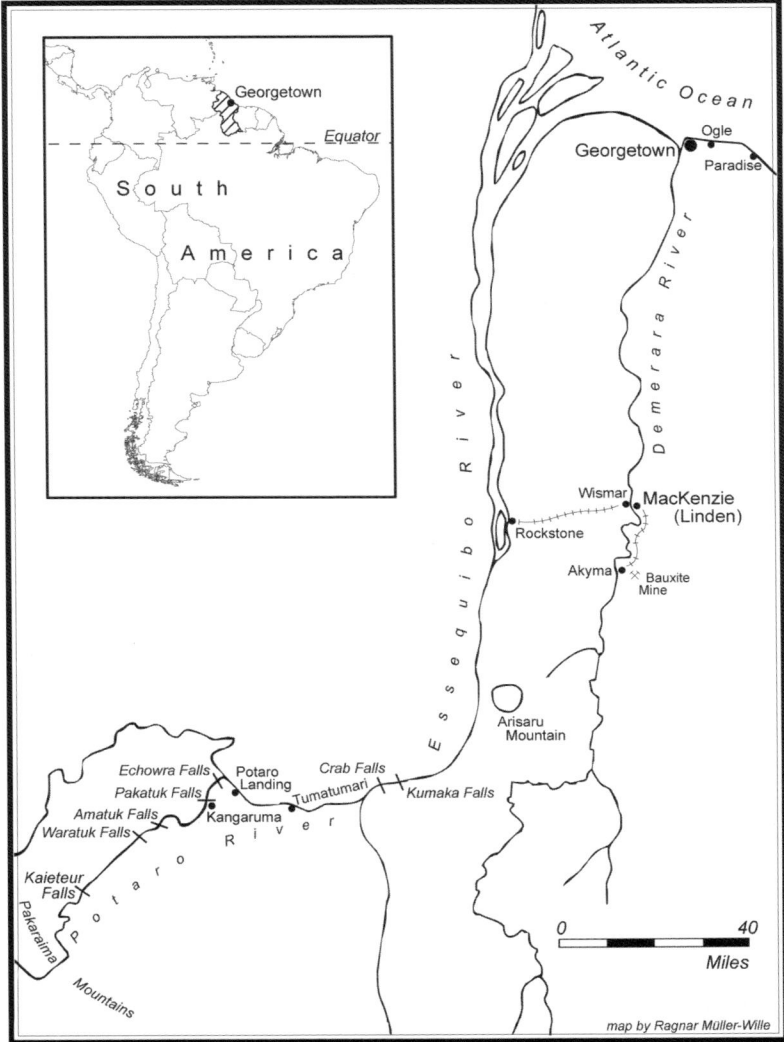

British Guiana (Guyana) 1928 - 1944

Foreword

About five degrees north of the imaginary line of the Equator, a little short of the Guiana Highlands in an unnamed place no more than 500 feet high, a thin blue line appears on the map of South America where it has no business in the world to get started. The new line marks the river of my childhood that forever defines the place where I was born. At first a mere leisurely trickle through the rainforest, by the time the Demerara reaches our home in Mackenzie, the river has grown wide and deep and tidal so that sometimes it continues swiftly, and sometimes it goes backwards, and sometimes, like it did in the beginning, it seems not to move at all.

All my memories begin where the river flows past the wharf-like stelling where we used to swim, past the airy house on stilts where we used to live, past the hospital where I was born and the bauxite plant and office where my father used to work, past the cricket field at Cockatara where my first world ends. Down and past us the Demerara flows through the green rainforest where the tangled roots of the mangrove come down to the riverside to drink, down to the city of Georgetown and out to the wide muddy sea.

Without the river, we would be trapped like statues in this place where my mother feels trapped, where everyone feels trapped occasionally, because our world is so small. Surrounded by the impenetrable rainforest, our only link with the outside is by water, and, to travel it, we must take the river steamboat that makes the voyage down and back every other day but Sunday. On one never-to-be-forgotten trip to Georgetown when I am small, the Captain lets me hold the steering wheel. The wheel is wooden and almost as big as I am, and I have to stand very tall so I can reach up to the smooth round rim. I am bursting with importance because I believe that I am steering this big ship all by myself. The Captain is standing behind me so I cannot see the smile of conspiracy that he shares with my watching parents. "Hold her steady," he tells me. "Keep her going straight ahead." His arms are arced around me so that at any time his big capable hands, that have smoothed the surface of the wheel to softest satin, can seize command if something untoward should happen. He is tall and strong and gentle, like all the adults of my childhood, who are there to be kind and keep me safe from harm.

It is all such a long dream ago, belonging to a time when I believed that we would live here forever, but of course in this world there is no forever. Once upon a time, we say, implying that time has only briefly stood still. After we leave our time by the river, Mackenzie will become Linden and the little colony of British Guiana that those of us who live here always call BG will become the independent country of Guyana, but when I am a child and nothing in the world changes, Mackenzie has always been and always will be Mackenzie and I am sure that BG is the biggest and most important country on earth. Certainly it is the center of my universe.

I lie in bed at night and try to imagine the universe. I tell myself: "I am in a bed in my room. My room is in my house. My house is in Mackenzie. Mackenzie is in BG. BG is in South America. South America is in the world. The world is in the sky. The sky is in the universe. What is the universe in?" For a long time, this is a nightly puzzle, lying flat in the wondrous cave that is my bed draped in a tent of mosquito netting that has an ending like everything else I know has an ending, and for the life of me I cannot imagine anything that cannot be contained by something else. But at least as I lie here I know that I am rooted securely where I am, in the heart of everything that is important, and I never wonder how we got here, and I do not know that one day we will have to leave.

Eventually we will sail down the river on the dear old steamboat for the very last time. We will go to live in Georgetown, and then Jamaica briefly, and then the war will be over and we will be able to go Home. Home is confusing to think about because BG is the only real home that I have ever known. This is what I know, what I love, what I am. But I cannot call it home. Officially, my birth certificate says that I was born here but it also says that I am 'white', and I am English like my parents who are also 'white', and one day we will all get onto a bigger ship and go Home to England where we belong. Only I don't. Who made these labels, who made these rules? We have to go, they say, and I will leave my heart behind.

We will cross the impossibly vast Atlantic to the cold, grey place that is home to my parents but not to me. There I will be told that I have to stay, for my own good, and learn to be English, and forget all the things that I ever learned before. In my cold, elite boarding school, I will be told without being told that I must forget the joyful colours, the brown laughter, the white-hot heat and dreamy languid shadows, and I must learn to be sensible and thick-skinned and physically strong. I must lose the lilting accent that I learned from my nurse and speak instead in dipthongs and unmusical prose. I must forget that I ever hugged people who were black or brown or khaki, and learn to be discriminating and proper and beastly, instead of open and natural and kind. And above all, I must learn that I will never be able to go back to the river that fed my dreams. It is only much later, when we move to Canada and have to start all over again, that there is the slightest chance of un-learning and reconciling my worlds, but the way will be long and sometimes very hard, and there is yet another long, long river to trace on the map of my inner world.

Until then, there is only the remembered dream. If I go back to it, for now, it is enough to stand proudly on the deck of the steamboat when I am small. I can see no further ahead than the bend where the big, kind Captain will take the wheel once again. The smell of newly picked bananas and mangoes is wafting up to me, the river flows forever, there is no other world but this one, and I cannot even begin to imagine the faraway place from which my parents came, let alone the one to which we are going.

Wendy and Maud

Brown hands I remember
From my childhood
Brown as old banana skins
Voices I remember
Like molasses
"Me na love you, Miss Windy,
Ef you na behave."

A Sense of Place

"Guiana!" my mother exclaimed, and the famous British author Evelyn Waugh wondered, when they first heard the name of the country of their destination. "Isn't that the White Man's Grave?"

Of course, this was not in unison. To my knowledge, my mother and Evelyn Waugh never met, but they each had the same misconception when they looked at the possibility of going to this relatively unknown British colony. Both of them confused South American Guiana with Guinea in British West Africa, an area known for its high death rate for Europeans from malaria, yellow fever and blackwater fever. In spite of the error in place name, they were not wrong about the Grave however, for malaria was very prevalent in what was then British Guiana, and one of my earliest memories is of all of us children being lined up for a dreaded injection because one of the mine men had died from suspected yellow fever.

The timing of my mother's words was between the two World Wars. A year later, in 1929, she sailed out from England to join my father in the bauxite mining camp up the Demerara River where he had started work in 1928. Evelyn Waugh, on an unrelated mission, followed in 1932. My mother and the writer went as outsiders to a strange country, and strange they both found it. Waugh hightailed it back to England in very short order, but my mother had to stay because she had a husband who had found work in the colony when times were tough elsewhere. Until my father's term of duty was finished, she and the children who were born there had to remain in what she always later called 'That Awful Place'.

Of all the places in the British Empire that my parents could have chosen, British Guiana must have been close to the bottom of the list of countries that appealed to emigrants in England in the years between the Great Wars. Few people knew or cared about the relatively unimportant colony, roughly the size of the United Kingdom, that was wedged into the flat northern coast of South America just east of where the curve of the West Indies begins and ends. Only the sound of the name Demerara, which conjures up moist brown sugar and excellent navy rum, seemed to breathe the slightest hint of interest into any part of that country. With no spectacular quarrels for His Majesty's Government to settle, or horrendous happenings to titillate the curious or challenge the adventurous, most people looked instead at exotic India or mysterious Africa or the free, wide spaces of Canada and Australia for a more interesting destination.

The lack of knowledge about my unimportant birthplace was confirmed by Evelyn Waugh when he first thought about visiting British Guiana and found that neither he nor any of his English friends and acquaintances seemed to know anything at all about the place. None of them knew of its chequered history of settlement and ownership, beginning with the Dutch around 1580, and continuing with a confusingly frequent turnover of ownership between the French and British during the Napoleonic Wars. Eventually, in 1812, the British took permanent control, uniting the three original Dutch colonies of Demerara, Essequibo and Berbice into the one colony of British Guiana.

Before his trip, Waugh managed to track down a minimum number of contacts who could be of some assistance to him in his travels through the colony. A friend had an uncle who had been a missionary there, another man had adventured to the remote and beautiful Kaieteur Falls, another had business interests along the coast. The writer found a few books about the place ~ a very few ~ and pored over all the available maps and statistics to get a picture in his mind of a long skinny land, with a low swampy coastal strip where sugar cane grew and most people lived, connected without rail or road by ribbons of rivers through the heavily forested interior back to their origin in the high savannah lands and mountains bordering Brazil. "Gradually a vague, general idea began to take shape in my mind of a large empty territory stretching up three great rivers and their tributaries to shadowy, undefined boundaries," he said, "most of it undeveloped and unsurveyed, large areas quite unexplored; except for a trace of grass land on the Brazilian frontier, and an inhabited fringe along the coast, it was all forest and swamp; there was no railway or road into the interior, the only means of communication being by boat up rivers broken every few miles by rapids or falls; the coast population contained every conceivable race, chiefly Portuguese, Negro and East Indian; the greater part of the colony had no permanent inhabitants, except shy little communities of aboriginal Indians; except on the coast there had been practically no European settlement and little enough there; and a few place names, later to become real, stuck in my mind as words ~ Bartika, Wismar, Rupununi, Takutu."

Against the advice of the businessman, who thought his plans were reckless, Waugh decided that he would leave the populated coast and explore the partially unmapped equatorial rainforest and highland interior as far as the Brazilian border. He duly set out on his own to accomplish this self-imposed task. At the end of a trying journey, fraught with all the perils and discomforts typical of such a tentative, solitary trip though inhospitable tropical terrain, he returned to England to write a wry account of his misadventures in *Ninety-Two Days* published in 1932. Later, based on a thoroughly unlikeable character with whom he travelled part of the time, he incorporated a short story he had written on his bunk in the bush, called 'The Man Who Liked Dickens', into an unhappy part of his novel *A Handful of Dust* (1934) where his hero ends his days miserably at the mercy of a religious maniac who has trapped him forever reading Dickens aloud in the Guiana rainforest. "I wanted to discover how the prisoner got there and eventually the thing grew into a study of other sorts of savages at home and the civilized man's helpless flight among them," he said.

Most of Waugh's adventures were uncomfortable rather than romantic and exciting. There were no feathered cannibals or warring warriors to be found in the hinterland, and certainly no fawn-like Amerindian girls like Rima in W.H. Hudson's *Green Mansions*, the classic naturalist Romance of the Tropical Forest that was set in British Guiana at the end of the 19th century. Of course there was no sign of El Dorado, the fabled city of gold for which Sir Walter Raleigh combed the Guiana Highlands in vain in the Elizabethan age. Apart from the one peculiar individual whom Waugh later immortalized, he reported that for his taste he found only shy unattractive native Indians living uninspiring lives in the bush. He also found, panning for gold in a remote riverbed, a determined white man who was quite satisfied with a few shining nuggets instead of the imagined abundance.

Evelyn Waugh went to British Guiana to find material for a book; my parents went to escape England. At least, my father did, and my mother dutifully followed him as all good wives did in those days, except that like Lot's wife she could not resist looking back over her shoulder at the country and people she loved.

At the time of their major decision, my parents were living in Newcastle-under-Lyme in North Staffordshire, a town described by novelist Arnold Bennett as a clean and conceited borough with long historical traditions, on the very edge of the industrial, democratic and unclean Five Towns of the Potteries. Despite the apparent absence of any sign of the river Lyme for which it was named, Newcastle would have been mentioned in the guidebooks as a not unattractive market town on the edge of some of the loveliest countryside in England – the unexpectedly beautiful corners of otherwise industrially-ruined Staffordshire, the clean, green fields of Cheshire, the gently rolling lands of Shropshire, and the rocky peaks and lovely dales of Derbyshire ~ were it not for the fact that most of its departing roads ran immediately or before very long into the dismal, straggling 'Five Towns' that were actually six ~ Stoke, Hanley, Burslem, Fenton, Longton, and Tunstall ~ that came to be part of but never fused into the conglomerate city of Stoke-on-Trent.

It is hard to imagine an area that was worse affected by the Industrial Revolution than the benighted Potteries area before the Clean Air Act and electrification of the china-making industry that transformed the region to flourishing green in the 1960s. Under the pall of low-hanging smoke lay a strange soot-covered landscape of row upon row upon row of small, blackened, brick houses interspersed with dirty iron foundries, grim coal-mining slag heaps piled in unlikely pyramid hills, and surrealistic clay-firing bottle ovens, neat as wasps' nests, each with a chimney billowing black effluence into the sky. Visitors commented on its unbelievable ugliness. George Orwell, passing through in 1936, found Hanley and Burslem "about the most dreadful places I have seen." J.B. Priestley, who had grown up in industrial Yorkshire, was equally appalled when he visited the Potteries for the first time in the early 1930s. He found the whole place odd and unlike any other area he knew, with more smoke than he had ever seen before.

In the china-making places that he visited, Priestley marvelled at how the self-respecting people that he found there could live in such unattractive surroundings when they were so engaged in producing the beautiful delicate china that was valued all over the world, but Potteries people knew only too well that to make the china, the clay had to be fired, and for that you needed coal that had to be mined and fires that produced smoke and soot. Like all the practical people of the North of England, soot meant jobs that were needed, and what was the use of loveliness when the soot covered everything? Potteries men and women were made of pretty strong stuff. Their humour was kind but disrespectful of all authority and pretence. One man told Priestley politely but bluntly, "Oh, we often read you round here, and sometimes we'd like to give you one on the nose." They had no patience with Southern England's fancy ideas and ways. People like these writerly visitors were 'nesh', they scoffed, meaning that they were soft in the head and body. They had little time for anyone who was temperamentally unable to cope with their common difficulties of soot and cold. If you were 'mardy', meaning sick, or in real trouble, your neighbors would do what they could to help. Beyond that, there was the jovial cameraderie at work, the regular pint in the pub, the hearty singing in the chapel, the love of gossip over the garden hedge, and the sense of robust humour throughout.

Like Arnold Bennett, my father was a man of the Potteries region born and bred but, like so many young men of his era, his experiences in World War I had changed him. After a brief spell in the Dardanelles, he was lucky enough to have spent most of it in Malta, away from the trenches that took the legs of one of my uncles, away from the ugliness of men killing and men dying. When he talked to his young daughters about his army life, he mentioned only that the nurses were very pretty. He had his characteristic honourable twinkle when he said it so we knew that he had had a good time with them but it was all very sporting, very decently English. He had been too young when he joined up, for he lied about his age when his country said it needed him.

After he came home from the war, my father started an apprenticeship with an accounting firm in Newcastle. He was still living at home, where things began to get difficult. My grandfather had remarried after his first wife died leaving two small children. His second wife, my grandmother Toft, who had seven children of whom two died early, died in her 40s. My father was the oldest of the second brood. Before my grandfather died a few years later, he called my father to his deathbed and made him promise that he would always go to chapel and always look after the younger children after he had gone. Becoming a surrogate father to his unwilling brothers and sisters was a hard promise to keep for a young man in his 20s, just home from the war and finding his own place in the world. Things did not go well under the new arrangements. No one knows today exactly what happened except that in the end there was a huge family bust-up. The older siblings moved away, if they had not already left. One of my uncles walked out and he and my father never spoke to each other again, the two younger children were farmed out to older relatives, and my father sold the family house amid all sorts of acrimony and upset. He never mentioned a word of this to his daughters. Mother hinted at it but did not say much, except that somehow we came to believe that he had done what he thought was the right thing and been misjudged. This was the start of my father wanting to leave England.

The second reason for his unhappiness with England had to do with his place of work after he finished his apprenticeship. He loved to tell the story of arriving in London to take his accountancy finals. The city was shrouded in pea-soup fog and he was completely unable to find the numbers on the buildings. In growing desperation, he asked a man on the street to help him find the address where the examiners were waiting for him. "I'll give you a guinea if you can help me find the place," he said, naming what for him was a huge sum he could ill afford. The man took his outstretched hand with his own right hand and guided him over to his left. Then he reached for the cash. They were standing right outside the door of the building for which my father was searching.

He passed the exam with flying colours. Now officially acknowledged as a fully-fledged accountant, he naturally expected that his firm would give him an appropriate increase in pay, but in these stringent years, it did not happen. Unfortunately, he was not in a position to leave the company and set up on his own. The terms to which he had agreed in the beginning stated that he was not allowed to start a new practice within an area of 40 miles. In the England of the twenties, 40 miles might just as well have been the moon, so this was a seemingly impossible situation for an ordinary man without substantial means to establish himself in a far-away, unknown community.

Meanwhile, during his time of family struggle and apprenticeship, my father had met a pretty redhead who was working in the municipal town office. After he had settled the affairs at home and passed the final exams, he felt that he was at last in a position to marry. So, in 1927, in St. George Anglican Church in Newcastle-under-Lyme where my father later teased his daughters that he made the biggest mistake of his life, Joshua (Jos) Whalley and Gladys Hilda Parsonage were married. They bought a little house on a quiet avenue within sight of St. George and settled in comfortably.

Although my father was now happy at home, at work it was the same old grind for very little pay. He would travel into the Pottery towns and do the audits for the china factories. He would bring work home and brood over figures deep into the night. Winter came, and he always hated the cold and damp of England after the warm Mediterranean sun. The winter of 1927-28 was one of those typical English winters with sometimes snow and sometimes rain, sometimes frost or fog or feeble sun, and often bitter wind and a moist chill that seemed to creep into one's bones and set up house-keeping. Most English offices and shops and houses in winter were cold and damp and miserable inside. Even in what should have been cozy homes, the parlour fires warmed only a few feet away from the hearth, and unheated bedrooms were so cold that people lay in bed and watched their breath steam over the blankets. In the Potteries, the soot hung lower and blacker than ever, holding out the tentative sun. It was not a place for people who were 'nesh'. People like my father.

In the spring of 1928, there was an advertisement in the newspaper for the position of accountant with a bauxite mining company in tropical British Guiana.

Newcastle-under-Lyme

the Whalley family ca. 1911

back row (l to r); Edith, Jos, Reg
front; Geoff, Syd, Cissie, parents Joshua & Matilda, Bill
children not present; Ralph, Irene.

Jos in Uniform

The Promise of Bauxite

The letter that my father needed for his London meeting with the bauxite company interviewers was dated 7 June 1928. From his home in 'The Hollies' in Newcastle, Staffs, his employer, Mr. C.H. Steele, none too pleased to be losing his newly-trained employee so soon, had still managed to write graciously: "I have pleasure in stating that I have personally known Mr. Joshua Whalley of 5 Mayer Avenue, Newcastle, Staffs, for over five years. I can testify him to be capable in his Professional Duties, and is a man that can most conscientiously be highly recommended to your consideration. His general character is beyond reproach, and can be absolutely relied on to fill a position of confidential trust with integrity, and I am sure, satisfaction to his Employers."

Anxiously waiting outside the inner office for the door to open, my father was not to know that his prospects of being hired were very good. The Guianese-based companies of Sprostons and Demerara Bauxite Company Limited were actively looking for English personnel to join their management teams. They needed English staff for political reasons, since British Guiana was still a British colony. They were looking for men who were fully qualified and not easily daunted by tropical conditions, men who could be relied upon to be responsible in isolation, who could adjust to British colonial expectations but still be able to be taught North American ways of doing business.

The London interview was all-important. Charles Allen, whose trilogy on the lives of British colonials through firsthand interviews is an invaluable source of information for this period, noted in his *Tales from the South China Seas* that, for most young men wanting to go overseas from Britain in the 1920s, this initial contact was the only real hurdle that job applicants had to face. There were many young middle-class men like my father who wanted to escape from offices, factories, streets of houses, and the general hubbub of life in England. A career abroad often offered a higher standard of living than they could achieve at home, with the added lure of adventure and excitement. Whether the interview was for government services or for business firms, it followed a similar pattern. No one was expected to know very much about the conditions of the place where they would be going. That knowledge could easily come later. The most important aspect that emerged out of the interview was that "as long as you could play games and mix with people that was the sort of person they wanted... They asked the sort of questions which nowadays a lot of people sneer at. You ask a chap if he plays games. If he does and he's got a reasonable academic record as well, you're not going to go far wrong, because chaps who are good at games are usually well-orientated overall." They preferred men from a good family who had been to one of the major public schools, particularly if they had demonstrated a degree of leadership, so that they would be 'the right sort' to go abroad.

My father could happily answer their questions about games. He loved cricket and played a good game of tennis, as well as having a passion for billiards that nearly lost him his final accounting exams. His school was not one of England's finest but was given high marks scholastically. He was certainly qualified for the position and he had had some experience of living outside of England. The only real drawback might be that he was a married man. At that time, most companies abroad had rigid rules about marriage. They were not always explicit but it was soon understood that they preferred bachelors. The men chosen would often have to ask senior officials for permission to marry and then only after a certain period of time, in some cases as long as ten years. This was certainly true of the sugar planters in British Guiana. Sometimes the reason was the lack of married quarters but mostly it was assumed that they were expected to spend their early years learning about the country and their work without distraction.

My father was lucky that this was not a problem in his particular situation. He was older than many young men trying to go overseas, some of whom had only just left school, and he had already completed his professional training in England. The company officials who were interviewing him were looking for a stable, trained man and the job that they were about to offer him was in Mackenzie, a small mining community in a clearing in the rainforest, 65 miles up the Demerara River from the capital of Georgetown on the coast, where married quarters were already available. He would be one of 12 white staff and some hundred black employees who were opening up the bauxite mining operations. He would be supplied with a company house and be able to bring out his wife if he proved satisfactory. He would be allowed occasional trips down to Georgetown and once every four years he would have several months' leave in which he could go back to England on holiday. All the company asked at this time was that he would go out alone for the first three months on a trial basis. If everything was satisfactory at that time, the company would pay for his wife to go out to British Guiana to join him.

My father was definitely interested. The living and working conditions and salary sounded completely satisfactory. The whole adventure appealed to him ~ the change of place, the new challenges at work, and above all the warmth after the dreary winter in the smoky Potteries. He was sure that he would enjoy the experience and looked forward to learning more about the company.

Historically, bauxite mining in British Guiana was still in its infancy, although the ore that was the principal base for making aluminium (aluminum in North America) had been known to be there as long ago as the 19th century. It was mentioned in a British scientific journal in 1910, after Sir John Harrison, the autocratic Director of Science and Agriculture, reputedly poked his walking stick into the ground and barked "Bauxite! The future of British Guiana!" But it was not until demand rose for the end product in World War I that the Aluminum Company of America (Alcoa) began serious geological exploration.

Bauxite is a rock that is largely composed of a mixture of hydrous aluminum oxides, formed by the weathering of many different rocks. The name comes from Les Baux, an area of spectacular rock in the area of Provence in France. It is found in most countries but the larger deposits are usually found in the tropics, especially in the adjoining Dutch-settled Guianas that include British Guiana and Suriname.

The general history and development of bauxite mining in the area has been well covered by Duncan C. Campbell in his comprehensive *Global Mission: The Story of Alcan*. The first man to arrive in British Guiana, in December 1913, was Edwin Fickes, an engineer-geologist, who spent about ten days up the Demerara River in the area around Wismar, the highest point upriver for ocean freighter navigation. Aided by three strong men with machetes to cut through the rainforest tangles, Fickes discovered several sites with good bauxite deposits close to the navigable part of the river. On his return, he recommended that the company send out a good man to quietly buy up the most likely bauxite properties in the vicinity.

The man chosen for this legendary real estate transaction was George Bain Mackenzie, a Scot who had made his home in Arkansas for many years. Most of the desired properties that he looked at were old plantations with wonderful names like Fair's Rust, Amelia's Ward, Lucky Spot, and Three Friends. All of them had been abandoned and all had owners who were anxious to sell. To keep the price down, Mackenzie cannily claimed that he wanted the land to grow oranges. The experienced plantation men, knowing full well that the sandy bauxite soil would never support orange groves, laughed heartily as they took his money at an average price of about $2.00 an acre. It was only later that they learned that the joke had been at their expense.

The Demerara Bauxite Company Limited (Demba) was incorporated in 1916. The first shipment of bauxite, stripped out from the overlying sands, went out from the old Three Friends plantation at Akyma in 1917. By 1918, the company was looking at blueprints for the construction of a large mining, processing, and residential complex on a site 15 miles downriver from Akyma on the opposite bank from the settlement of Wismar. The community was to be called Mackenzie, after the man who had claimed to be an orange grower and had recently died.

The development was an ambitious undertaking, especially given the distance from Georgetown and the coast, the lack of roads through the enveloping rainforest, the broiling overhead sun so close to the equator, the heavy rains, the difficulty of obtaining building materials, and the lack of suitable labour. Yet the plan called for the creation of streets, suitable houses for the company employees, power and water supply, sewage disposal, school and hospital facilities, along with the necessary office and laboratory housing and the huge multi-use plant needed to treat the raw bauxite before shipment, wharves for the bauxite-carrying freighters, and a 12-mile standard-gauge railway needed to carry the ore to the plant.

The construction of Mackenzie proceeded slowly for the next three years. However, just as it began to be fully operational early in 1921, Alcoa ordered the whole thing closed down due to the post-war drop in aluminum demands. It was not until late in 1922 that the plant and mines were re-opened. Because everything deteriorates so rapidly in the tropics, there was a lot of work to be done to repair the damage caused by the heat and high humidity during the 20 months of neglect, but as early as 1923 the bauxite shipments were off and running again and had mounted steadily ever since, looking as if the prophecy of Sir John Harrison would certainly come true for the future of the colony and the company.

Five years later, the company officials in London enthusiastically assured my father that everything in Mackenzie was in full production. Optimism was running high in aluminum circles in June 1928. That was the month that the giant U.S. parent company, Alcoa, the single largest producer of aluminum in the world, was dividing like an amoeba. From that date, Alcoa would concentrate its energies on the U.S. market. The Guianese companies, and 32 other small companies outside the United States, mainly in the British Empire, would be run by the Canadian-based Aluminium Limited (later to become Alcan). The move was seen to be partly for convenience and partly to take advantage of British trade influence in the British Commonwealth.

So, if my father accepted the job, he would be going out to a British colony to work for a company with a head office in Canada, staffed with a residue of Americans who had not yet been recalled and an influx of Canadians yet to arrive, with a few local people to assist him in the office, and in association with a handful of Englishmen like himself who were part of a different breed to go out from England in that period after the Great War. These men were not Government officials or planters, doctors or missionaries, explorers or hunters, scientists or scoundrels, writers or dispossessed younger sons. My father was going out to the colonies as a fully-trained professional to work as a Company man. In India, he would not have counted for much socially because he was in trade. In British Guiana, he was part of the projected future.

Was he the right man for the job? He would be taking with him his idealism in spite of disillusion, his uncompromising honesty where a little relaxation of the rules might be more to his advantage, his hatred of flattery where there were many wheels that could be oiled. Many men went out to the tropics with high hopes for a better life, but in the indolent sun their ideals quickly faded. It remained to be seen whether Jos Whalley could make his mark in another kind of unkind climate.

But first he had to persuade my mother that this change in their lives was a wise decision. Even if Guiana was not the White Man's Grave, it was still a very long way from home, in a strange world where malaria and yellow fever were far from unknown. They would be marooned upriver in a little mining camp in the middle of nowhere, surrounded only by tropical jungle. What was in this for my mother, who loved her present life surrounded by shops and cinemas, friends and family, and her beloved English countryside? In Newcastle, they were all close at hand, and she had only to walk down the hill past the site of the old castle and up another hill in the opposite direction from the sooty Potteries and she was soon out in the beautiful clean country where she was so completely happy. Both my parents loved to walk and it was nothing for them to walk ten miles, play a good game of tennis, and then walk home again. She loved flowers, especially the English wildflowers that my grandfather had shown her and taught her all their names. She loved her garden, and the little house for which they had saved so long. She had so much to lose if she left this behind and he must have wondered whether it was fair to ask her to make the sacrifice.

My parents could not have been more different. Jos was dark and quiet and serious, a man who looked at life carefully but with a leavening sense of humour. Gladys was an open, impulsive, outgoing girl who stood out from the crowd with her bright auburn hair and her fair skin with a mass of freckles from her tomboy out-of-doors life. She had strong, often headstrong, ideas, and what she believed she believed fiercely. She loved an active life. She loved to dance, once borrowing my grandmother's wedding slippers without permission and ruining them by dancing all night. She loved to sew and she was a good cook. My father said that she took cooking lessons in their courting days at a place just up the road from St. George Church and he used to meet her on the corner afterwards. "She used to bring me what she'd made and make me eat it," he said, "and if I turned up again next week she'd know she hadn't poisoned me." There was one time, however, when she refused to cook for him. He had innocently suggested that they should spend a holiday in a houseboat on the Norfolk Broads with his friend Albert. Gladys hit the roof. There was no way, she fumed, that she was going on a holiday with two men sitting around doing nothing while she was left to cook and clean and wash up after them. She reminded him forcefully of Arnold Bennett's famous short story about a new wife who had been disappointed in her husband's miserly ways after their marriage, until the day he came home and threw a lot of money on the table. It turned out that he had been saving for an expensive holiday all the time, so off they went on a lavish seaside trip that kept them happy for the rest of that year and all their future years together. My father got the point. They all went to an expensive hotel where Gladys could be waited on to her heart's content.

My father's sense of irony went completely over my mother's head. If he teased her, she rose to the bait without suspicion and was quite perplexed when she found that he was pulling her leg. One of my uncles remembered the time that the whole Whalley family got into the teasing act. They were talking about a bed tick and Gladys thought that they were referring to an insect instead of a mattress. When they realized her mistake, the entire clan joined in with relish, embroidering the fantasy and watching her guileless reactions with helpless laughter. When they finally explained the joke, she simply did not understand what it was all about.

There must have been much about my father's desire to move that my mother did not understand. But she did understand that he was unhappy in his work and this was an opportunity for him to get out from under his difficult situation. She could see that this was something he really wanted to do and she was completely convinced that a wife went with her husband, whatever he decided, and whatever sacrifices that might mean that she had to make. Bravely, like the good English trooper she was, she said yes.

Jos and Gladys on
honeymoon in Switzerland

engagement
photo

Farewell to England

My father sailed for British Guiana on the first available freighter. My mother was left to wait until word came from him at the end of the three-month trial period that all was well and she should put their little newly-wed home on the market. She had no idea how great her sacrifice would be for she would never again have a real house and garden of her own as she always dreamed. As it was, it took all her present courage and tested all her faith in him to follow his instructions.

As soon as she heard that he had arrived at Mackenzie, my mother began to think of getting the house ready for selling. She still had no idea of the conditions that she would be facing if she was to go out and join him. It is doubtful if anyone they knew in Newcastle had ever been in the West Indies or South America. Their contact with the company in London had been brief in the extreme. Unlike the civil servants who usually went out to the colonies after at least a preliminary indoctrination into what they could expect and how they were expected to behave, my parents appear to have had no preparation at all. On the other hand, they were free to go and make their own decisions about what they saw, based on their own firsthand impressions and coloured only by their own prejudices, and they had the option to return if they were too appalled by what faced them, even if it meant starting all over again in England.

During his trial period, my father also does not seem to have given my mother much information about where they were going to live, although it is apparent that he quickly decided that he was happy there and felt that my mother would find ways to enjoy it too. With company approval, soon he was able to assure her that it was time to sell the house and make the journey. Gladys immediately threw herself into a frenzy of activity. Once the house and possessions were sold, she spent the rest of the time before sailing in shopping for clothes and saying her goodbyes. She was in her element shopping for things to wear and her tropical wardrobe was soon extensive, even if she was to find later that she had made many mistakes because there was no one to advise her as to suitability.

The goodbyes were more difficult. Friends and family were equally distressed by their decisions. Why was Jos throwing up a perfectly good job to go off to a strange wild place where goodness knows what he would find? What was Gladys going to do out there all alone? It was so far away! People got sick in those foreign places and sometimes they died out there. In Chesterton, her parents agonized over whether they would ever see their daughter again. What was Jos thinking of, taking Gladys to that godforsaken place? But of course by now all the protests came too late.

My mother left England on a large passenger-freighter in the spring of 1929. My grandparents accompanied her to the docks in London and tried to put a brave face on the leave-taking. Goodbyes were tearfully swallowed and my mother went on board, only to lean over the rail and wave again and again. She stayed at the rail for a long time as the ship moved out, wanting a last look at the Thames, a last look at England and everything she knew and loved. As she stood there, she became aware of a young black boy in Scout uniform standing beside her. He was a nice lad who had been in England for a Scout Jamboree and had obviously had the time of his life. He said something to her. Wrapped in her sadness at leaving England behind, she did not reply, but later she was ashamed of herself for her incivility. She always remembered the incident because he was the first black person she had ever seen. She did not see him again on board to apologize.

Traditionally, the voyage out from England on the Empire shipping lines was considered to be instructional for newcomers to the colonies. For a start, there was an immediate separation of passengers, according to colour and rank, by cabin arrangement and meal sittings. On her ship, Gladys noted that there were about 75 white passengers, including many sugar planters and Colonial Servants who had been home on leave. She furiously resented the latter as they appeared to her to feel themselves superior to the other passengers and tended to hold themselves apart. In fact, their backgrounds in England and positions in the colonies qualified them for a superior ranking, but my mother was from the democratic Potteries and she had not come as far as she had to take any snobbish intolerance lying down. In her journal she wrote scornfully: "I should write about them 'in capital letters'. They seem to be very happy going back to a life of ease and privilege!"

Of all the passengers on board, the sugar planters were the most friendly and easy to get to know. One of these sun-tanned men was Jim Sutherland, a charming Scot who became Manager of Ogle Sugar Estate and a lifelong family friend. Like the other young men on board, he enjoyed teasing the innocent redhead who had been given into the bluff Captain's charge. "Gladys was a lot of fun on that ship," he said. "She was a kind, happy girl who soon became very popular with everyone. She was a good sport."

"I was 24. Two years married, and with my flaming red hair and freckles, all the men tried, and succeeded, to make me blush. I'll never forget the Captain recommending a real Madras curry made by the all-Lascar crew ~ winking while I tried it and laughing when I bolted to catch my breath and wipe away my tears. Mean!" She did get her revenge on him, however. One day after he had completed a routine inspection of the ship, including the crew's quarters, she noticed something on his shirt. "What is that insect on your collar?" she asked innocently. The Captain flushed angrily. "My God, a flea!" he roared, turning abruptly back to his cabin. No doubt, she added dryly, he would string up his suffering crew by the toenails for this offence. But he did fulfill his guardian duties and always asked with whom she was going on subsequent trips ashore before they reached Georgetown.

Most of the passengers were male, but there were a few women going home from leave or going out for the first time. My mother soon befriended Iris, a girl from the West Indies who had been in boarding school in England and was on her way home for good. She and Iris joined a group that used to meet in the Doctor's office in the evening for endless cups of tea. At night, Gladys had a cabin to herself in an alleyway. In the cabin opposite her door were two young English girls, both pretty, one dark and one fair. They struck her as not being very bright and seemed to be in the charge of an East Indian lawyer who rapped on their door to give them orders to wake up or dress for dinner. As the voyage progressed, they always sat or walked with him and the other men had to ask his permission to dance with them after dinner, duly returning them as soon as the dance was over.

Dressing for dinner was mandatory on the ship. As they neared Barbados and the weather got hotter, Gladys felt sorry for some of the men in their black wool suits with the obligatory starched shirts and stiff collars. (On the P&O, the first-class shipping line to the East, Charles Allen said that newcomers were told that they had to bring no less than 18 'boiled' shirts and 36 stiff collars for the voyage out.) My mother thought it was Prince Edward who later introduced the soft shirt for dinner. She was happy to see that the old hands dressed in lightweight, short, white jackets, impolitely called 'bum freezers', with a wide cummerbund or sash. For the women, it was still the Roaring Twenties and all of them wore the hip-low waists that were the hallmark of the period.

My mother's favourite evening frock was a silk georgette creation covered with beads and scalloped around the hem.

The trip took nearly three weeks. Once they had passed the grey and stormy Bay of Biscay, the sea became calmer and bluer every day until on a sunny day it was a deep Reckitt's blue. As they neared Barbados, she was delighted to see her first flying fish. Reaching Bridgetown, the ship dropped anchor some distance out, unable to go further into the shallow harbour. The passengers went ashore in launches. Those who were returning to the ship afterwards went mostly to swim at the yacht club and marvel at the clear turquoise water and white coral sands. It was here that my mother nearly lost her life in a foolish incident. To tease her, the two young officers sharing her small boat, knowing that she could swim, deliberately upset it for the fun of it. Unfortunately, they did not realize that her feet were crossed under the seat. It took her a while underwater to free herself and come up to the surface. I dread to think what my furious mother, with a temper that matched her red hair when aroused, said to the embarrassed young men when she was safely on land after her silly scare.

By now Iris was having so much fun that she asked her family if she could stay on the ship as far as Georgetown and its return to Barbados. With her parents' consent, the girls, setting out for the bank for more money, impulsively boarded a decrepit local bus, packed with black people going home from the market with live chickens and other produce. Gladys thoroughly enjoyed the trip with all the good natured banter as the bus rattled and roared through the tropical scenery, so new and green to her appreciative eyes. When they reached the bank, they met a young clerk who had come out on the ship with them. Laughingly, they told him about their adventurous trip. He was horrified at their recklessness, and Gladys was suddenly face to face with white mores in the colonies. The pompous young man who was so angry with them quickly made her aware that they had overstepped the bounds not just of female safety but of white propriety as it was to be defined for her. She who had always been friendly with everyone was now supposed to draw a line between the people with whom she was supposed to be friendly and the people she was supposed to keep at a distance, and the line was not to be based on character or aptitude or shared sympathies but on colour, that separation of people that is such an obvious flag of difference that it could not be missed. This was her introduction to the prejudice that underlay colonial living. She was soon to learn that in the Guiana of 1929 the colour-bar was complete, making most whites treated as superior beings, irrespective of rank, job, background, class, education, or personality. It was a strange new idea for a girl who still regretted being unintentionally rude to a nice young black lad as they left

England, and prickled at the upper class snobbishness of the white civil servants travelling with her.

Another problem still bothered her and she was obviously not alone. Before the ship arrived in Barbados, some of the men had become concerned about the two girls in the opposite cabin and felt that they should have a formal interview with the Captain about them. It was decided that he should take them back to England on his return trip, but one of the girls did not return from an excursion in Barbados and the other disappeared ashore in Trinidad. My mother always wondered what happened to them.

Meanwhile, she and Iris were having the time of their lives. Between Barbados and Trinidad, the ship called at Grenada. Interested passengers toured the lovely island in a hired car and went swimming. On all these shore trips, my mother arrived back aboard with assortments of local fruit, for which her sugar planter friends scoffed that she had paid too much, and armfuls of flowers that they scornfully called 'weeds'. Ginger lilies maybe, she conceded, but not the beautiful hibiscus, frangipani and Barbados Pride.

In Trinidad, it was normal for docked ship passengers to be entertained ashore in the evening. Evelyn Waugh, who went there in 1932, dourly described a heavy evening at the country club, which was all stiff shirts and white waistcoats and saxophones and as urban as the Embassy. My mother, on the other hand, was overwhelmed. "In Trinidad," she said, "we women got a shock. We went to a dance at Queen's Park Hotel and all the women there were wearing floor length evening gowns with natural waists, copied no doubt from *Harper's*." They were way ahead in fashion, for this style was only adopted in England the following winter. My mother's beautiful silk dress, so quickly out of date, completely disintegrated soon after her arrival in Mackenzie. In the humid tropics, silk was a no-no. Her white silk tennis dresses and my father's white tussore suit would soon turn a deep beige with constant washing. Her best investments were to be the Irish linen and cotton Tobalco dresses that she had bought from 'Robinsons' in London. She later hiked them up to a natural waist.

The ship left Trinidad on its last lap before Georgetown. The voyage was choppy. Some 12 miles off the Guyanese coast, the water turned from blue to brown where the rivers of 'The Land of Many Waters' were pouring mud into the sea. As they waited at the Georgetown bar for the tide to allow them to enter the estuary of the Demerara River, my mother's excitement grew. Soon, she would see Jos again. Soon, she would see her new home. Sadly, she would have to say goodbye to Iris and all the fun she had had on board the ship that was her last clear link with her homeland. In a sense, although she had no idea of this at the time, this was to be the dividing line in my mother's life between her carefree English girlhood and the woman she was going to become, but she was not in the mood to look back. Ready or not, she was eager to see what lay next and where life was going to take her.

Gladys with her parents,
Mary and Thomas Parsonage

last glimpse
of England

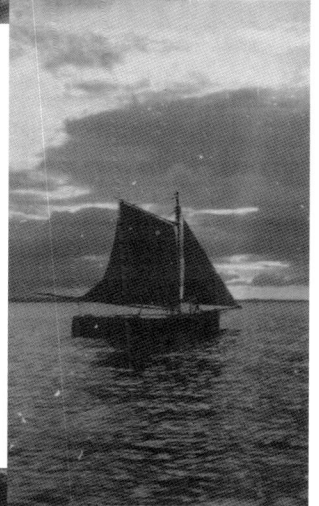

sunset in
Port-of-Spain
Trinidad

street in
Grenada

market in
Grenada

Georgetown Introduction

My mother's first glimpse of her new country was not inviting. At the rail with her new friend Iris, gazing south over the soupy sea, at first there was nothing to see but a taupe horizon under a brilliant blue sky. The sun, straight overhead, beat down on the frying decks as the passenger-freighter waited for the tide to lift them over the shallow bar that protected the mouth of the Demerara River.

Inside the estuary, the view did not improve. The low-lying town of Georgetown barely made an impression along the line of the sea. Dull brown mudflats edged the shore on the town side of the river while mangrove roots crawled along the other. Of the docking area, arriving in the rain on 23 December 1932, Evelyn Waugh said three years later that he had never seen a less attractive harbour. "Hope dried up in one at the sight of it," he said. "Only the reek of sugar occupied the senses." As he described it, half a dozen small ships were tied up along the quay as their ocean craft steamed up and then drifted down to berth with the current. Low wooden sheds and low roofs lay beyond them. Everything was flat. Landing for him was simple, but there was none of the jaunty cross-examination that usually greeted a British subject when he arrived on British territory. "An elderly Negro in a straw hat glanced at our passports; the Customs officers opened nothing; we passed through the sheds, which were full of bees attracted to the sugar bags, and out into the water-logged street." A taxi, splashing and skidding, took him from the area around the docks known as Tiger Bay, noted for its rum shops, cheap boarding houses, and ladies of the evening, to his hotel in the business centre of Georgetown. He saw nothing of the drive because of the ceaselessly pouring rain.

The same scene was waiting for my mother, but her view of it was completely different. The sun was shining, her hopes were high, and there was someone special waiting on the dock to meet her, his face wreathed in smiles of welcome. My father was wearing his white silk suit and an item of clothing Gladys had never seen him wear before. He was wearing a *topee*, the light, hard, pith helmet that white male arrivals in the 1920s quickly adopted as protection against the burning tropical sun. It seems to me to be the only kind of headgear that I remember my father wearing while we lived in Mackenzie. He wore it when he cycled to work or had to stand outside in the midday heat. In our house, it was a symbol of civility and common sense. It hung on the hook with his bicycle clips that he used to protect his trousers against the oil on the chain. It was the hat that he tipped out of respect to all he met. Yet this was the head-dress that came to be so hated by the black race because of what it represented to them. With their long history of slavery and cruel oppression, the pith helmet, along with the whip, was a despised symbol of white abuse of power, abuse which my father, with his strict sense of fair play, would have found unthinkable. If he had known, I wonder if he would have discarded his topee with the white-hot anger that seemed to rise in him at the sign of any kind of unfairness. But at the time, unknowing, as for so many unthinking white colonials, it was simply the thing to do to wear one. Until it became unfashionable in the 1930s, for these men it was a different symbol. On the ships going home from the Far East, they had a ceremony where all the men gathered on deck at a certain point on the voyage and threw their helmets overboard to officially mark the ending of their time of service away from England.

At the Georgetown dock, innocently complete with his topee, my father looked handsome, tanned, and happy. When he bent to embrace my mother, she was amused to find that he reeked of mothballs and insect repellent. His silk suit had been hanging in a wardrobe ever since he arrived the previous year and was well impregnated against marauding moths and cockroaches. Gladys was soon to learn that all their clothes had to smell of disinfectant if they were to survive. She learned that she could not leave a food stain on any garment for more than a short time or the roaches would eat a hole in the material. She was also to find that her new wardrobe contained light bulbs to fight the mildew that otherwise would turn all their shoes a bright verdigris green in the tropical dampness.

So this, at last, was British Guiana. "They call it BG here," she wrote to her parents. "It is very hot as we are only six degrees from the equator and the mid-day sun is right overhead (they say you could fry an egg on the pavement at noon) but there is a pleasant on-shore breeze during the day. At night, it dies down and then watch out! But everyone seems to have big fans in all their rooms."

They stayed in Georgetown for a few days before going upriver to Mackenzie. The company had arranged for them to stay at the select Tower Hotel where the travellers undoubtedly found themselves like Waugh in a clean but bare white room faintly scented with 'Flit' repellent and furnished with a rocking chair and large bed draped with mosquito netting. Zahra Freeth, in her book *Run Softly Demerara*, wrote that, even 20 years or so later, everyone who arrived in the colony still stayed at the Tower for a period of brief acclimatisation. Before new English employees started work, she said, before houses were prepared for wives or men bound for the backwoods were asked to cut their links with civilisation, they were given a few days in the hotel to recover from their journey, to grow acquainted with Georgetown, to "get the feel of the place."

The feel of the Georgetown of the time was aptly summarized by Duncan Campbell when he described British Guiana in the twenties as still being very British, a colony of Englishmen and of Guyanese of various racial backgrounds living under a 19th-century British colonial governor, playing cricket, lunching in the Victorian atmosphere of the Georgetown Club, their ladies drinking afternoon tea on shaded verandahs preparatory to black-tie dinners in each other's homes. No wonder Waugh was disappointed in the place. He went for a walk in town and found it hot and tiring, noting without interest "some quite considerable villas, sordid emporiums, and the Scotto-Flemish town hall in match-boarding and cast iron." He changed from the Sea View Hotel, a large but too quiet boarding house that had been booked for him by the agent of the businessman in England, and moved to the Tower Hotel on Christmas Eve because it had a noisy bar where he could learn something of interest to a writer. But there was little in Georgetown that appealed to him at first glance. "I had pictured the place small and solid like the town at St. Helena. Instead it was all made of wood and very large; large in the tiresome sense that everything was a long way from everything else. The main streets were very broad, with grass and trees down the centre, and the houses all 'stood in their own grounds'. The shops were large and departmental stores and seemed all to be called either Booker's or Foggarty's; the club, for which I found a temporary membership card awaiting me, was a vast barn entirely empty. The museum took some finding; it was an upper floor smelling of must and containing a few cases of Indian work, some faded photographs and the worst stuffed animals I have seen anywhere. There was a large Catholic cathedral, concrete and unfinished, and numerous timber churches in the box-of-bricks style of architecture. The people seemed all black or brown; the black noisy and shabby, the brown subdued and natty. There had once been trams but they had ceased working. That at first sight was Georgetown." Not to seem completely ungracious, he added: "Doubtless some local patriot will complain that I give a wrong impression; that there is a cricket club, a promenade along the sea front and a spacious botanical gardens. That is also true. I have nothing against the amenities of the place. Just the reverse, but it is disappointing to travel a long way and find at the end of one's journey, a well-laid out garden city."

It is hard to imagine that Waugh was not royally entertained by all and sundry during his stay. He was interviewed on arrival by two black reporters from the local press so that his presence was known immediately to the entire community. He was an interesting single male visiting Georgetown over the Christmas holidays, when visitors would be imagined to be lonely and everyone was having house parties. On New Year's Eve, Georgetown was alive with celebrations. He went to a ball at the elitist white Club, where everyone was in fancy dress, and drank whisky and had dinner before returning to the Tower Hotel to find a scene of Scottish orgy, complete with pipers, and quite elderly men sitting on the floor. He was knowledgeable enough about travelling abroad to observe the protocol of signing the Government visitors' book on arrival, and was immediately asked for lunch on Christmas Eve and again on New Years Day and dinner on Christmas Day at Government House. He did acknowledge the kindness he received, along with cordiality and help from every kind of person in the colony, including Governor and Lady Denham with whom he spent a pleasant three days on their launch on an expedition up the Essequibo River.

For exactly the reasons that Waugh was disappointed, my mother liked the town at once ~ clean, attractive and spacious, the houses set apart in their colourful tropical gardens. She learned that Georgetown was built below sea-level. "Only the Dutch would have built a town on the confluence of sea and river at below sea-level," she wrote in amazement. Although the town had been founded and named after George III by the British when they took control in 1781, it was first named Stabroek by the early Dutch settlers, and later Longchamps under a brief French rule, before it regained its British name in 1812. The whole urban area was laid out in a grid system on top of what had once been old sugar plantations. Drainage was accomplished by digging a series of narrow canals intersecting the layout. Many of these had been covered over, accounting for the width of the streets about which Waugh complained. When the tide came in, the main canals going to the sea were closed off by dropping heavy wooden barriers, still called by the Dutch term of 'kokers', which were opened twice a day when the tide receded. For additional protection, the sea around Georgetown was held back by dykes like the ones found in Holland. Like everybody else, my parents promenaded along the Georgetown Sea Wall, enjoying the cool, onshore breeze, and found it, with its bandstand, to be a favourite afternoon meeting-place, although they felt that it was a shame that the sea and sands were the same unattractive muddy brown that my mother had seen from the arriving freighter. Gladys learned that the retaining sea wall that was so impressive in town petered out to the east of the civic boundary, but the drainage ditches and kokers remained all along the coast among the sugar estates, going 'aback' for miles.

From their hotel, my parents could walk down Main Street, a prosperous thoroughfare lined with hotels, offices, and large private houses, with a broad grass-edged footpath running down a central avenue between the lines of traffic. From here they could see Government House, set back in spacious grounds, through a screen of trees. The entrance was marked by two uniformed sentries standing smartly at attention by the road. "Everyone in uniform is very smart," my mother observed. "The policemen directing traffic are a sight to behold."

They were also within easy walking distance of the large Anglican cathedral, St. George's, designed by Sir Arthur Blomfield and said to be the tallest wooden structure in the world. It is odd that Waugh did not mention it, for the graceful Gothic building was centrally located and considered one of the sights of the city. Zahra Freeth wrote that although the cathedral had no pretensions to great architectural beauty, it was a notable and conspicuous feature of the capital. "In certain lights its silvery white outline, and the metallic sheen of its aluminium roof, give it an insubstantial ghostly quality against the grey-white tropical sky," she said, "almost creating the illusion that the tall mass of the spire and nave is dissolving before one's eyes into the bright haze above the city."

Some distance along Church Street, east of the Cathedral, lay the pride of Georgetown ~ the Botanic Gardens, which had been created between 1879 and 1884 from an abandoned sugar plantation. The soil was heavy clay and badly drained so an elaborate system of irrigation and drainage had had to be constructed before the planting could begin. In spite of this inauspicious beginning, the garden planners had worked ceaselessly to create a peaceful, natural setting with a magnificent collection of tropical plants. I am sure that my father would have taken my mother to see the Gardens, knowing her passionate interest in flowers. Here she would see many of the plants that she had gathered in the islands when the ship allowed her to go ashore, and get a chance to look at the magnificent royal water-lily, *Victoria regia*, which she had noticed in some of the canals, up close in its native habitat. The leaves were huge, measuring up to eight feet across, and tray-shaped with interior bracing resembling an iron grill, with lethal spines underneath and around the upturned margins to protect them from aquatic predators. My parents would have left the gardens before sundown, so they would not have witnessed the wonderful spectacle of the large white waxy

flowers as they slowly opened at dusk, but if they had stayed into late afternoon they would have seen the dramatic arrival of hundreds of herons, egrets, and bitterns coming in to roost in the shrubbery and trees at the edge of the pond.

The pond was renowned for containing a family of manatees, that rare and ugly water mammal which, incredibly, is supposed to have been the origin of the myth of the mermaid because of its tail-fin and human-like breasts for suckling its young. William Beebe, the famous naturalist and Director of Tropical Research for the New York Zoological Society, who extravagantly compared his feelings about the Georgetown Botanic Gardens with seeing the Taj Mahal in India, took Theodore Roosevelt there to see the manatees on his earlier visit to the colony. "A guidebook will doubtless give the exact acreage, tell the mileage of excellent roads, record the date of establishment and the number of species of palms and orchids," he wrote in his lyrical account of Guiana in *Edge of the Jungle*. "But it will have nothing to say of the marvels of the slow decay of a *Victoria regia* leaf, or of the spiral descent of a white egret, or of the feelings which Theodore Roosevelt and I shared one evening when four manatees rose beneath us. It was from a little curved Japanese bridge, and the next morning we were to start up-country to my jungle laboratory. There was not a ripple on the water, but I chose to stand still and wait. After ten minutes of silence I put a question, and Roosevelt said 'I would willingly stand for two days to catch a good glimpse of a wild manatee.' And St. Francis heard, and one after another, four great backs slowly heaved up; then an ill-formed head and an impossible mouth, with the unbelievable harelip, and before our eyes the sea-cows snorted and heavily gamboled."

Those were the days when Georgetown was proudly called the Garden City of the Caribbean and my mother loved the private gardens in the residential area near the sea. She observed that the private Dutch Colonial–styled houses were all wooden, painted white and standing on tall columns above the ground which gave them a great sense of height. They had jalousied shutters at the windows, opened by a long stick and closed if raining. The windows were open to the air, with no glass or netting. The gardens were well tended, with crushed shell paths and lovely trees and bushes of hibiscus, crepe myrtle, yellow alamanda, and Barbados Pride. There were long wide avenues, lined with red Flamboyant trees. Some of the trees, like the Saman trees on Main Street, had been planted as long ago as 200 years earlier by the Dutch colonists. A lot of the public buildings were survivals of Dutch architecture. They were usually long and multiple-gabled with red roofs, sometimes with an open balcony running along the front of the upper

floor. The most famous example of this style was Stabroek Market, built in the 1880s, framed in iron and painted red and white. Its most noticeable feature, apart from the gables, was the central clock tower, topped with a wrought iron balcony and a red pyramid roof raised on slender posts.

Days in Georgetown began early while it was still cool. The shops and offices opened their doors at eight o'clock and it was not long before the shopping streets near the hotel were in full swing. Gladys was sorry that she had done all her clothes shopping in England when she saw the stylish dresses in shop windows and the number of dressmakers advertising their skills. She was not very happy when it came time to do the food shopping for Mackenzie. She burst into tears in one grocery store because all the prices were in BG dollars (five to a British pound) and she had no idea which items were expensive and which were not. She did realize that liquor was cheap at $1.68 for Gordon's gin and $1.00 for local rum. Butter, sold in sealed tins, was invariably rancid, and there was no dried or any kind of yeast in the colony so the bread was incredibly awful. She was beginning to learn that life in the tropics, without the fresh and familiar foods of home, was not going to be all that easy.

She was also suffering from swollen ankles caused by mosquito bites. She was lucky that she did not come down with malaria for this was prevalent in the colony at the time. She noted that as soon as darkness fell around 6.p.m. there was a cacophony of sounds caused by insects and many kinds of frogs whistling and croaking. When my parents were entertained at different houses or went to the Club, they heard the welcome sound of ice in a canvas bag being pounded small on kitchen window ledges to make the ubiquitous 'swizzles', a frothy pink cocktail that was tossed off at one go each time the tray came around. Long a midday favourite of the Demerara sugar planters, swizzles were a famous Guiana drink created by adding copious amounts of rum, a small glass of water, a dash of Angostura bitters, a little sugar, and lots of crushed ice. To make the foam, the mixture was whipped with a tool called a swizzle-stick, made from a local bush that had numerous twigs radiating from a central axis, which was twirled around between the palms of the hands. Once the ice had melted, the result had to be drunk immediately before the foam subsided.

Evenings in Georgetown were hot when the wind died down, but there was always a big fan somewhere to imagine being cool. Whether they relaxed in company or alone, this was the best time of the day for my parents to sit back and enjoy being together again, and look forward to their new life upriver.

fan palm

palm

paw-paw tree with fruit

Botanic Gardens

bandstand

Georgetown

old Dutch-
style house,
Georgetown

Up the Demerara

There was no road to Mackenzie when the time came for my parents' departure. The only way for them to reach the mining camp with all Gladys' luggage was to take the Demerara River steamboat, the *R.H. Carr*, which ran thrice-weekly, three days up and three days down, with no service on Sunday. The trip could take six to ten hours, depending on whether the steamer was bucking the tide or going with it. The river was tidal for 75 miles, all the way up to Mackenzie. The water ran down for seven hours, and up, slowly, for four hours, with one hour of slack tide between changes. The ocean ships that came up for bauxite ore had to wait for high tide in order to leave when loaded.

As the steamer moved out into mid-stream on the day they left Georgetown, Jos and Gladys leaned over the railing of the bridge deck to watch the proceedings. Suddenly, there was a gust of wind and Gladys lost her most expensive and much-loved item of clothing, her made-to-measure, Henry Heath–designed, white fur-felt hat. There was nothing to do but watch it being churned up in the muddy waters while my father tried in vain to console her.

The waters stayed muddy for at least half of the way, eventually turning to a clear dark brown, stained by the rainforest vegetation. At first the river was bordered by banks of shining mud out of which grew a tangle of mangrove. Egrets perched on branches over the water and caught the eye in paint strokes of white. They could see the pale green sugar cane fields stretching back to the chimneys from the factories, some emitting the sweet-sickly smell of lees (the dregs left over from the sugar-making process), but these petered out not far from the coast and then there was only the rainforest, locally known as 'the bush', growing down to the edge of the river. The steamer passed the small island of Borsselen which had been the capital of Demerara in the days of the Dutch settlers. It had been completely abandoned at some point in the past and had reverted to bush like the surrounding riverbanks. The rainforest trees were tall, a mix of palm and shiny broadleaf, and they were thickly tangled with liana and undergrowth, impossible to see through. Now and then, above the canopy, there would be an especially tall cabbage-palm or a huge silk-cotton tree draped with spreading epiphytes. At water level, the banks were hidden by a lush growth of aquatic plants, stout aroids with huge leaves submerged at high tide but visible at low water at the edge of the river, plants like the giant caladium or large-leaved mucka-mucka, but as the forest grew denser and the banks less muddy, they were replaced by clumps

of manicole palm, corkwood, trysil, wild nutmeg, wild cocoa, and the trumpet tree. The higher up the river they went, the more the impression was of travelling between walls of solid green.

Although my mother had been excited with her first sight of tropical garden flowers, she was not enthralled by the tropical flora as a whole. The rain-forest screen that they were passing was too big, too dense, too luxuriant, too green, and the few glimpsed flowers high in the canopy too wildly coloured for her English taste that cherished the small, the dainty, and the subtle paler tones of the northern countryside. But it interested her at least to see the difference and know the names. My father could not help her. His interest in plants was dismissive, to say the least. What a pity that Gladys could not have travelled out from England with a group of men who arrived in the colony a few weeks later, in August 1929, and were soon boating up the Essequibo, a much larger parallel river to the west of the Demerara, en route to their camp at Moraballi Creek, which was a long way away because of the route that had to be taken but as the crow flies would probably be only about 25 miles west of Mackenzie. The group was the Oxford University Expedition to British Guiana, consisting of a number of biologists who hoped to continue and extend the work done near Bartica by Dr. William Beebe, the American zoologist and naturalist. They were particularly interested in the life of the canopy at the top of the forest trees.

As they travelled up the river to the west, their leader, Major R.W.G. Hingston, noted much that would have fascinated my mother, for above Bartica the Essequibo narrowed to resemble the Demerara, flowing between two walls of luxuriant forest. Sometimes the green cliffs were fronted with mangroves but more usually they seemed to rise up directly to an average height of about 120 feet, although now and then one tree would send its crown about 40 to 50 feet higher. Said Hingston: "It was too uniform to be picturesque. Not an acre of ground was anywhere free from it. It clothed in a magnificent tangle every square foot of river-bank and every island or small lump of rock that projected above the water. In this mass of vegetation we saw many trees that later were to become better known to us. There was the mora, silk cotton, iteballi, trysilo, and other unrecognized but impressive species. Draping the face of this wall like a curtain was a tangled mass of interlacing creepers that hung down from their attachments to the canopy carpet. The drapery both spread to the water-level and climbed up to the summits of the highest trees which it covered with a suffocating burden of festoons. It presented to the river so dense a front that only rarely could one get a glimpse through it into the darker solitudes behind."

Because of the enclosing vegetation and lack of settlements, there was not much to see on the Demerara. Now and then the *R.H. Carr* would pass a raft loaded with greenheart lumber, heading downstream. Of all the vast number of rainforest trees, greenheart was probably the only one being exported at the time, noted for its hardness and resistance to rot, which made it useful for making wharves and pilings as well as fishing rods. Because the wood was heavier than water and would not float, the logs were lashed under a large open punt, which had four sweeps for guidance, and floated with the down-tide and tied up at the side when the tide flowed up. The journey to the coast could take weeks, going only a maximum of 14 hours a day very slowly, so that whole families lived on board, men, women, children, and dogs, sheltered at one end by a palm-thatched area with hanging hammocks and cooking utensils. Gladys impulsively waved to the families as they floated past while Jos smiled at her naive excitement.

From time to time, the steamer passed small clearings between the trees, with little wooden houses in ragged, haphazard groups, and they made several stops mid-stream where the occupants paddled quickly out in corials (dugout canoes) to collect or deliver passengers, goods, and mail. At one clearing where the steamer waited, my father could not resist teasing my mother. He pointed to the women along the shore, pounding their clothes on logs and rinsing them in the river. Trying to keep the telltale twinkle out of his eyes, he said, "That's how you wash your clothes here." When she did not reply, he went on to bigger and better things. Around another bend in the river, the steamer passed an Amerindian encampment with an open, palm-thatched hut strung with hammocks like a spider's lair. Little brown children with shiny naked bodies watched them solemnly from the bank. When my mother waved, they did not wave back. "They call them Buck Indians here," Jos said. "I suppose to distinguish them from the East Indians from India." He watched my mother's face and a grin spread across his own. It was too good to miss. As they watched the scene, trying to keep his voice light and his face straight, he said brightly, "We live in a hut like that. Only ours is a little bigger." All the way up the river, Gladys believed that this was how she was going to be living.

The bauxite company had a small first-class cabin on the foredeck of the steamer, with a private deck from which they watched the river go by. The cabin was available to staff if the General Manager was not travelling. The second-class deck below them was strewn with people and their belongings. Sometimes there were also live chickens, or even tethered cows or goats. The smell of bananas and unwashed bodies wafted upwards as everyone made themselves comfortable. There were people sitting, sleeping, talking, laughing, or just silent. There were patient old black faces, wrinkled and crinkled from care and laughter. There were big African-black women nursing their small babies or cuddling young children until they fell asleep in their arms. There were neat brown East Indians going to Wismar ~ the women, adorned with gold bracelets and noserings, pulling their shawls around their shoulders or over their heads in the midday sun, the men smoking and discussing affairs of personal importance as they crouched on sacks or on the floor of the deck. Amidst the huge piles of bundles, Gladys noticed a sack with water melting from inside. My father told her, truthfully this time, that this was Mackenzie's meat supply.

In the comparative luxury of the cabin above, it was the invariable custom for Jones, the kindly steward, to serve 'breakfast', the traditional 11 a.m. mid-day meal in BG, shortly after boarding, after which the travellers usually took a rest. In the afternoon, he brought in tea and toast, both tasting of smoke from the charcoal brazier. With the toast, he proudly produced imported cheddar cheese, standing in a pool of grease from the heat, and guava jelly. After breakfast, Gladys was reading the newspaper. Knowing that their steamer destination was Wismar, across the river from Mackenzie, she asked my father, "What is a water camoodie?" She had just read that one over 30 feet long had been killed on the pier. My father said, "It's a snake. Native name for a boa-constrictor." Gladys thought longingly of Iris returning on the ship without her.

It was only when the steamer blasted her horn as she rounded the last bend of the river that my mother realized that my father had been pulling her leg all along about where she was going to live. From the deck as they drew near, Mackenzie looked immensely civilized compared with what my father had given her to expect. It resembled almost any newly-built Canadian company town, built according to company hierarchy, well maintained and carefully organized. Before her was the wide view of the black workers' village of Cockatara with its neat, stilted wooden houses. My father pointed out the playing fields where he played cricket. Beyond lay the big bauxite-crushing plant and adjacent buildings and freighter wharves, which separated the workers' community from the pleasant white staff village of Watooka, with its raised bungalows and tidy lawns, that beckoned attractively in the distance.

The *R.H. Carr* completed her journey at Wismar, on the opposite bank from Mackenzie, in the mid-late afternoon. Wismar and neighbouring Christian-burg were all that remained of two old sugar plantations once owned by a family named Patterson. The area had been government-acquired since 1896 when a dispute arose between the Scottish landowners and Sprostons Company over the building of part of the Demerara-Rockstone Railway across the private estate land. Wismar was now important enough to house a Government Rest House, the local Magistrate's Court, and the only railway station from this point on into the interior of British Guiana. The settlement had a large number of East Indian residents left over from estate days and there was an area of primitive shops that sold meat and fruit and colourful cloth and bazaar articles.

The bauxite company usually sent an official launch over from Macken-zie to bring back arriving staff and important visitors from the river steamer. A Demba representative came on board to greet my father and mother and assist them down the gangplank and into the smaller craft. The outboard motor on the launch made it too noisy to talk as they moved out into the river, so Gladys sat in excited silence as she looked back at the green rainforest bank, reflected in the smooth river mirror that now loomed high above them from water level. Ahead lay Mackenzie, her new home. The highest structure to be seen was the tall water tower, but the plant was easily the largest and most obvious feature in the land-scape. A plume of steam rose into the air from the bauxite washing and crushing process inside the building but it was all very clean after the dirty black Potter-ies. Several freighters, large by river standards but small and shallow enough to cross the Georgetown Bar, waited in line along the dock area to receive the dusty cargo of processed bauxite to be poured into their holds. She squeezed Jos' arm as he shouted to her and proudly pointed out the window of the office where he worked, the small hospital, and their bungalow in the village of Watooka to the right of the plant where the launch was heading.

Did my mother have any idea what a small world she was going to? Com-pletely surrounded by the imprisoning rainforest, with no access to the outside except by the river steamer she had just left, Mackenzie had a population that had not grown much since my father had arrived in the previous year. She would be one of four white wives in the clearing ahead, to bring the total of Watooka occupants including the staff men up to 16, and her only other contacts there, apart from the occasional visitor, would be the black domestic servants and main-tenance workers around the community, and the East Indians who occasionally served her at the bazaar stalls across the river in Wismar. Although the community would grow slightly in size, it would change little, and this would be her entire world for the majority of her time there, time that would stretch into long months and then into seemingly endless years. Gladys, who had grown up so tomboyish and carefree in her native England, was about to enter a world where everything she did would be open to scrutiny and criticism, and nearly everyone around her would be older, including her husband, and where freedom was a minimum of a day's journey away and seldom available. It was perhaps just as well that she could not see into the future on the day she arrived at what a later arrival from Canada complained was a 'dinky little mining camp'. Ever the optimist in her youth, before she gave in to the bitterness and regrets of old age, my mother that afternoon was all ignorant smiles as Mackenzie drew nearer.

Mackenzie

R.H. Carr at Wismar

Demerara River

Watooka, Mackenzie

Watooka

timber barge
timber is below the water,
tied to the arms sticking out.
The greenheart wood is too
heavy to float.

A Home on Stilts

The company launch completed its journey from the steamer by pulling up to a wooden jetty that was always referred to by its Dutch name of stelling. Jos and the representative offered to help Gladys to climb ashore but, used to rowboats, she sprang lightly over the side and up the steps. At last, she was in Mackenzie! Was it here that she had her historic meeting with Mrs. Rucker? It was not unusual, with so few women in the camp, for all the wives to go down to the stelling to greet new arrivals when they heard the steamer whistle blow. If this had been the case in 1929, there would have been only three wives to meet my mother, with the plant manager's wife in charge. Mrs. Rucker was a square-bodied woman with a mannish short haircut and plain, intelligent face with expressive, honest eyes. She spoke with a broad Arkansas accent and she said the first thing that came into her head as she shook hands with my mother in greeting. "Oh, Miz Whalley," were the first words that she said to her, "You have all your teeth!" My 24-year-old mother thought this was hilarious.

The area of Mackenzie assigned for white staff, officially called Watooka but always referred to by the inhabitants as 'the camp', was laid out along a single straight road parallel to the river, bordered by drainage ditches and neat houses on either side. Typical of Canadian one-industry towns, all the houses looked as if they had been stamped out by the same company machine, except that here, instead of having basements, they were raised wooden bungalows with corrugated aluminum roofs that gleamed in the sun and were thunderous in the heavy tropical rains. Like many of the houses that my parents had seen in Georgetown, they were built on high concrete pillars which reduced the risk of snake and insect invasion. Unlike Georgetown, the windows and verandahs were screened against mosquitoes and other flying insects.

Although all the buildings were similar, there were smaller bungalows for bachelor staff on the far side of the camp and larger models closer to the plant. Only one dwelling was different. Nearest the plant was the Managing Director's large house, built on a grand colonial scale and surrounded by spacious, well-kept grounds. As they passed this imposing mansion, Gladys noticed a large pond filled with the famous *Victoria regia* waterlilies that she had admired in Georgetown, and a jacana, a bird with splayed feet, strutting on the huge lily pads. Further down the road, ever observant of gardens, she was disappointed to see that the staff area where she was going to be living consisted mostly of unfenced coarse grass, scythed by company workers, with a few tropical trees and shrubs and one or two flowerbeds near the houses containing just one kind and colour of hardy roses and a few straggly zinnias and marigolds.

Gladys described her arrival at their new home. "We mounted the steps of our bungalow to a long verandah furnished with cane chairs and the inevitable 'Berbice' chair which had folding pieces which could be opened for a man's legs to rest on. There were straw mats everywhere, and a few plants, and inside was a long room, one end being the dining area. Off this room were two bedrooms divided by a bathroom with a shower, then the kitchen at the end." There was of course no air-conditioning, despite their proximity to the equator and the intense heat, but the open plan allowed for a leavening breeze to cool the interior. It was hard at first for northerners like my mother to get used to the lack of privacy in the open curtainless space, especially after dark when the lights were on. As in Georgetown, there were wooden shutters that could be closed against torrential rain, but if there were any drapes they were placed at the sides of the window where they would not obstruct the cross breeze. When Zahra Freeth arrived in Mackenzie about 25 years later, she said that she and her husband were quite unprepared for the open airy house in which they found themselves. "In general the effect was somewhat like living constantly on an open verandah," she said. "At night when we sat in the living room with the lights ablaze we were completely exposed to the gaze of the passerby, like birds in an illuminated cage." One of the common sounds at night, apart from the barking tree frogs, was the slam against the screens of beetles that were attracted by the lights inside.

The houses were entirely furnished by the bauxite company. Gladys remarked that the furniture was English in style, made of crabwood, a local mahogany, with the varnish somewhat furrowed by the heat. She hated their bedroom, which contained twin beds with 2" deep, lumpy flock or horsehair mattresses placed on very rusty cup springs that twanged alarmingly when weighted. Like Freeth, she was discomfited by the lack of privacy and worried about the noise they made on those tell-tale springs because she felt everyone around could hear them. "I hope they didn't keep diaries!" she wrote later in embarassment.

She did not mention the obligatory mosquito nets over the beds. Even with screened doors and windows, there was a constant fear of the *anopheles* mosquito at night because malaria was so prevalent in the colony and many newcomers suffered badly from it. Old colonials often shrugged off intermittent fever attacks as an expected part of living there, and in some quarters it was even given as a reason for the traditional passivity of the Guianese people as a whole because so much of the population endured constant and recurring bouts of the disease. I doubt if my mother thought of those mosquito nets as anything but a necessary evil, but when I was a child I thought they were wonderful, softly draping and enclosing the bed, creating that romantic private space that children crave when they crawl under tablecloths or make tents all over the place. We always felt that although we could see out clearly, somehow we were hidden and secret and safe inside.

Water from the shower was brown because it came from the Demerara River; however, unlike the Georgetown water which came from the dirty Lamaha Canal, Gladys was relieved to find Mackenzie drinking water pure and clean, as it was collected from rainwater off the aluminum roof. Again as children, if it rained at night as we lay in bed, there was a double feeling of security under our mosquito nets, snuggling down and being dry inside while the heavens rained down tomtoms that played percussion on the corrugated metal over our heads.

Jos had collected a household staff of cook, maid, and washerwoman from Cockatara. They arrived in the morning after the train had left for the mine, giggling and happy, and they sang and joked as they worked. They left before nightfall, as the train came back from the mine bearing their menfolk, and they still sang and joked as they swayed down the street towards their families, still wearing their prim cotton uniforms with starched white caps. My mother enjoyed them. She found some of their skills rather primitive but was happy to teach them what she knew.

In the kitchen, she showed Cookie how to make things to please her fussy husband, who, like so many of his countrymen of the time, liked his food bland and as English as could be arranged. Gladys soon learned that between them they had to make compromises that would fool him into thinking that his food was the same as at 'home'. As Jos did not care for the tropical vegetables, they had to make do with imported canned ones, but there was no problem persuading him to eat the local fruit. Although the rinds of the oranges stayed green when ripe, on the whole she found the fruit excellent and safe to eat, for all of the citrus family, guavas, avocados, bananas, sapodillas, mangoes, and the delectable paw-paw or papaya were grown on trees. These were mostly bought either at the kitchen door, or on the Saturday launch expedition to shop at Wismar on the other side of the river, where there were a few Chinese-owned shops. The trip to Wismar could be made by the company launch or there was a more exciting way to travel there, going out from Cockatara in a long dugout canoe ferried by a Chinese man in a wide straw hat who charged tuppence per passenger. Sitting in the low craft just above the level of the water, the trip across could be quite an experience if the tide was changing, as the current ran very fast.

The Chinese shops at Wismar were quite similar to East Indian shops in Kenya. There, in addition to local produce that was brought in by African growers, the shopkeepers had a surprising range of tinned and bottled goods imported from Britain that included Eno's Fruit Salts (in the old-fashioned wrapping with the children climbing the wall handing the grapes down to each other), Borwick's Baking Powder, and Ovaltine which was found in every shop. There was also Reckitt's Blue. Everything white that was washed in Kenya and Guiana in the early days always came out a bright blue as it was used in enormous quantities by every dhobi and washerwoman. "Every household had any number of Reckitt's packets lying about," said Charles Allen in his *Tales from the Dark Continent*. The Chinese shops in Wismar also sold cloth but there was not much choice. As one new arrival said when she bought some to make a dress, she chose plain material because everyone had to buy the same stuff and she thought it would be awkward if she and all the maids had the same.

My mother was as fussy as my father when it came to buying fresh food. It was lucky for her that they had not ended up in the Far East, for she avoided the East Indian sellers at open stalls in Wismar with a shudder. "There were higglers who displayed their produce on a dirty sack on the ground ~ cucumbers, shallots, wilted lettuce and tiny tomatoes, etc. ~ but unless one liked playing Russian roulette, it was dangerous to buy and eat them if grown in the ground where unscrupulous gardeners emptied night pots on them, or deliberately used the patch as a place to pee, to encourage growth. They must have developed an immunity to typhoid, but were still carriers." It was hard not to be appalled by the smells and lack of sanitation in this open marketplace where people, dogs, goats, chickens, and bulls mingled and jostled together in the narrow street that was no more than an alley in width.

Back in the kitchen at home, all the fresh food was carefully washed and peeled or cooked before eating, but perhaps because of my mother's scruples about where she bought her food and avoidance of food grown in the ground, she did not resort to treating everything with the strangely tasting 'pinky' (permanganate of potash) as was customary in English households in India.

There was one area in the kitchen that Gladys would not allow the cook to take over and that was making pastry. That was her job alone. Her cooking lessons in Newcastle had borne fruit and she was a skilled pastry-maker but she had to make her now famous apple pies from stale dried apples as no fresh ones were available locally. There was only one way she could get fresh apples and that was from the bauxite ships. Sometimes Jos would ask an officer to come home for a drink or a meal, usually both, and they never came empty-handed. Sometimes they brought a bottle, but more rapturously accepted would be a familiar food from home, like a cabbage or a cauliflower or a bag of apples. On one occasion when a visitor had brought apples, Gladys made a pie and asked Cookie to sprinkle it with icing sugar. As they didn't have any icing sugar, Cookie thought it would look just as good sprinkled with salt!

The kitchen drove my mother crazy. "And the kitchen!" she moaned in letters home. In it were a monstrous wood stove, which smoked and was terribly hot in the oppressive tropical humidity, and an icebox that leaked. The ice for the icebox came from Georgetown three times a week on the *R.H. Carr*. Each family received a rapidly melting block of it, brought by 'Old Foxy' on his donkey cart. The icebox legs stood in cans full of liquid to discourage the ants.

There were ants everywhere, despite the fact that there was a moat filled with tar surrounding the base of each pillar under the house. I remember as a child watching the ants bringing material to build a bridge so that they could cross the tar and climb the pillars. I also remember leaving a hard candy on the dresser beside the bed one night. Next morning there was a long line of ants across the floor and up the dresser leg to the ant-covered sweet and back. The ones in the house were usually small ones that we called 'fine ants'. A lovely story went around Mackenzie about the Georgetown mistress who asked her cook how she liked the sermon in church on Sunday. The cook answered testily, "Missus, all he talk about was fine ants!"

Scorpions were a real problem for one staff member who occupied a bachelor house until his wife arrived. He found scorpions everywhere in that house, on the floor, under the bed, on the walls. Finally, he had had a man take up the floor, and underneath they found a nest with about 50 of them.

"My main memories of that place," said Gladys later, "apart from the heat, mosquitoes and interminable waiting three years for leave home, were of moving insects, to say nothing of snakes. Dozens of kinds of ants, also a minute beast in the grass called 'bete rouge' which burrowed under one's skin, as did the jiggers. As for our cockroaches, they were enormous, and since they were able to fly they could always get in the house somehow. In fact, I have seen one enter a closed match-box. It was quite acceptable at a party that if one ran in sight, the nearest lady whipped off her shoe and bashed it. Our motto was, 'If it moves, kill it'." She wondered what her English mother would think of it all, she who hated frogs and insects. "She would have had a fit to see a Rhinoceros Beetle at least 4" long staring at her from our mosquito netting where it was enmeshed. A beast not to be batted in the eye when cycling at night to the movies, or wobbling home from a smorgasbord dinner on board a bauxite ship, washed down with copious amounts of Aquavit and Tuborg beer!"

The movies were shown in the workers' village. They were old black and white films, with much flickering on the screen and much enthusiastic participation from the audience. The staff sat on a raised platform at the back. One evening, Gladys turned around to see a large hairy tarantula spider on the wall behind her, as big as a man's hand. She had no later recollection of the movie.

Mrs. Rucker and
Mrs. Kerr on stelling

the Managing Director's house and pond

Watooka village. House on left ~ Gladys
& Jos' first home in Watooka.

back view

my parents' home

Jos on the verandah

Grant and Irene

Gladys with
Rodney

Watooka Ways

Slowly, Gladys began to adjust to her new life in Mackenzie, so different from her life in England. The heat was the hardest thing to adjust to at first. "August and September were so hot I thought it couldn't get any hotter," she said. "But it did." The average shade temperature in August and September was 90 F, but in October it rose to 91 F. But shade temperatures had no meaning when the sun shone, especially at noon under the direct equatorial glare. Gladys had arrived in a dry season when the sun beat down every day. The rains would not come until December and for two months they would be drenched, then drying out from February to April and wet again from May to July. Like temperature, 'dry' was a relative term in the rainforest as it was always humid due to condensation. "Shimmering heat all day, very humid, but thankfully a heavy dew came down at sunset and it was almost bearable." Evenings after sundown were relatively pleasant, as were the nights for sleeping, and early mornings, when everyone arose, were damp and cool before the mist burned off the river and the sun began to bake the land.

Her mornings seemed very strange to Gladys at first as she supervised staff instead of doing everything herself but she quickly learned why local people were hired to do the jobs she would have done easily for herself back at home in Newcastle. The women who worked for her were used to the conditions that she found so dreadful. Cook struggled cheerfully with the fearsome wood stove and did not seem to mind the additional torrent of heat which Gladys found impossible to withstand. The maid happily made the creaky beds and stirred dust around the furniture and cleaned the shiny floors on her hands and knees, ordinary tasks for Gladys in England's brisk climate but debilitating for her in the equatorial heat. She was perfectly happy to leave the laundry to someone else rather than cope with the primitive conditions. The clothes were washed under the house in galvanized tubs filled with clean water from a large vat, which in turn was filled by rainwater from the roof. Coloured clothes were hung up to dry once rinsed in clean water; white clothes were rinsed in the blue Rickett's water and then laid out flat and bleached on the grass in the sun. When dry, the clothes were brought upstairs and ironed with a flat iron heated on a brazier.

The ironing was done in a room beside the kitchen where Gladys set up her sewing machine. The first thing she did was to alter the length of the too-short skirts she had brought out from England. That was the room where Gladys spent most of her mornings while the staff worked around the house at their separate tasks. She was either sewing or writing letters home, letters that would take weeks to arrive and more long weeks to be answered so she was careful to keep them cheerful and tell her family things that she thought they would find interesting about her new life. She, like everyone else who lived far away from their homeland, lived for the letters and newspapers with news from 'Home'. When the mail came, she would open everything with great excitement and she and Jos would pore over them in the evening, and next day she spent hours in her room answering the comments and queries and news of family and friends.

The sewing machine brought Gladys into her first memorable encounter with the second of the Watooka matrons. "No account of BG is complete without mentioning the incredible 'Peachy'," she wrote. "I've met a few of her kind since but none with such 'crust'. My introduction to her was on the night I first arrived at the camp, to dinner at their home, both being 'dressed' for it. I mentioned that I'd brought a sewing machine, and the very next morning she arrived with an assortment of clothing for me to fix, including her stays!"

The only other wife in the camp at that time was Mrs. Kerr, a sweet-faced, soft-spoken woman who was always my idea of an elderly angel. It was impossible not to like Minnie Kerr, and her husband Archie was given to gruff teasing which appealed to my father, so the two couples enjoyed each other's company. But my mother particularly liked the bluff and honest American manager's wife who had greeted her with her extraordinary comment on arrival. "Our indefatigable American Manager's wife," Gladys called Mrs. Rucker. "She was a delightful lady, extremely energetic and capable." Later she was to compare her to Eleanor Roosevelt, for whom she felt the same admiration. Mrs. Rucker had started a Girl Guide Troop in Cockatara, also one of Brownies. Mrs. Kerr was Brown Owl, and my mother was soon conscripted to be Tawny Owl. The little girls always called her Tony Owl. "The Brownies, with skins of all shades from beige to black, were so sweet," Gladys said. She was interested in the fact that sisters who had a different father were always called by their father's surname, unlike similar situations in England when they would have to take their maternal name. The Brownies met one afternoon a week, at 3.00 p.m., and she complained that, although young and normally active, she was exhausted by all the games and exercises in that awful heat.

While the everyday routine of the women in the camp centred around their homes and servants, the male routine depended on the working activities of the mine and the plant. The day began early with the departure of the train to Akyma. As Duncan Campbell described it: "When the Mackenzie plant whistle blew at 6.00 a.m. all who worked at the bauxite mines, staff men and hourly-paid workers alike, had to be aboard the small railway train, with its puffing steam engine, which conveyed them to the scene of their labours. Three hours later the 'breakfast train', carrying the food buckets of hot food for the men's 'breakfast' was dispatched. Dutiful wives or servants carried the food buckets to the train, employing wooden trays balanced on their heads. After a long hot day in the mines, drilling, blasting and loading the ore, the men returned on the train at 6.00 as darkness was descending." It was a very long day for the mine men and if there were breakdowns, washouts or derailments, they might not get home until 8.00 or 9.00 p.m. but still had to be ready to start the next day at 6.00 a.m.

Work at the plant and office started at 7.00 a.m. Like all the other staff men, my father rode a bicycle to work, and I can remember as a small child watching him reach for the customary clips for his trousers and giving me a hug before he donned his topee. The mornings when he rode away were always cool and misty, with a white cloud rising from the brown river and over the tops of the rainforest beyond, before the hot sun rose high enough to burn it away. By the time he returned for 'breakfast', the sun was high and the oven of the day was reaching maximum temperature.

After their pre-noon meal, as was typical in the tropics, it was time for an afternoon nap until the sun had passed its worst. It was William Beebe who noted: "It is a fetish of belief in hot countries that every unacclimatized white man must, sooner or later, succumb to that sacred custom, the siesta. In the cool of the day, he may work vigorously, but these hours of rest are indispensable!" Even inside the rainforest, Beebe said, when the sun neared its zenith, a hush settled over the jungle proclaiming that most of the wild creatures were also resting. "At this hour the jungle shows few evidences of life, not a chirp of bird or song of insect, for pursuit and killing are at the lowest ebb, the stifling heat being the flag of truce in the world-wide struggle for life and food and mate."

For my parents, this period of rest would last until about 2.00 p.m., when the full heat of the middle of the day was deemed to be over. Jos returned to work on his bicycle, back to totting up long columns of figures by hand (he added very quickly in his head), working in the sticky heat with fans blowing his papers, until he left to pedal home at the end of the day, if not detained by extra paperwork for the waiting freighters.

Meanwhile, after the midday nap, the ladies spent their afternoons socially. Other than the once-a-week afternoon spent with the Guides and Brownies, and despite their small numbers and the fact that they usually had nothing to offer by way of news, they walked together, visited each other's houses, had afternoon tea, and sat by the stelling at the river bank where they used to swim. Gladys found this time of day rather boring unless there was some kind of physical activity involved. She was young and restless and she needed something to challenge her mind and body. She did try, like so many English women marooned in lands without familiar flowers, to plant a garden, which would have given her much pleasure if she had succeeded, but the soil was heavy clay that lacked nutrition and the plants that came up were sickly and sad and she soon abandoned the project. She decided to try fishing and sent to England for her tackle. She found she had to pay out long yards of line to be successful at catching anything from the stelling but at least it made a change in her deadly routine. She was so eager to learn, to grow, and this tiny outpost offered her so little. She felt stifled by the smallness.

Boredom was the worst part of life in the camp, particularly for the wives. The men at least had their jobs, which most of them enjoyed, although even they sometimes revolted. Gladys remembered that the bachelors in the era of the British were called by their surnames and lived in small bungalows, but later moved to the Clubhouse. One night there was a huge racket when they, in a fit of desperation, smashed all the windows. "I felt like joining them," she said. As well as impatience with anything slow-moving, patience with bureaucracy was not among her finest qualities. "The niggling pettyfogging rules!" she fumed. She particularly resented the company method of shopping for household items. "We had a ration-store book in which we wrote our orders and these were delivered though we could easily cycle down there ~ everyone had a bike though many had to learn to ride one." The books were examined from time to time by the 'Powers'. It reminded her of Merle Travis' 'I Owe My Soul to the Company Store'.

Gladys missed her family and her girlfriends far away, but she was far from alone in her situation around the world. Most colonial outpost wives throughout the Empire were in the same position. Some were even more isolated, on distant stations or farms or plantations where they were the only white woman for miles. These women had gone overseas to be with their husbands and they knew they either had to put up with the conditions they found there or go home and leave their mates behind. They usually had too little to do around their houses, they had few diversions and little choice of compatible female companions, and often their husbands worked long hours or were away from home, leaving them to their own resources. Yet they were expected to be good wives and mothers, to be ambitious to further their husbands' careers, to be gregarious with company and a good sport, and to be cheerful and 'chin up, old girl' in every situation. In spite of the later impression that the memsahibs or their equivalents everywhere were servant-spoiled, lazy, useless women, these women had to be made of pretty stern emotional stuff in order to survive. It was a rare woman who could break out of the traditional mold and succeed on her own terms and the choices for most of them were stark and unbending. 'You made your bed, you have to lie in it', was the philosophy of the times. Some of them failed and went or were sent back home to England. Some of them died, or were carried out, too sick and unable to stand the climate and disease. Some of them had affairs with the ever present bachelors, who waited in hopes for the availability of pretty wives. Many more of them would have succumbed to drink if it had not been for the fiercely maintained taboo against drinking until the sun had set. Under the circumstances, women like Mrs. Kerr and Mrs. Rucker and my mother, who fought the loneliness and boredom and found ways to survive with kindness, decency and usefulness, were nothing short of splendid.

Because of the rigid rule about not drinking 'until the sun had set over the yard arm', an old naval rule often carried to ridiculous lengths in the tropics at the time, drinking was usually done in the evenings as a social affair. There was an unwritten rule against getting drunk, which was neither 'ladylike' nor 'gentlemanly'. By the same rules, bachelors who did any more than harmless flirtations with a lady were written off as 'cads'. In Mackenzie, these social get-togethers were most frequently at the Watooka Clubhouse, which also combined sporting activities. When the men at last came home from work, the entire white community congregated at this convenient and congenial location. What would Mackenzie have been without the club! Later there would be a little six-hole golf course, but when Gladys arrived, "there was a Clubhouse with two concrete tennis courts, and a decent billiards room to my husband's delight, he being a good player who had spent many hours at his Conservative Club in Newcastle playing snooker." Gladys and Jos enjoyed playing tennis. Gladys said she had a very good underhand service but there she finally learned to serve overhand. They played for one hour before sunset. "We did try with overhead lights, partly for the mine staff, away until nearly dark. However, the lights attracted so many flying critters, to say nothing of frogs underfoot, that it was hopeless. Also that was the time of day when the deadly malarial mosquitoes were prevalent." They changed into dry clothes immediately after playing tennis because "one's clothes dropped with a thud, completely saturated." I seem to remember her telling the story of one young man, recently arrived, who did not change out of his wet clothes in spite of her pleading with him about its importance. He sat on the verandah having drinks with them all as the humid night air settled around them and he got a chill that was so severe that he went back to his bungalow and actually died. It might have been combined with malaria. She did not mention whether they drank pink gin with soda dosed with five grams of quinine that was considered customary in other parts of the Empire to prevent or reduce the effects of malaria. Somehow I doubt it. Somehow I think that in Demerara the only drink of any importance was one with rum.

The importance of the clubhouse in colonial living is best described by Charles Allen in his *Plain Tales* series. "It was said that wherever there were two Englishmen there was a club, sometimes station clubs that were little more than a meeting place with a bar and a snooker or billiards table, sometimes gymkhana clubs where officials and non-officials alike could gather in the late afternoon to play scratch polo or a game of tennis or squash ~ or even a round of golf on a rough course that had browns instead of greens. It was always considered vital for one's health to keep fit and active, however unsuitable the season might be for violent exercise, and sport in one form or another provided the means, coming naturally to young men who had been brought up to regard sporting activity as an integral part of their social life." The only sporting activity at Mackenzie that was not centered around the clubhouse, apart from swimming in the 'waterhole' beside the stelling, was cricket. My father loved the game, having played at school and in the army, so he regularly played on a team in the black village of Cockatara.

The clubhouse served another important social function, as Allen pointed out. "What was just as important from a health point of view was that the club provided the opportunity to drink in company ~ because 'drink was unquestionably a major factor of life in the tropics; it was a very pleasant thing after the heat and burden of the day to rest and have a long whiskey and this was a very common sort of relaxation'. The verandah of the station club also provided a natural setting for the exchange of shop and station news ... but for the newcomer probably the club's greatest value was that it filled the 'rather difficult hour in the tropics between six thirty and seven thirty', a melancholy hour which could be passed in congenial company before he returned through the darkness to his own bungalow to have a bath and late supper before retiring to bed'."

In Mackenzie, they often had dances at the Clubhouse and the few women were kept busy dancing with all the men unless there were female visitors to the camp. A favourite bachelor partner for my mother in the early days was the mine manager, Gil Wallwork, who came out from England the same year that she did. He was a Lancashire man, from Wigan, and he endeared himself to everyone with his gentle good humour. Both Jos and Gladys enjoyed his company and they became firm friends with him, and later his wife, for a lifetime.

It was at one of the club dances that Gladys found a man standing at the bar in a filthy temper. He was the man in charge of providing household equipment for the staff houses and he had just had an encounter with the opportunistic Peachy while they were dancing. She had asked him for more sheets, which were all supplied by the Company. She must have just come back from a trip because everyone knew that she was in the habit of tearing up all her sheets before going on leave so that she would get new ones on her return. "She was the cause of us all having to buy our own," said Gladys. "We have a saying in my native Midlands area that people like her would skin a gnat for its hide!" She was incensed when Peachy tried to beat down the prices of a pitiful few vegetables and fruit grown by a dear old white-haired woman who supported a blind husband in a little clearing up river. "She often arrived in her corial when we were swimming and knew she was welcome in any of our kitchens for a meal, except one!"

Peachy's reputation for meanness and opportunism went with her when she left Mackenzie. In Georgetown, one of my mother's friends would avoid doing her usual Saturday shopping when she knew the lady was in town because she felt that Peachy lay in wait for her, hinting broadly for an invitation to stay at her Estate. On short trips to the capital, like many of the wives on a shopping or dentistry trip, Peachy always stayed at one of the cheap boarding houses run by estimable but impoverished widows. The overnight charge in these places was $1.50 a day and everyone knew that the women who did it were barely making a living out of the operation. For breakfast, the custom was to send up an assortment of fruit to the guests' rooms, from which people could choose what they wanted. Usually, they tactfully left the rest of the fruit for their hostess, whose needs were greater than theirs. Peachy became even more unpopular for packing each day's supply into her basket to take home full at the end of the week. But the final straw to her reputation came after her husband had retired from the company and died in Georgetown. Peachy, before she left the colony, went around Georgetown buttonholing every male she knew, trying to flog her husband's clothes. "Even," one bachelor said, "his false teeth!"

the Doctor's wife, Mrs. Giglioli, with Mrs. Rucker; ca. 1930

cricket field at Cockatara.

Akyma clubhouse, Watooka

party at Mrs. Rucker's house

Cil Wallwork

bachelors' quarters

Minnie Kerr

Cockatara Brownies & Guides

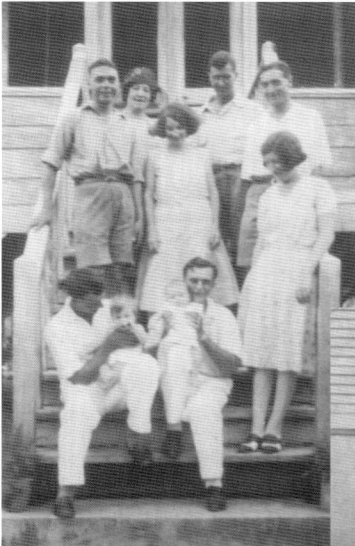

Guide &
Brownie
leaders

Mackenzie Cricket Team
cup presented by Mrs. Rucker.

All Creatures Weird and Dangerous

Under the Mackenzie Clubhouse, my mother found, to her great distress, two beautiful English racing skiffs with outriggers and sliding seats. They had been left propped under the building and allowed to rot away. "They must have cost the earth," she mourned, "and should have been carried upstairs after using." However, they inspired her to find an answer to her boredom.

Having unhappily decided that the racing skiffs under the clubhouse could not be saved, and finding that her fishing off the launch landing was limited, she decided to order a dugout canoe to try her luck further out on the water. "I had to settle for my own corial," she said, "made from the entire half of a tree, tapered at each end and hollowed by burning coals before the seats were installed. I had two paddles, one double and one single. These boats never sank, but as they had only two to three inches of freeboard they could easily tip over if you were careless. Mine arrived still marked by burns and I had to get it registered and numbered and kept it chained to a tree near the stelling. It was easier to fish from the corial by floating with the tide."

I can imagine how anxiously she was watched from the riverbank when she first went out in her new craft. The Demerara, among other South American rivers, is noted for a species of fish that has a reputation as fearsome as that of the shark; in fact, it is often referred to as a freshwater shark. It is the piranha, or cannibal fish, that travels in schools and has the reputation of causing more loss of life to man and beast than any other aquatic monster. Despite their fear of this fish, the early inhabitants of Watooka were convinced that the Mackenzie side of the river was safe for swimming because they believed that the piranha congregated on the Wismar side, attracted to the blood when the East Indian butchers threw their offal into the water. It was, however, one thing to feel that it was safe to swim close to the riverbank in Watooka but another to go out to midstream. Local Guianese said that many swimmers had disappeared further out in the river. There were dark legends not only of piranha in those waters. There were stories of the masacuraman or water tiger, a fearsome fanged creature unknown to biology but said to be seen by some people, that was held responsible for many drownings where the recovered bodies were found to have been savagely mutilated.

Whatever the stories, and she must have heard at least some of them from the servants or on the verandah of the Clubhouse, my mother as usual paid no attention. She certainly had heard the legend of the Fair Maid's Daughter, who lived at the bottom of the river and dragged her victims to their death below, because she mentioned it in a poem. But once her mind was made up, my mother was a very determined woman. Gladys loved to fish, Gladys wanted to fish, and Gladys was going to fish, out in the middle of the current, from her corial, and no one was going to stop her! It was soon made obvious to her that she was surrounded by piranha out in the deep river, but even overturning the corial brought only a mild comment as to her safety. "At first I lost all my hooks to piranha fish (or pirai as we call them), even though the hooks were attached to wire," she said blithely, "but I was told of a dodge that worked. I had to thread a strong gill over the yard of wire down to the shank of the hook and as pirai needed to twist, the quill twisted too so they were foiled." And then she added, with a touch of pride, "I don't recommend hanging on to a tipped over corial for very long because of the pirai, so one should hurry and reverse it, and swish it back and forth to empty it and climb in, not easy."

She was proud of her equipment, sent out from England at her request, that included a split-cane rod, a Greenheart rod (it was ironic that the wood had probably been imported from Guiana), and a stiff-topped sea-rod for the large bony-headed lukanani that took live bait. She also had a landing net and a gaff and line-dryer for the mostly surface fishing. She found that the best time for fishing was at slack tide, the hour between the changing of the tides.

Apart from the lukanani, my mother did not mention the names of the fish that she caught. Most of them were quite good tasting but none were very plentiful so she might be out on the river for a long time alone without bringing anything home for dinner. Some of the local fish could not be hooked in the traditional manner. The Amerindian technique of catching fish with bow and arrow, often celebrated as a cherished symbol of primitive man in Guiana, was shown to zoo-collector Gerald Durrell by Tiny McTurk, the celebrated pioneer-rancher in the Rupununi Savannah area, and carefully described in *Three Singles to Adventure*. "He unhitched a small bow he had been carrying, a frail and useless-looking weapon, and fitted a slender arrow to it. Then he waded out knee-deep in the dark water and stood motionless for a few minutes. Suddenly he raised the bow, the string thrummed, and the arrow plopped into the water about 15 feet away from him and struck there, some five inches of the shaft showing above the surface. Almost instantly, the arrow appeared to take on a life of its own: it twitched and trembled, moving fast through the water in a vertical position, tracing a wavering path. After a minute or so, more and more of the shaft showed above the surface, until the arrow tilted and lay almost flat. On the end of it, the barb and part of the shaft through its back, a large silvery fish was gasping its life away in a web of blood." Durrell marvelled that although he watched McTurk carefully three times, he could never see the fish before it came to the surface. "Years of practice had made his eyesight abnormally keen, and he could see the faint blur beneath the water that indicated a fish's position, work out which way it was travelling, allow for deflection, fire his arrow and hit it, all before you could see any sign of life."

Although Gladys was brave where fishing in the river was concerned, she was far from courageous when it came to snakes and other land dangers. She told the story of Gil Wallwork, the staff man in charge of the mine, who had been trapped upriver by the changing tide: "This business of the river being still tidal, even ten miles further up than Mackenzie, had a strange sequence for a friend. He lived alone at the mine, and one evening decided to go up one of the many creeks, maybe to fish or hunt. Our physical activities were mainly done during the last hour of daylight because it was a bit cooler then, so, as it was getting towards dark, and being a good Scout, he followed the creek water in the direction that he thought would take him back to the river. By the time he was deep in the bush in the wrong direction, he realized that the creek water had backed up with the tide, and it was dark. He spent the night there, being found by his foreman in the morning. My hair would have been white with fright and I'd have been a gibbering idiot. I think he climbed a tree—not many man-eating creatures about except perhaps a herd of peccary, but all those creepy poisonous biting things!"

The snakes were her worst fear. "The snakes were bad ones," she said, "the worst of course being the Bushmaster, an arm-thick, diamond-patterned ten footer, one of the three most poisonous snakes in the world, also fer-de-lance, coral and parrot snakes." According to Durrell, the fer-de-lance is the most venomous snake in South America. The bushmaster is the dreaded Guianese equivalent of the Indian cobra. It is feared more than all the other snakes because it is reputed to lie in wait and strike suddenly at its victims, and the venom takes effect so quickly that a bite from a bushmaster spells certain death. Although it is usually less than ten feet, closer to six or seven feet in length, "A bushmaster was shot under a neighbour's house and it filled a large bucket," my mother said with a shudder.

Gladys saw a lot of snakes during her time in Mackenzie, where they were more often seen than in the forest that surrounded them. Not all were venomous but so many were that they were all feared as a possible danger. She never saw the large anaconda that was on the dock at Wismar just before they arrived. "It was not poisonous, just a constrictor, but still don't fancy being near one and never saw a live one." Many small snakes chose to live under and around the houses. "Once my husband and I went for a walk after dinner with our cat who kept to the ditches, alarmingly, while we carried torches. On our return we were astounded to find a snake-skin hanging on our door. We must have banged the door on a live one, and it escaped by shedding its skin."

Everyone in Mackenzie had a snake story to tell because they were so common. One resident was relaxing on the stelling and about to stretch out when she saw a snake lying there. Without thinking, she flicked it with her hand and brushed it off. One of the men rushed up screaming and killed it ~ it proved to be a laborea, next to the fer-de-lance in deadliness. People riding bicycles at night were careful to raise their legs if the wheels ran over a snake that had been lying on the road where the surface was still warm after dark. Gladys was not above killing snakes herself if she saw one when Jos was not around. "I have killed smaller snakes with a handy flexible branch of bamboo." Later, when there were children in the camp, it was routine to beat the baby pram to scare out sleeping snakes before putting the mattress and baby inside.

Some of the men in Mackenzie were very fond of hunting. Before Gladys arrived, Jos had enjoyed going on trips into the bush to camp and hunt. I remember one of the hunters only as 'Mr. Jack'. He was the man who taught my mother how to fish in the Demerara. Somewhere we have a faded brown photograph of him standing proudly with his prize kill, a huge capybara, or waterhaas as the Dutch colonists christened it. Known to be the world's largest rodent, there is something appealing about this odd, unlovely animal with a rough shaggy coat, but it was a prime hunting target for its meat. At the Oxford expedition camp at Morabelli Creek in 1929, the visiting scientists pronounced that it made an unusually tasty dish, quite like beef in flavour and appearance.

The other enthusiastic hunter was Fitz, the doctor who arrived in Mackenzie just before I was born, a crazy, sports-loving Irishman who at one time brought back a hunting horn and pair of hounds, and proposed breeding them into a pack. What he would have done had he succeeded is beyond imagination, for the image of hounds and horses and men in hunting pink riding off into the jungle is just too much. So it is hard to say that it was sad that his impractical plan did not succeed. The hound pair were isolated for breeding purposes, and at the right time the female duly produced her litter, but something had gone terribly wrong in the process because the puppies were all mixed-breed pi-dogs with vaguely hound-like ears. It was not long before both the original dogs developed bad skin troubles and had to be flown home. Gladys and Jos missed the sound of the hounds braying madly when Fitz blew his horn to summon them.

Fitz and Mr. Jack provided the residents of Watooka with a good number of wild provisions ~ meat, fowl and fish ~ which made a welcome change from an otherwise boring menu. As well as capybara, the Great White Mackenzie hunters brought back carcasses of the red forest deer, which made good venison, a small agouti called accourie that tasted like rabbit, and labba, or paca, that tasted like pork. There was a saying attributed to the colonists of Demerara that 'he who has eaten the flesh of the paca and drunk the water of the forest creeks will return to end his days in the colony'. One is reminded of Evelyn Waugh's sad hero in *A Handful of Dust*, trapped in the rainforest to the end of his days, doubtless eating paca and drinking creek water as well as reading Dickens to his dying gasp. The scientists at Morabelli made the interesting observation that all these animals could swim, which they attributed to the need to do this in the rainy season when the area where they lived could be flooded at any time.

The hunters also brought in wild turkey, sometimes called curassows or powis, which weighed about eight to ten pounds and were much sought after as they made very good eating. Other game birds were considered as tasty as the game birds of Europe, birds like the lesser tinamou, or maam, a small flightless bird that resembled a bob-tailed partridge. Gladys said that apart from their friends' trophies, there was one "rascally Indian who appeared occasionally and sold us a Ma'am ~ a great treat, a small game bird with a lot of breast. This was the same man who was later asked to locate a Harpy Eagle's nest by a bunch of visiting animal collectors from an American zoo. However, he was discovered building one!"

The game birds were welcome as fresh food in Mackenzie because the company did not allow anyone to keep poultry for fear they would awaken the neighbors. My mother felt that this was unjust because the mine people were up and away at 6.00 a.m. and the rest at 7.00 a.m. Someone in the camp once tried to keep a lovely trumpet-bird as a pet, reputed to be a good watchdog, but it was outlawed for the same reason. So the only live hens near the house were those that had been bought to be cooked. I suppose I was about four years old when I followed our cook to a small enclosure kept for this purpose and watched with horror as she wrung a hen by its neck, after which it ran around headless. As if this was not enough for one day, on our way back with the limp chicken body we noticed a small snake, about four feet long, lying along a branch of the hedge that grew next to the house. We woke my father from his afternoon nap and he grabbed a golf club and hit it. The snake coiled rapidly and looked as if it would strike before the second blow killed it. Two deaths in a small person's day made it a memorable one.

Since Mackenzie had been cleared of forest, the inhabitants rarely saw any of the wild animals except for the snakes and frogs. My parents, like everyone else, usually went for their walks along the only road, lined with ditches where frogs bred in abundance, that ran the whole length of the community. One day, however, they ventured onto a trail into the forest instead and suddenly saw a baby jaguar in the clearing ahead. It was fluffy and endearing, like a large kitten, and Gladys, who loved cats in all shapes and sizes and had absolutely no fear of even the largest of them, wanted to stroke it, but Jos restrained her. It was lucky that he did. As they stood quietly watching, the mother jaguar appeared from the shadows beside them. With the slightest sideways movement to show that she knew full well that humans were standing there, she joined her cub and they silently melted into the vegetation, leaving my parents feeling awed and privileged.

If the folks in Watooka did not usually see any wild animals, they certainly heard them. Across the river from the surrounding bush, around the camp at night or sometimes by day, there was a sound like an approaching gale that got louder and louder as it got nearer until it became like the roar of a cheering crowd. This was the sound of the howling monkeys, red-brown long-haired monkeys that resembled baboons, traveling in packs through the forest canopy, the loudest sound in the tropical rainforest. Scientists know that there is a cuplike structure under the chin, containing a sac near the larynx, that makes the noise possible, but no one knows why they do it. Almost anything could set them off ~ a storm, thunder, an intruder ~ and then the earth-shaking choir would start, led by a dominant male, over a treetop territory of six to eight square miles. When our first teacher arrived in Watooka, she heard a noise like a hurricane one Sunday night and found that it was about 150 of them coming down to the river to drink.

The howling monkeys are not the prettiest of monkeys. Their bodies are covered in long chestnut hair with a golden streak down the middle of the back. Their faces are hairless and slope backwards from a projecting muzzle circled by a long conspicuous fringe. They have a distinctly unfriendly look to them, unlike my mother's favourite, the night-monkey, a kind of lemur with very large eyes and soft fur. A more attractive but not really friendly monkey which the hunters often saw around their camps was the sakiwinki or spider monkey, a delicate-looking monkey with a thin, elongated body and very long prehensile tail which made it look like a spider in its web. Sakiwinkis also travel in troops in a noisy bunch, although not as loud as the howlers, chattering to each other in a high-pitched squeaking sound as they keep up an endless search for food in the trees, shaking branches and turning over leaves, checking crevices and picking blossoms and fruit. They are very demonstrative, gesticulating freely, and very agile as they leap from branch to branch and across spaces as far apart as 20 feet or more. They are not noted for being good pets, however, which brings us to another story about the Irish doctor.

For as long as everyone had known him, Fitz had been the bachelor life of the party. He was given to practical jokes, like the time when Mrs. Kerr had had to send her false teeth to the dentist in Georgetown for repair and was hiding in the house until they returned. Knowing she was shy about her toothless appearance, the doctor appeared at their door one evening. Archie opened the door. Fitz said "I've come to pay you a visit." He laughed. When he opened his mouth he showed his bare gums. He had taken out his dentures to keep her company.

All this changed when his English wife decided to come out to the colony to join him. The sudden materialization of a wife came as a shock to everyone. They had always felt there was something mysterious about Fitz, something he wasn't telling them. "We thought he had done something disgraceful at home and been packed off to get him out of the way," said Gladys. "He liked his bottle, maybe it had to do with drinking. Or gambling. It was obvious that he came from a good family and had had a good education ~ presumably he was a younger son or he would have inherited an estate in Ireland ~ but we thought he'd probably got in some trouble with an unsuitable woman or some other kind of scrape. We never dreamed he had a wife!"

'Mrs. Fitz' arrived on the steamer. There was no doubt that she had come to stay. Her trunks and suitcases filled the launch, which had to go back for more. Twenty-three pieces of luggage were finally carried into the doctor's house.

The lady turned out to very grand. A Lady in her own right, but she was far from gracious. Haughtily, she stayed at home and ignored everybody. The change in Fitz was unbelievable. Now instead of partying he went straight home from the hospital. He who had been all smiles and jokes and friendly chatter to everyone now avoided them or spoke hardly at all. Weeks went past and everyone said how miserable and morose Fitz was these days and would that woman ever come out of the house and become a little more friendly. Any polite overtures in her direction had been rudely snubbed so no one went to call on her. Then one day my mother saw Fitz walking down the street carrying a spider monkey.

"Where are you taking that thing?" she asked. Fitz beamed at her. "I'm taking it home," he said proudly. "Home?" said Gladys. "They bite, you know!" Fitz looked at her happily. "I know," he said with a wink. Within a month, her Ladyship and all her luggage were on a ship back to England and Fitz was once again the life of Watooka.

six-foot snake

Jos with cartabac

Mr. Jack with capybara

Fitz with powis

spider monkey

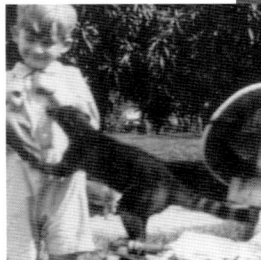
Marco Giglioli with popski

Old Man Falls Expedition

About a year after my mother arrived in Mackenzie, my parents were offered the opportunity of a lifetime. An invitation came from Sprostons, the subsidiary company in Georgetown, to join a party going to Kaieteur Falls in the interior, all expenses paid. It seemed almost too good to be true. The mighty Kaieteur, featured on Guianese postage stamps and in tourist brochures everywhere, was considered to be one of the most beautiful falls in the world, ranking with Niagara Falls in North America and Victoria Falls in Africa, and since this was a trip made by only a few people a year to British Guiana's most interesting destination, the offer was irresistible. Unfortunately for my father, he was not able to get away from work, but my mother jumped at the chance.

At that time, few people ventured into the interior without a special reason. People like the 'pork-knockers' (Afro-Guianese men looking for diamonds or gold) or white prospectors went up the back rivers to seek their fortune, but they were believed to be slightly crazy to do it. Once inland from the coast, there was some ranching activity in the Rupununi highlands, there was the occasional missionary or District Commissioner who would head upriver to work in isolation with the aboriginal peoples, and now and again a handful or so of explorers and adventurers made the difficult journey up the Potaro River to see the falls and came back singing their praises, but they too were felt to be out of the ordinary. Most people in Georgetown thought that Kaieteur was pretty when you got there but it cost a great deal and you might be drowned or get fever if you tried to make the trip. It was not until the days when the pioneer bush pilot, Art Williams, ferried people directly to the falls and back with some frequency that more local people got to see them. Sprostons officials were anxious to promote the trip as a tourist destination, using their hotels and rest houses en route, but the idea somehow never reached its full potential, and my mother was incredibly lucky because it appears that her trip was the last large overland expedition that the company organized.

Gladys met the group at Wismar as they came off the steamer on 28 February. The party at first seemed to consist mostly of women, ten young females and only two men, but they were joined by a District Superintendent and an elderly magistrate, a cook, porters, and guide, all male. The group reassembled at the railway station with their gear, all set to board the waiting carriages for the eighteen-mile ride to Rockstone, on the east bank of the Essequibo River. Gladys had been there once before with Jos and Mr. Jack, the men hunting while she fished in the river, transported there and back on a pump-trolley used by the workers to repair the rails. She thought that her present group took one of the last Wismar-Rockstone return trips on the toylike train. The little wood-burning engine was christened 'Leona' after Mrs. Rucker, to my mother's delight, and all the carriages were equipped with wire gauge windows to keep out the sparks.

On arrival at Rockstone, travellers usually stayed at the rambling Sprostons-built Hotel, with accommodation for about a dozen guests, looking out over the Upper Essequibo River at Gluck Island. Gladys said the old place was on its last legs by then. She was intrigued to find several interesting entries in the guest book, including the name of 'Teddy Roosevelt' who had gone on the same trip some years before. It is not hard to picture the expedition party, like Teddy Roosevelt, relaxing in the old hotel in the same way as another group in the same year. Wrote Graham Cruikshank in *A Trip to Kaieteur Falls, British Guiana*: "There is much worse fare than the familiar beef brought on ice from town, and, as we reclined in a Berbice chair after dinner and watched the smoke curl upwards from a cigarette, we were at peace with ourselves and all the world. From the surrounding swamps, and from the creek near the hotel, we could hear the constant whistling and croaking of frogs, led, fortissimo, by the throaty cronk-cronk of the great tree-frog while a hum and buzz of insects arose from the bush. Before dawn, the light of a lamp moved along the gallery; there was a sharp rat-tat at the door, and a voice said: 'Five o'clock, sir!' A thick mist covered the river and almost hid the heavy forest on Gluck Island. We could hear the distant roaring of the howling monkey. It was damp and chilly, and we were glad to get a cup of fragrant, and hot, coffee by lamplight in the dining room. Before long the mist on the river slowly dispersed, rising from the water like stream from a boiling cauldron of tar. From Gluck Island came the sharply-repeated call of a number of birds ~ hanaqua-hanaqua-hanaqua! Diurnal bush-life was awaking."

An old steel-hulled launch was moored at the river landing by the Rockstone railway station at daylight, ready for the next step of their journey. Gladys said that their conveyance next morning beggared description, being a large, cumbersome, ancient boat, mostly open, reminiscent of C.S. Forester's *African Queen*, rapidly filling up with trip members and gear, as well as sundry other passengers and freight. It is reasonable to assume that it was the same boat that Evelyn Waugh took downstream to Rockstone three years later, owned by an elderly East Indian who made the trip regularly but whose timetable, apparently, depended on the caprice of the bosun. "Him starts when him likes," they said. "De captain very old and him can't see much!" It was powered, from all accounts, by an old Kelvin engine that had to be heated with a blow torch before it would start, and it chugged loudly and belched forth smoke and flames as it headed up the Essequibo toward their next stop.

The Kaieteur group made themselves as comfortable as possible on the cramped deck. One young man made himself comfortable to my mother's alarm. "One male of our party, a blonde Englishman, ensconced himself, clad in shorts, astride the prow, dangling his bare feet in the water. I warned him," said Gladys, "that he would get a bad burn from the sun and reflection, but was ignored, and afterward he had to limp around with bound feet and legs, big help to us!"

The weather was dry and the river level down so that progress up the Upper Essequibo was slow. The route took them through winding channels between high banks of yellow sand, as well as dark granite and greenstone dykes lying in the river, which had to be navigated carefully as the launch chugged its way onwards. Now and again they could see the results of the forest fires of five years earlier. Soon they had their first glimpse of the highlands of Guiana. In the distance to the east they could see Arisaru Mountain, 1 300 feet above the green riverbank. Other than that, there was little to see but the forest walls.

They were soon to be in rapids country. They managed to get up the ones at Kumaka Falls, and reached Crab Falls in the late afternoon, hoping to get over the turbulent water before dark. After several tries, it was decided that the old boat could not make it because of the low water level. There was nothing to do but tie up below the rapids and spend the night on board, with everyone attempting to sleep somehow on the open deck with little room to stretch out. Luckily for them, it did not rain, nor did they have trouble with mosquitoes. But it was still very uncomfortable. "I had a hard bunch of plantains for a pillow,' said Gladys. It was a rough night, but, "Imagine at dawn, our good luck and astonishment to see a few howling monkeys come down to a sand-spit for a drink." Since the howlers were far more often heard than seen, it was a rare treat for the expedition members to see them that morning.

Eventually, after offloading some of the cargo to be fetched later, the boat was able to scale the rapids. Reaching the mouth of the Potaro, they turned up this important tributary of the Essequibo, famous for its gold and diamond workings, and reached the Rest House at Tumatumari, high on a hill top overlooking the river and surrounding country. "Here we bathed, breakfasted and left most of our luggage," said Gladys. From the wide open gallery, they could see the first of the waterfalls that make the Potaro the most picturesque and unnavigable river in Guiana, looking up at a great dyke of greenstone with a rocky treed islet in the middle, on either side of which great masses of water tumbled and foamed down and past them, sounding like the roar of ocean surf.

It was at Tumatamari that Gladys had her first real encounter with the original people of Guiana. The District Superintendent who accompanied them on the trip received an invitation for the whole party to go to a nearby Amerindian village for their Harvest Festival or Piwarri. This was undoubtedly the Patamona village that Matthew French Young had visited earlier, as described in *Guyana: The Lost El Dorado*. The village consisted of four or five large-leafed huts into which were packed men, women, children, dogs, and fowl. The men and boys were naked except for a red sallow cotton cloth tied around their waists and passed between their legs. The women, with bare breasts and buttocks, had only a small bead apron, 18 inches wide by 12 inches deep, worn in front and tied at the waist, and strings of coloured beads around their necks. Traditionally, their upper arms, wrists, and legs below the knee and ankle were bound with strings of coloured beads, said to give their limbs a good shape, and their faces were heavily tattooed, considered their beauty mark. Their babies were carried in a woven shoulder hammock. My mother reacted indignantly when she was told, "don't know if true, that when an Indian woman had a baby, she went alone into the bush and produced it, then placed it into a shallow part of the river-side. If the baby swam, as I was told a healthy infant can before 24 hours old, she fished it out; if not, she left it. Meanwhile, the baby's papa, wailing like a banshee, was tenderly cared for!" She also learned that if a white man got an Indian woman pregnant, the law at that time made him marry and be responsible for her.

In her account of the expedition, Gladys did not mention whether they were offered food in the village, but there would certainly have been a communal clay pot kept hot over the fire and added to as meat or fish was procured, which also contained a mixture of casareep (a black substance similar to molasses in appearance) and fiery red pepper. If Gladys had tasted it, she certainly would have mentioned it because Young had only one mouthful. "Tears ran from my eyes, my nose started to run and I imagined smoke coming out of my ears." Hot red peppers, the hotter the better, have always been eaten in quantity by the inhabitants of tropical America. The other flavouring in the tribal pot, casareep, was made from bitter cassava root, or manioc, the staple food of the rainforest

Indians of South America since pre-European times. The Indians cultivated it by making a clearing in the forest to allow it to grow, moving on to another clearing as soil was depleted. In its natural state, bitter cassava is virulently poisonous, but over time, and with that incredible ability of indigenous peoples to understand and treat poisonous plants, the Amerindians evolved a complicated method of rendering it fit to eat. The root was grated and placed in a long squeezer called a matapee, made of soft pliable basketwork with a handle at each end, and the poisonous liquid was squeezed out. The expressed juice, allowed to settle, deposits a large quantity of starch known as Brazilian arrowroot, or tapioca. The juice becomes edible after being boiled and furnishes the cassareep used in the tribe's cooking pot or made into a sauce. The solid residue, from which they made bread, was baked on a large iron plate, dried, and stored in the roof inside their palm-thatched benabs (open shelters) for further use. Apart from bread, the cakes were used for ceremonial occasions to make an intoxicating beverage known in Guiana as cassiri.

My mother and the rest of the Kaieteur party were given a cooling drink of cassiri in a calabash (gourd). Gladys emptied her calabash and pronounced the unfamiliar drink very good ("it certainly had a kick!") and, feeling no pain, was happy to accept another one. It was only then that the District Superintendent gleefully told them all how it was made. To make cassiri, the old women in the tribe who had lost their teeth used to chew the dried cassava cakes until they had turned into mash. They spat this into a large pot. Water was added and the mixture was left to ferment for three days before it was ready to use. On hearing this, Gladys was left holding a full calabash to dispose of as she felt fit, surrounded by dozens of curious eyes.

They left Tumatamari at noon the next day. There was not much to see in the village, a few ramshackle dwellings and shops licensed to buy gold and sell rum, and a straggling road, buttressed by a low wall of loose stones on the waterside and lined on both sides by flourishing cashew trees, which led to a landing area above the falls where a smaller launch waited for the expedition party. It took them about four hours to reach Potaro Landing. Beyond lay two more falls, Echowra and Pakatuk, which were avoided by taking to a six-mile trail to Kangaruma on top of a Ford truck that carried 17 people, stores and baggage. The road through the damp, green rainforest went up- and downhill on a sandy track that was corduroyed in parts. It is doubtful if they saw much more than a lizard scuttling across the road or a brilliant blue morpho butterfly before it disappeared in the bush, or heard the greenheart bird call 'pi-pi-yo-o', because of the sound of the engine and the laughter and chatter of the group as they bounced along.

Because of their late start, the party probably arrived in Kangaruma after dark. The Rest House was a plain, long, two-storey, wooden building, little more than a shed with windows, which was part store on the ground floor, and part dormitory above. There were no screens on the windows but there were real beds available, which the women in particular were happy to see. Something, however, made them pull up the bedding at the foot of the beds and to their horror they found that the bottom ends of the mattresses were covered with patches of dried blood. En masse, they descended on the owner down in the store and demanded to know what was going on. He was quite unshaken by their assault. Matter-of-factly, he told them that it was only where the vampire bats had bitten people's toes in the night and sucked their blood. Nothing to worry about, he said blithely, the bats usually sealed up the puncture afterwards and this was only where they had been interrupted and this was the after effect.

Needless to say, there was an instant change of plan. "All the Rest Houses were equipped with heavy hooks for visitors to hang their own hammocks," said Gladys, "usually bought from the Aboriginal Indians who made them either from their own cotton, rolled into twine on their hips, or from palm leaves for a lighter, cooler version." The group immediately strung up hammocks and hung mosquito nets over them. They put on thick socks and pillows over their feet. Gladys wrapped her feet in her husband's thick Jaeger dressing-gown as well. She had learned that the trick of sleeping in a hammock was to lie across it, not lengthwise. They all settled down to an uneasy sleep but no one complained the next morning of having been visited by 'Mr. Blair', the bushman's term for the unpleasant bat with an unsavory reputation for drinking animal blood.

The expedition left Kangaruma for the final run on the Potaro in a boat owned by Mickey McTurk. The family was well-known in British Guiana for their contributions to developing the interior. The boat passed Johnson's Island where the McTurks ran a shop that sold supplies to the pork knockers before they set off up the remote creeks to look for diamonds. "Those men slept in hammocks in the bush, with a lantern to scare away the evil spirits and vampire bats. I hope they used their nets," Gladys said, "as there was also a tiny vicious fly called a kaburi whose bite was much worse than that of a Canadian black fly." McTurk bought gold and diamonds from them, and periodically left for Georgetown to sell his purchases and get new supplies, leaving his small blonde wife to hold the store. "She was quite safe " my mother said, "those Pork Knockers were her guardians." The McTurks met the party at the foot of the next falls, bringing their pet toucan that had once swallowed $2000 worth of diamonds and had to be chained until the gems were recovered.

At Amatuk Falls, the group disembarked and walked up to a spot where they had breakfast while the porters busied themselves carrying their gear and supplies topside to another boat. Gladys said they had to bail out the boat for two hours. The scenery was changing. They were coming out of the rainforest blanket and beginning to look upwards. They were now at the foot of the Pakaraima Mountain range which marked the boundary separating British Guiana from Brazil. Beyond Amatuk, they would be entering the foaming gorge that would stretch back to one of the great natural waterfalls of the world. One last smaller falls remained, the Waratuk. The portage around it was about a half mile walk. On this and the later walk up to Kaieteur itself, my mother complained that "the whole trip would have been almost a dead loss to a botanist, unless another Bates, but possibly very rewarding to a rockhound, ornithologist, or zoologist, especially the last, who seem to attract specimens of all kinds." She thought they would have to go much further into the interior to hear, even see, the Red Bell bird with its haunting cry, but "Large macaws, both the red and turquoise ones, flew raucously squawking high overhead, always in pairs, and we saw a few long-billed toucans. No orchids which I always thought grew in great profusion in virgin forest. Someone pointed out a black cat briefly, don't know if it was a jaguar, usually spotted, or a puma, and thankfully, no snakes. There is also a kind of alligator there called a caiman, larger than an alligator but smaller than a crocodile. I scanned the rare sand-spits down the river ~ not one. I was sorry too not to see any trace of a huge fish found in the Essequibo river called an Arapaima, which, believe it or not can weigh up to 300 lbs and has 4" square scales. It can, and has, upset small boats."

Above Waratuk Falls, the river became narrower and deeper, encompassed by flat green mountains hung with clouds and mist. The water ran faster, swirling and foaming. Finally, rounding a bend in the river, they could see far ahead what looked like a white chalk mark running down a steep cliff face. It was Kaieteur, the mighty falls they had come all this way to see. The official discovery of the falls is credited to an Englishman, Charles Barrington Brown, while on a geological survey trip in 1870. The discovery was as impressive as it was unexpected. "I was prepared to meet with great falls on our way down the Upper Potaro," Barrington Brown said, "but nothing so grand and extraordinary a nature as this even entered my mind for a moment." From a tableland 1130 feet above sea level, with the river water 300 yards across the rim at the top of the falls, Kaieteur drops in a spectacular perpendicular column 741 feet straight down into a basin, from which it sweeps over an 81-foot sloping cataract and between great blocks of rock to the gorge beyond, with the effect of a mass of boiling liquid pouring into a huge cauldron that is tipped and overflowing on the far side. The geologist explained that a very hard conglomerate 25 feet thick overlying reddish-grey sandstone of less durability was the cause of this magnificent fall.

The name of the falls comes from two Patamona Indian words ~ Kai (meaning old man) and Tuk (meaning falls, as in Amatuk, fall of the ashen-grey waters). Although the oral history has evolved into heroic stories of an old man's sacrifice to save his people from the warlike Arawaks, an old Patamona Indian version may be closer to the truth. "Long, long ago, there lived in a village an old man (Kai) who was so feeble that he could not pick out the jiggers that constantly infested his feet but put his relatives and friends to the trouble of doing so. They wearied of the old man and determined to get rid of him. So one day they put him in a woodskin [boat made from tree bark], with his few worldly belongings, which he would want in spirit-land, pushed the woodskin out into the river, and left him to drift with the stream over the precipice. So the fall was called Kai-tuk, and is so known by the Patamona to this day." Whatever the true version, the name Kai is still enshrined in the water dropping over the precipice to the terrible gorge below.

There was no close way to reach the falls from the gorge, so the final expedition landing place was at Tukeit, about four miles further down. Here Sprostons had another Rest House, consisting of two rooms furnished with about ten cots, a makeshift kitchen, and a gallery facing the river, where they spent their last night before the climb up to the falls. It was raining when they started up the trail in the morning, moving fairly easily at first up an open slope through the woods and crossing on squared logs over two fast-moving mountain streams before tackling the difficult ascent, which was about a quarter of a mile straight up over smooth boulders and slippery wet tree-roots. When they reached the level grassy area at the top of the escarpment, they found where former travellers, thankful to have made it, had carved the one word, 'Amen!' (For modern climbers, the trail is now referred to as the 'Oh, My God' trail, and the top as 'Thank you, Jesus'!)

It was now a relatively easy walk of about three-quarters of a mile from the area above the escarpment to the Sprostons rest hut near the top of the falls.

Of the climb and walk, Gladys said, "I saw some passion flowers growing on wet rocks when climbing. It was raining, and by the time we had climbed to the top we were soaking wet." She added, "and we girls were herded into Sproston's shack and asked to throw out everything to be dried by a smoky fire. It was the first time I had seen females in the nude. Only two of us were different as we were redheads. My beloved English pigskin walking shoes were so shrivelled, even seared, by the fire, as to make walking from then on difficult but at last we had arrived at the head of the Fall."

The path to the falls from the hut led across a pebble-strewn plateau, scattered with the odd moss or flower. Almost at the edge of the cliff, they could not help seeing a large conspicuous plant with sword-like leaves, the endemic Tank Bromeliad, which is home to the minute, highly poisonous, bright yellow Golden Frog said to have been used by the Potomans for arrow poison. They could hear the falls before they saw them, the great volume of water that had gathered in the flat Upper Potaro to the point where it flowed over the lip of the tableland and down, a long way down, to the rocks in the river below in a great backspray of mist and foam. Every visitor to Kaieteur stands on that same platform and looks down with awe, and the Sprostons party were no exception. They gathered at the lookout point for expedition photographs, they hugged each other for their safe arrival after the long trip, and they looked down and back at the route that they had covered so adventurously, the river small and winding way down below between the flat tops of the Amatuk Range, over the endless cataracts into the distance.

What impressed my mother about the falls was the noise of the falling water and how beautiful they were when the sun made rainbows shining on the spray. She was interested in the seaweed-like vegetative growth in the river, just behind the head of the falls, because it seemed so strange that it could grow there and not be swept away. But most of all she was fascinated by the thousands of white-throated Guiana Swifts that flew in and out of a great dark cave about halfway down behind the cascading water. They would fly backwards and forwards in front of the falls, wings drenched in spray, and then suddenly dive behind the curtain into what one visitor thought was surely one of the dampest, darkest, noisiest, and most protected haunts ever chosen by bird.

After seeing the falls, there was nowhere for the group to go but down, down the slippery climb they had come up, down the river of many rapids to Kangaruma and Tumatamari where they had one last adventure before going home. "Our return down the gorge and river was much easier than the journey and climb up," said Gladys, "as was our uneventful journey down the Potaro to Tumatmari." On the 5th of March, going by land about five miles out of Tumatamari, they spent the night at Tiger Creek at the invitation of a Captain Lamport, an Englishman who ran a gold mine. My mother found him very charming. "We were transported in a Ford lorry to his nice house and entertained royally. We had a three- to four-course dinner, the works, cocktails, wines etc. It appeared that his Amerindian employees could conjure up anything to eat from the bush -- fish by throwing certain berries or lianas into a creek, causing them to surface and be easily netted, or by using bent spring traps -- birds and beasts by imitating their voices, bringing them near enough to shoot." At the dinner table, the conversation, as usual, got around to snakes. Captain Lamport regaled them with his story of one occasion when he went for his shower in an enclosed lattice-work stall standing outside his house, fed from a tank of rainwater on the roof. After divesting himself and showering, he reached for his dressing-gown which had hung outside, put it on, then felt a cold slimy thing twisting round his bare leg. He stood stock still, afraid to move, thinking it was a fer-de-lance snake. Eventually, he cautiously parted his dressing gown to find the thick damp cord of his gown snared around his calf.

Lamport called his gold-dredging operation 'Minnehaha'. The retrieval process consisted of digging up mud and gravel in a stream bed and pouring the excavated material down a sluice and through a series of sieves to separate out the gold dust, nuggets, and also diamonds, found in the residue. There is an expedition photograph of my mother standing in front of the dredger holding what she always believed to be a brick of solid virgin gold. Lamport may have melted down his gold dust and nuggets but it was more normal to seal them in a metal cartridge which could be weighed and shipped for sale. The diamonds in the district were of good quality. They were cleaned with hydrofluoric acid and boiled in aqua regia before they reached the market.

After bathing in Washerwoman Falls on Tiger Creek, the group returned to Tumatamari, where they duly re-embarked on the noisy old scow for Rockstone and the last trip on the train to Wismar. "The only excitement was caused by one clever girl producing real chocolate fudge made in the dark, smoky, Rest

House kitchen!" Their trip had taken nine days. In that time, they had been forced to sleep on an open deck in acute discomfort, lived with the threat of vampire bats and learned to sleep in a hammock, been bumped along rail and trail and rapid water in cramped and crowded conditions, spent hours waiting at portages, climbed a terrible climb and been completely drenched on the way up to the falls, endured sunburn and a host of discomforts - but they had seen Kaieteur and much else to remember. By the time they got to Wismar, my mother said, "we were very scruffy, our clothes were dirty and smelled smoky, and we were sunburnt too, but it was a very worthwhile trip, seeing much more of the interior than by flying there and back in one day as is done now."

The land trip to Kaieteur was still being advertised in 1932. In the *Geographical Journal* that November, the son of the discoverer of Kaieteur Falls said: "The journey to it from Georgetown can now be made in comfort in six days by the same route up the Essequibo and Potaro rivers."

Group on truck to Kangaruma

Kaieteur expedition in front of train

the launch at Crab Falls

Kangaruma

Mr. McTurk's toucan,
who swallowed $2,000
worth of diamonds!

Tumatumari Falls

portage at Waratuk Falls,
had to bail the boat for 2 hours.

group - Kaieteur Falls

Kaieteur Falls

Gladys with gold bar

Indian in charge of rest house, Kaiteur

the party at Washerwoman Falls. Tiger Creek.

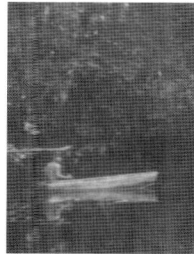

the gorge

A Break from Bauxite

1932 was a banner year for my parents. That was the year that came like Leap Year, once every four years, for which they lived all the long years in between, the year when the Company gave my father four months' leave from work, giving them time to go Home to England.

How they longed to see and be in England again, to see and hug the relatives and old friends, to find themselves again in a land that was familiar and beloved! I do not know what date they left Mackenzie, although rifling through the old albums I found some photographs taken on the outgoing boat they took from Georgetown, the *Ingoma*, and there are the usual shots of people playing shuffleboard or sitting in deckchairs, and one female passenger who huddled in her ready-for-England overcoat as she and Gladys and Jos posed beside a smoke-stack with a friendly officer. There are undated photographs that suggest that the boat called in Trinidad, and Barbados, for there is one of Gladys with her first shipboard friend Iris, obviously no longer a schoolgirl, although some of these could have been on the return trip. In England, there are the photos, much mixed up with the next leave in 1936, of friends and family members, and one of my grandmother standing at the gate of their new house in Chesterton. The name on the gate is 'Watooka'. There are also photographs of a holiday on the Isle of Wight, possibly to see people they had met on the ship. Otherwise, the details of their leave are up for speculation.

I can only imagine that my parents chose to return in Spring, so that my mother could see her beloved wild daffodils and bluebells again, and that April was as treacherously lovely as it always is in England, that May was as seductive, and June and July as close to heaven as the poets sing. And as hard to leave behind again. There is a poignant comment in Philip Gibbs' *England Speaks*, published in 1935, which I am sure came very close to how my parents felt three years earlier, a sentiment echoed by so many colonial wanderers when they came back on leave or forever. It came from a man who had been abroad for years and was home for the first time: "England is still beautiful. I find it so beautiful that I want to shout out or burst into tears. It's a beauty which is like an old song. Having been out of the country for several years I just wallow in it and feel as sentimental as a schoolgirl." He wanted to keep talking about England because he was looking at everything "with fresh eyes and a heart that bled" when he thought that he would have to leave it again.

I know how much my grandparents were longing to see Jos and Gladys again and how much they wanted them to stay. My grandfather no doubt worked hard in the garden before they came to make sure it was in good shape for Gladys' critical appraisal, with a wide grin on his face as he told the man next door when they had their usual get-together over the fence, how grand it was that she was coming home from foreign parts. After they arrived, he stoked up huge coal fires in the grate to keep them warm after the hot tropics and made sure the bed was warm with hot water bottles and their bedclothes warm by the fire before they went upstairs. I can imagine how hard my grandmother worked beforehand to clean and decorate the house, ready for when Gladys came home, only to have my mother look at the results in horror and start immediately to do it all over, if she was to follow true to the form of her later visits. The usual pattern was that my mother would launch herself into an orgy of redecorating and Granny would meekly go along with all the changes ~ and then replace Gladys' dull wallpaper with something more bright and cheerful for her taste as soon as my mother left the country.

My grandmother also looked askance at the strange presents her daughter had brought her from that outlandish place where they lived, which confirmed her opinion that Jos and Gladys were much better off in England where there were things you could understand. A necklace of alligator teeth made by those naked Indians? "They're caiman teeth. The scraped powder from these are supposed to be an anti-venom for snake bite," Gladys explained. Not in her house, thank you. Tanned ocelot skins ~ dirty things! ~ and bits of jewelry made of virgin BG gold ~ they looked like brass! And balata, what was that? "A kind of local rubber," her daughter told her. Now what would she do with ugly things that looked like horrible creepy-crawly lizards and snakes made for the tourists? As soon as my mother left, those things would all go to the nearest taker or out in the rubbish bin. Valuable? Not as far as my grandmother was concerned!

For my parents, back in England, it was home at last, with all the old tensions and pleasures, and the ease of old slippers by the fire. I am sure my mother longed to stay. The Potteries were as black and sooty as ever, but outside lay the lovely fields and woods of her childhood. Very close to her parents' new house was the land that was and is now Wolstanton Golf Course. Years later, when she presented the Club with two oils she had painted from memory, she said that she used to walk to work across the area when it was nothing but fields, and I can imagine that she was not at home very long in 1932 before she went for a walk in that direction. Over the nearby Talke road, she had to go through a stile to follow her old route. "I passed between a field of corn on one side, and roots on the other, then came to a dip in the path to a tiny stream [which probably joined a tributary of the River Lyme] on the left side, deeply wooded further on, where I used to pick both red and white raspberries, alas no bluebells, then it passed beside a hedge which marked the boundary of the golf course ~ it was there even then. The farm near the old clubhouse was adjacent to some quite ancient stone ruins, sequestered among tall old trees. Don't know if they were of any consequence in history, though both Wolstanton and Chesterton date back to Roman times, and Newcastle-under-Lyme is mentioned in the Doomsday Book."

Although he had his doubts, my father also wanted to stay but he was realistic enough to know that he probably would not be able to find a job, given the present state of affairs in Britain. From the one comment my mother made in her BG memoirs, I do know that my father tried without success to find a job in England while they were there. But how and where did he try and how hard? Were there just no jobs in his field or only in places where they did not want to be? Did they want to stay in the Potteries? And how did they find the England that they had magnified and glamourized in their minds while they were far away? Did they really fit in there now that they themselves had changed? We will never know. People are so interesting. We think we know them, and yet how much is guesswork? I can only put pieces of the jigsaw puzzle together and hope they make sense.

One thing is certain. The England that my parents had left was not the England to which they came back. Although things did not seem to be too bad down South, in the North and Middle of England, times had been tough when they left and they were tougher now. The heavy industries of the North were particularly badly hit by the crash in the world economy, which had occurred a few months after my mother had left for South America. Mines, factories, shipyards ~ the lifeblood of the economy ~ were all closed down for lack of business, and there were people out of work everywhere. If they weren't out of work, people were haunted by the fear of possible or inevitable unemployment. In the Potteries, the china factories were holding on but had been cutting back ever since the New York stock market crash of 1929 when they lost their lucrative North American sales, and they had also to face strong competition from countries that were selling cheaply made china at cut-rate prices. Sneer as they might in the Potteries

89

at the poor quality of this foreign ware, it was not a time when buyers could afford to be choosy about good but necessarily higher-priced products.

Things in the countryside were no better. Gibbs said that the year before 1932 was the blackest year of English farming, with either no market or prices so low they lost money on everything. Things were to be not much better for the next few years as prices kept dropping and the home market was flooded with dumped products from Denmark and other countries. One farmer blamed it all on the Empire. "The Empire is our enemy. Those Ottawa agreements were dead against the British farmer. We're swamped by cheap meat and cheap wheat. Look at Argentina meat coming in at cut-rate prices. How can the British farmer pay the wages of labour and make a profit for himself? It can't be done!"

In the South of England, the bankers in the City, the reporters on Fleet Street and even the theatre managers in the West End who had suffered from the lack of American tourists, were relieved that they seemed to have pulled through the Depression without too much difficulty. Strange things had started to happen to improve the job situation down south. Industry had begun to move down from the north, bringing more employment, but it was a new type of industry that was suddenly blooming – light, clean, and relatively trivial. J.B. Priestley in his 1933 *English Journey* noted that the Great West Road looked very odd. Being new, it did not look English. It was more like California with the line of new factories on each side, decorative little buildings, all glass and concrete and chromium plate, producing potato crisps, scents, toothpastes, bathing costumes, and fire extinguishers behind nice painted signs and coloured lights. Products that were fun and cheap instead of solid and good were the hallmark of the times. People who worked in frivolous occupations took themselves very seriously, he said. "It looks as if this age were only frivolous about its values, which are the only things sensible people take seriously." In Southampton, he found that money was being spent freely but not sensibly, as it was going mainly on cheap things. The better shops were not doing very well. They had been struggling since 1930, mainly because they catered to people of means who could not spend as they did before. It was the decaying landed gentry country folk, with their rattling old cars, their draughty country houses, their antique bathrooms and cold tubs, who were the Spartans of the time.

When Jos and Gladys arrived, they could not help but notice, like Priestley, how many other things had changed as they travelled up to Staffordshire. England had been transformed by the motor coach and the picture theatres, each offering plush comfort and a form of seductive escape for all but the very poor. Hairdressers were doing a roaring business since the women had cut their hair short in the latest fashion. It was the new electric age and everyone had or was getting a wireless set as prices came down and quality went up. Villages all over England were being transformed by electric light, and in small and larger towns along the road there were rows of new redbrick little villas in standard new suburban roads, hundreds of them everywhere, all alike. In the South Midlands, Coventry had been changed beyond recognition by factories making motor cars, bicycles, electrical gadgets, machine tools, wireless apparatus, and some planes. In Staffordshire and the rest of the Midlands, there were new neat brick houses for workmen, who drank their beer in gigantic new public houses and took their wives to gigantic new picture theatres. "These pubs are a marked feature of this Midlands landscape," said Priestley. "Some of them are admirably designed and built; others have been inspired by the idea of Merrie England, popular in the neighbourhood of Los Angeles." Huge new Blackpool-style dance halls were to be found everywhere. Even the Potteries had got an enormous new one. If there is one thing of which I feel certain about my parents' visit, it is that my mother, who dearly loved to dance, dragged or tried to drag my protesting father into one of these new dance-halls!

No holiday in England could be complete for my parents without a week in London, which they both loved. It was an easy trip on the train from Stoke to Euston Station. There was something about London that was different from anywhere else in the world, and going up from the grim Potteries was like suddenly walking into Alice's Wonderland. Gibbs quotes a man from Newcastle-on-Tyne who said: "There is a different spirit down south. It's almost gay. One is aware of a general sense of well-being and happiness. Life seems easier and softer." While there, Jos was expected to visit the London office of his company, where he had been hired, and he also had an old army buddy, Albert, whom he was always happy to see. They all went to the theatre together to see J.M. Barrie's ever-popular play, *Peter Pan*. They went to small, old pubs for warm beer, and walked in Hyde Park where my father loved to watch and listen to the impromptu orators on soapboxes surrounded by the heckling crowds. They usually walked everywhere, for they both loved to walk. Gladys spent as much time as her husband would allow to go shopping. Not only was she a born shopper, but she was suffering from typical isolation fever. There is nothing like living in a place with few or no shops to create an insatiable greed when faced with a dazzling array of new and previously unobtainable goods. This time, she knew what to take back with her, what kind of clothes would be suitable, what kind of cloth she could take back that would stand up to the climate which she could sew into dresses that she could wear in Mackenzie and Georgetown.

One of the biggest ordinary joys of being back home was the pleasure of eating fresh English food again. My mother relished going into the greengrocer shop that smelled of apples and plums and pears, the butcher's with the rows of appetizing, pink slabs of meat (minus flies), the fishmonger's with the flat smooth flesh of fish delivered that morning from the North Sea, and raiding my grandfather's garden for luscious strawberries, raspberries and currants. Lettuce that was safe to eat! And bread, real bread, that had taste and body and satisfied the soul. And gardens, full of all her favourite flowers! She went around smelling them all, inhaling the fragrance of the English roses and her absolute favourite wallflowers, and my father stood back and watched her, smiling at her pleasure.

There were so many relatives to see and catch up with, and old friends in Newcastle who all had news to tell them. The time, alas, went much too quickly. All too soon, it was time to leave again, and once again there were the agonizing goodbyes and the long reluctant trip back to Georgetown on the first available passenger freighter. There are no photographs of the return journey unless they are the ones already mentioned. This trip, which probably took a similar route to drop off passengers and cargo in the West Indies, was very different for Gladys from the one she had taken so many innocent months and years ago. She was now one of the experienced colonials who could advise the newcomers what to expect. She had my father with her for support. After dinner, instead of going for tea with a girlfriend, she and Jos were soon deep in a game of bridge for they both liked to play. "At first we only, and had always, played Auction Bridge," my mother said, "then to avoid losing our shirts to the guests of our Managing-Director's house-party members, we both learned Contract from a Culbertson self-teacher." They were both good at it, Gladys with a natural aptitude and Jos with a quick and retentive grasp of numbers. When they played it was serious business because they always played for money, no matter how small the stake. My mother liked only bridge but my father loved all kinds of cards, including solitaire (patience) and poker which he had played a lot in the army, and he loved crossword puzzles and mind benders of all kinds. I was once told that he wrote an essay when he was young on '100 Kinds of Patience' which he sent to an editor somewhere, but nothing seems to have come of it and the text soon disappeared.

Once they arrived in Georgetown, there would be no Tower Hotel for them this time. Instead, they were invited to Ogle Sugar Estate, five miles out of town. Gladys' shipboard friend of 1929, Jim Sutherland, had been made manager the previous year, and with that raise he was able to send to England for the girl he had met in a convalescent hospital when he had been injured in World War I. He had seen her in England on various leaves, and in 1926 he had taken her and her sister to Paris, but there was no hope of marriage for them until his promotion. As soon as he became manager, which ensured him a house and company approval, Ann came out to join him and they were married on her arrival. With their baby, Donald, they welcomed visitors with open arms to their large and gracious house, set in the lovely garden that was Jim's pride and joy.

While my parents very much enjoyed their visits to Ogle, the sight of a baby was difficult for them. For some time, they had been trying to have a child without success. They had secretly hoped that the trip to England, the relaxing sea air, the happy vacation, might make it possible for them to conceive, but so far there were no signs of success. Gladys began a series of visits to doctors in Georgetown which finally ended in a stay in hospital the following year to have her appendix removed and remove a blockage in the uterus or fallopian tubes. In the spring of 1934, they had a secret when they walked together along the ditch-edged road in Watooka.

the Ingoma

Mr. Francis, wireless
operator

Events in the Big House

Times were not good in the British Guiana to which my parents returned from England. The Depression was having a disastrous effect on the two major exports, sugar and bauxite, which did not sell well in those years of economic stringency. As Evelyn Waugh noted on his arrival in Georgetown at the end of 1932, bags of sugar were lying everywhere on the docks, going nowhere. As for Mackenzie bauxite, Duncan Campbell outlined some of the problems the company was facing in the early 1930s. "Demba stumbled its way through the Depression years, barely producing and selling enough bauxite to keep the wheels turning. Its shipments of bauxite went mainly to Alcoa, some for conversion into alumina for Alcan's Quebec smelters, but these needs of course were dropping too. The failure of the dry ore plant at Arvida in 1930 didn't help its bauxite sales either. Demba's total shipments plummeted from a high of 185,000 tonnes in 1929 to under 40,000 tonnes in 1933."

With the dismal shipment and sales figures dancing in his head, my father often did not sleep very well at night. In addition to his professional concern, he worried about what would happen to them personally if the company should have to cut back or fail. He had so recently explored the lack of accounting jobs available in England. As usual, he tried to keep his business problems away from my mother, with the consequence that he suffered from frequent and inexplicable headaches and upset stomach. But everywhere, people were just hanging in and hoping for better days.

In Mackenzie, there were a few changes in the white staff, which was now essentially British in origin. Gil Wallwork, the shy young mine manager from Lancashire of whom my parents were particularly fond, had moved from the mine into bachelor quarters in Watooka, a move welcomed by all. Of the original white community, the Kerrs were still there, but, to the sorrow of Mrs. Kerr and my mother, the Ruckers had returned to the States. Mrs. Rucker's sturdy enthusiasm was sadly missed in their small circle as they struggled on. However, in their place, fresh out from England, were the Hendras, with Mr. Hendra taking over as manager from Mrs. Rucker, and another couple with a young son, Mr. and Mrs. Sharpe and five-year-old Derek, who were welcome additions. The telling of the arrival of the new wives was a story not to be missed in the camp. As recorded by Carolyn Harder in her personal diary, Messrs. Hendra and Sharpe arrived ahead of their wives, who traveled out together on a later vessel. The men went down to Georgetown to meet them and got to the dock expecting to find the ladies leaning over the rails in excitement. Instead, there was no sign of them. It turned out that the boat had got in earlier than scheduled so that, instead of being all dressed up and waiting when they docked, the wives were still in their cabins in their nightgowns. The husbands obtained the respective keys from the purser, and Mr. Hendra opened the first door. He immediately withdrew, saying "There's a strange woman in there." "That must be my wife," said Mr. Sharpe. To the horror of his nightie-clad spouse, he invited Mr. Hendra in to be introduced. Mr. Hendra retreated, tried the next key successfully, and promptly introduced Mr. Sharpe to an embarassed Mrs. Hendra, standing in her cabin in her negligee. Needless to say, this story was oft repeated with great hilarity.

The camp had need of hilarity. Try as they all might to keep everything civilized, it was hard to stay cheerful and pleasant every day in what my mother muttered was a "God-forsaken hole". It was hard enough when things were going well in the mine and at the plant, when freighters were lining up at the dock to take away the bauxite dust that the world was eagerly waiting for, and all the men were smiling. Now, not only did the uncertainties that the men were facing lie over everything like a pall, but for everyone it was the smallness and the sameness that eventually got them down, especially the women who had nothing to look forward to but day after day after day of the same weather, the same people, the same enclosing place. In a word, they were bushed, and in need of a change, any change, that would bring amusement. So it was with particular pleasure that everyone looked forward to the changes in routine and company that came via the Big House.

For no better reason than the fact that it was the biggest house in Mackenzie, in my childhood we always called Watooka House the Big House. It was the huge two-storied house that stood in imposing grounds, with a lily pond, that my mother had seen when she first arrived. It was more like a hotel than a house, with its wide enclosed verandahs with the splendid views of the river, its large downstairs rooms for entertainment, and ample bedroom accommodation for overnight or long-term guests.

The Big House was the official domain of the managing-director of the company when he and his wife periodically visited Mackenzie. Usually, they brought visitors with them, and the resident staff and wives would be invited for dinner or to play contract bridge with the house guests in the evenings. "We met at these gatherings some very interesting 'Visiting Firemen' from abroad," said my mother, "including a Labour MP from England, a famous woman writer supposed to be an intrepid explorer (but she wasn't), and of course Colonial Servants. Some invitations read 'Tails and orders' as though any of our men even if possessed of a tail suit had taken it to a mining camp."

For the period of the visitation, dignity and decorum and best behaviours reigned supreme. Both the Hendersons inspired awe and respect. Mr. Henderson was a tall, frail-looking Englishman who carried himself with the erectness that characterized not only his demeanour but his whole way of life. He was a chartered accountant who had come out from Yorkshire in 1911 and early shown his business talents in the colony. In time, he took over as Demba's managing director from Ralph Hamilton Carr, for whom the river steamer was named. He had been appointed chairman of both Demba and Sprostons Limited the year before Jos went out to Mackenzie and my father had a very high regard for him. Mrs. Henderson was a large and imposing woman who had been born in Georgetown but educated in England and 'finished' on the continent. My mother said she was fluently French-speaking and a wonderful hostess and organizer.

"One of the few big occasions in our camp was the Company dinner, run by the managing director's wife," Gladys said. "Each family was allowed to invite two guests from town. We each cooked a turkey, and lent one of our maids, correct in uniform, also we each sent a bunch of the only roses which bloomed there, a scented hardy cabbage rose." The roses could be sent even if the leaf ants had been down the camp overnight defoliating all the rose plants, leaving just the blossoms, which was a very strange sight. For the dinner, trestle tables were joined all along the verandah, covered with white cloths, flowers at intervals, and all appropriate glasses and cutlery. The menu was long, six or seven courses written in French and served with correct wines, ending with dessert, chocolates and petit fours or a savoury. "At this stage, we ladies left the men to their port and cigars and had our coffee and liqueurs elsewhere. Then, if we could stand up, we danced later. More drinks too. Next morning, after we had all staggered there and fell into the swimming-hole, I think it would have been dangerous to strike a match!"

The big annual 'bash' was held on a Saturday night, the day the steamer came and stayed until Monday, so the town guests had at least a day for recovery. Some, of course, stayed longer. Among these guests in the winter of 1933-1934 were Ann and Jim Sutherland, who came to visit my parents, bringing their little son Donald. Welcome as the Sutherlands were in the Whalley household, it was the visitors who came to the Big House later that year and stayed the longest who were the ones most remembered by everyone. The coming of the Harder family to spend nearly three months in 1934 in Mackenzie was the summer that my mother remembered as being one of her happiest times there. The American-born Harders were gentle and fun-loving and interested in everyone and everything, and the whole family quickly made friends all round. Dr. Harder was already a familiar figure in the camp because he had been to Mackenzie on business many times before, but his charming wife and daughters were with him for the first time. My mother not only found an instant rapport with the senior Harders, but as the youngest wife in Watooka for so long, often disapproved of for her light-hearted behaviour, she delighted in the company of their girls, Carolyn and Jean. Of the two sisters, Jean was the younger and still a child in many ways while Carolyn was a grown-up 15-year-old who reminded my mother of her young friend Iris, so the two had many happy walks and talks together. However, it was to Mrs. Harder that Gladys first confided the secret that she and Jos had been keeping from everyone, the secret that would soon be obvious to everyone: that she was expecting a baby in October.

My father also enjoyed their visit. Apart from the enjoyable social evenings he and my mother shared with the family, he was able to see Dr. Harder at the office during the day, giving him a chance to talk to someone with a wise perspective about the business worries that were never discussed at home. As Secretary of Demba and Alcan's chief geologist, Dr. Harder was a good listener and interesting to listen to. He was a quiet, thoughtful man who had travelled widely, and his views were usually optimistic as well as knowledgeable, which was reassuring. His background in the company was extensive, having played a key role in the secondary bauxite exploration in BG, and been active in the design and building and growth of Mackenzie.

On the female side of the picture, it was simply time for a delightful social whirl. The Harders had no sooner arrived in Mackenzie than they had to prepare for the arrival of the Acting Governor of British Guiana and his wife, Sir and Lady Douglas-Jones, and their 18-year-old daughter, Marguerite, who acted as her mother's secretary. As was to be expected, the whole place was in a state of high excitement and had been for some time. Mrs. Kerr and my mother had been preparing the Brownies for weeks, and the Guides and Scouts were similarly being trained to be smartly on hand. The mine and the plant had been spruced up and readied. The residential areas of Watooka and Cockatara had been mowed and weeded, painted and trimmed. The little bauxite train had been freshly painted, as had the pullman car that, sporting a Union Jack at each end, would carry the official party to and from the dock and the mine. At the Big House, the Harder family had to move bedrooms to accommodate Their Excellencies and were given instructions as to the proper mode of address during their stay.

On the afternoon of Saturday, 23 June, the entire welcoming assembly, suitably dressed for the grand occasion, gathered on the main Mackenzie wharf to await the important arrivals. Carolyn Harder wrote in her diary: "The dock was crowded with Brownies, Girl Guides and Boy Scouts. Also all the staff was there. In the middle of the dock were the newly painted pullman car and the newly painted engine. I felt sorry for the Guides and Brownies who had to stand in position in the glaring sun for the longest time. We had to wait an hour for the arrival of Their Nibs, because the Governor had gotten out at the pineapple canning factory. Finally we heard the welcome whistle from Christianburg. Mrs. Hendra, Mrs. Sharpe, Derek, Jean and I went to sit on some special armchairs provided for us at the end of the dock under a canopy. To the front of us on the left was a long line of Guides and Brownies, and to the right, a line of Boy Scouts. The Guides and Scouts both had flags and looked quite resplendent in spite of the heat. Mother and Daddy stood in front of everyone, waiting to receive our visitors. We could see the Governor, his wife and their daughter at the rail.

"When the boat stopped, they stepped onto the dock and the whistles started blowing ~ the shrill sharp train whistle, accompanied by the factory whistle and the boat whistle, was deafening. After the Governor and his wife and daughter had shaken hands with Mother and Daddy, the Governor inspected the Scouts, and Lady Douglas-Jones the Guides and Brownies. As she walked down the line she talked with Mrs. Whalley and Mrs. Kerr, and now and then said a word to a wide-eyed Brownie. The Governor also stopped now and then to ask a scout how he was, etc. Then they came and shook hands with us and Jean said, 'May I present these flowers?' (as instructed) and gave Lady Douglas-Jones a big basket of flowers."

From all accounts, it was a most successful Royalty-style visit. The official party was taken by rail in the pullman car from the dock to the station. From there, the Douglas-Jones and Harders walked to the Big House for tea and then were transported in relays in the Hendersons' Austin (the only car in Mackenzie) to the plant for inspection. There was doubtless a smile or two at the plant when the second carload arrived, with Carolyn, the daughter of a senior company executive, and Marguerite, the Governor's daughter, gaily riding on the running boards when their turn came around. In the plant, the party looked at the crusher which handled the crude bauxite ore on arrival, followed by the steam washer and dryer, and finally they walked along the high bridge beside the conveyor which carried the fine resultant material to the storage house to await transfer for shipment. After the inspection, they all walked back to the Big House, meeting my mother and Mrs. Kerr on their way home from dispersing the Brownies.

The following day, the party went out to the mine in the pullman car pulled by the little engine. The trip took about an hour through the rainforest. The weather was fine when they arrived at the mine. "Daddy and the Governor went ahead," wrote Carolyn, "Daddy explaining it all to him. Marguerite, Jean and I walked with a young man whom I later learned was the only bachelor on the staff. His name was Mr. Wallwork and he explained to us how the overburden of sand and clay is taken off by a high-powered hose, exposing the bauxite underneath. The overburden can be from a few feet to 35 ft. deep. They discover new bauxite deposits by looking at the pebbles in the creek for bauxite pebbles. We climbed up to a high piece of land and then they blasted a large wall of bauxite for our benefit. There was a deep rumbling sound and then a large side of the mine slowly collapsed." By now the sky was overcast and Lady Douglas-Jones retreated to shelter, not a moment too soon. "Sure enough, we had not gone far when it suddenly started pouring in torrents," said Carolyn. "The Governor lent Mother his rain coat and Marguerite put hers on, but Jean and I had only our umbrellas to protect us, and in these tropical downpours an umbrella only keeps what is above your waist dry. The water slushed in and out of my shoes while my wet dress flapped uncomfortably around my legs. In spite of all that, it was fun. We stood in the rain and watched them blow up a boulder with dynamite. Then we turned back and finally came to the shelter where Lady Douglas-Jones was standing quite dry. I envied her."

On the way back with its damp cargo of passengers, the train stopped briefly at the house of a missionary. Mr. Bavistock was not at home but they were welcomed inside by Mrs. Bavistock and their six-year-old daughter. My mother once looked after this little girl when her mother had blackwater fever. She had found the experience completely exhausting. Little Gwennie may have been tiny but she was incredibly lively, and full of acquisitive curiosity which my mother attributed to the severity and lack of other children in her isolated religious outpost. It was probably just as well that her worthy, plain-living parents did not see their child during the week when she was under my mother's frivolous influence. That week, Gwennie loved nothing better than to trip around the house in my mother's high heels, draped in cascading jewelry and clothes that were sleek and shining and highly unsuitable for a good little Christian missionary.

Back at the Big House, dry and comfortable and changed, there was a big BG breakfast for the official party, followed later in the day by afternoon tea with all the residents of Wismar. Both evenings were spent alone in the privacy of the Big House, with the families relaxing together, playing games, and chatting informally. Carolyn accorded her approval of their imperial visitors. "They impressed me at once as very nice people, just like any other family and not at all cold or dignified as one might expect a Governor's family to be." At their leave-taking ceremony the next day, Jean presented Lady Douglas-Jones with the usual armful of flowers, Derek gave Marguerite a little bouquet, and my mother presented the Governor with a small bunch of violets for his buttonhole. The whistle on the train gave a last ear-splitting salute as the boat sailed slowly down the river.

That afternoon, the Harders met a man carrying an enormous venomous snake, a fer-de-lance about six feet long that had just been caught. It was still alive, and about to be taken to an American who collected snakes and sent them back to zoos. The next evening, they met the friendly American 'snake man' in person. His name was Mr. Pinkus, and his mission in Guiana was to collect not only snakes but also small fish, lizards, tarantulas, and butterfly wings. He was staying with the Canadian minister in Wismar, a Mr. Archer, who collected monkeys, parrots, sloths, bush cows, boars, etc., for pets. The two men called at the Big House to invite the Harders to come and see their collection the following morning. "Mr. Pinkus had the snake which was caught in the Sharpes' yard," Carolyn said. "He had a great big orange-footed tarantula that he caught in Trinidad. It was in the same cage as the lizards, and Mr. Pinkus put his hand right into the same cage to haul out lizards for our inspection! He says that tarantulas are very sluggish and don't charge at you. I have heard that lizards lose their tails from fright but could hardly believe the story. Well, this morning I saw it happen with my own eyes! Mr. Archer took one out and it slipped away from him and he and his tail parted company."

After dinner that night in the Big House, Carolyn was writing a letter to a friend back home, telling her how they really felt they were living in the middle of the jungle, the one that William Beebe had written about when he lived not far away, because they sometimes heard wild monkeys across the river roaring at night and there were snakes too. She was interrupted by a commotion downstairs. Mrs. Harder had been rolling down the awning curtain when, not a foot from her hand, rolled up inside, she found a green, venomous parrot snake. Mr. Kerr and a policeman came and caught it with a lasso. The policeman said he would give it to their friend Mr. Pinkus.

It was in the middle of their stay that the Harders saw their largest snake. "We looked out from the balcony," said Carolyn, "and there, with a rope around his neck held tightly by two gardeners, was the biggest snake I have ever seen. It was a boa constrictor or Land Camoodie, as they are called down here. At first glance it appeared to be dead but it was really very much alive. I dived into my clothes and hurried out. The gardeners had just found it and brought it over to show us. It hadn't been harmed at all, and if the rope were taken from it, it could easily have wrapped itself around someone and crushed the person to death. It certainly was a horrible looking beast. It was about 16 feet long, one of the longest ever found in Mackenzie. Every time anyone came near it, it would let out a long drawn out hiss, which was very loud and threatening and lasted about 15 seconds." When Mr. Pinkus looked at the snake, he was not able to meet the going price per foot as asked by the gardeners. He said that he would have lost money on the deal, because of shipping costs and because the zoo would not pay more than three dollars for it.

The Harders saw quite a bit of the zoo collectors during their stay in Mackenzie. Mr. Archer gave them a pair of plantain birds that the girls christened 'Archie' and 'Pinkie' in their honour. Mr. Pinkus often came over for a meal in the Big House until he moved to Georgetown in July. As it happened, the Harders also had reason to go down to the capital on a brief visit, so in due course they went round to his boarding house to see him. "We were told by the landlady that we would find him out back in the shed with his animals," said Carolyn. "After greeting us heartily, he introduced us to his partner, the famous Mr. Guppy. I was very honoured to meet him, as Guppies (the tiny fish he discovered and which are named after him) are quite the fad at home. He is an old man with white hair. Mr. Pinkus and Mr. Guppy took us around the shed and showed us all the fish they are going to send away, including some with baby fish that disappear like lightning into their mother's mouth when she or they sense any danger. When the danger is past, she spits them out again. We also saw lizards and snakes, but the most entertaining of the animals were the baby toucans. We had them standing out on a box as they cannot fly or get away, and we got sticks and played with them for some time. Their great bills seem to get in their way all the time and they look so comical as they play with each other and bite each other's bills."

Carolyn's diary of that summer carefully recorded all the Harder activities from late June to early September, activities that went into every corner of Mackenzie life. With or without Dr. Harder, who was sometimes away on business, the family went to everything that was going on. Unlike the white British wives, who tended by custom to keep to themselves in Watooka, the outgoing Americans participated in a number of social activities with the black workers in Wismar and Cockatara as well as those in the white staff area, and they enjoyed them all. They went to an Amerindian settlement just outside of Wismar, to concerts and a dance in Cockatara, to teas and breakfasts and dinners in Watooka. They went to the club, played tennis and ping-pong, went swimming and rowing, took rides in the launch, went for walks, and played seemingly hundreds of card or board games nightly or by day. They were kind to Derek and Gwennie, who as only children without playmates were not always easy to get along with, and found amusement with people's dogs, monkeys and parrots. The last included my parents' parrot 'Laura' that loved to sit on my father's shoulder saying, "Left Right, Left Right," while he marched, and was known for shrieking with laughter at the end of a joke's punch-line, just one split second before everyone else burst out laughing. They also read a lot. To everyone, they extended gracious hospitality or enjoyed their return invitations. They were, in fact, the perfect visitors, and it is no wonder that by the time they left my mother was comparing Mrs. Harder favourably with her beloved Mrs. Rucker.

Before they left on 3 September, the Harders hosted an event at the Big House that was of particular interest to the Whalley family. It was Wednesday, 8 August, and Carolyn was out walking with my mother who said confidentially, "I suppose you know about my baby," and Carolyn said yes and asked if she would rather have a boy or a girl. "She said it didn't make any difference to her and that she would give a girl the same opportunities and education as a boy. I thought happily of the surprise she is going to get to-morrow, when all the ladies are going to give her a stork party at our house. She doesn't know anything about it but thinks it is just an ordinary tea party."

The stork party was anything but an ordinary tea party. It had been suggested by no less a person than Mrs. Henderson, the managing director's wife back in Georgetown. "Today is the big day of the surprise stork party for Mrs. Whalley," Carolyn wrote the next day. "After our nap Mrs. Kerr came in to help arrange the tables. Mrs. Kerr said Mrs.Whalley didn't suspect a thing. We couldn't for the life of us think of a place to hide the table on which all the gifts were to be piled. Mrs. Kerr said we couldn't put it in the front after we had finished our tea, because Mrs. Whalley always makes a dash for the cigarettes as soon as she is through eating, so she would get there first. At last the ingenious Mrs. Kerr thought of a plan that near the end of the meal she would ask to be excused. Then she would go and fix up the table with the stork and presents. After this had been decided, we arranged the table. The stork went in the middle. It was a great big stork, about 3 ft. high. It wasn't new, having been left over from a previous stork party. But now it had been painted over and looked elegant. Around the stork we placed the presents, one from everyone in Mackenzie. Then we hid the presents with large round water lily leaves. It looked splendid when completed, with here and there a purple water lily peeping out from the dark green leaves. After arranging it, we put everything in the kitchen. By this time all the maids had been over with their mistresses' respective offerings to the bounty on the table. And such delicious looking things there were! They made my mouth water."

As hoped in all the plans, the stork tea was a great success. Carolyn said it was all delicious "and I could have eaten more if I hadn't been so excited. After a while Mrs. Kerr looked around innocently and in the most serious voice asked to be excused. No one knew what she was really going to do but Mother, Jean and I. It was all I could do to keep from laughing. Mrs. Kerr returned and finally we finished tea and went excitedly out to the porch. Everyone looked at Mrs. Whalley as she walked out talking to Mother. When she saw the table with the stork she gasped and her mouth fell open. The next minute she was all smiles and almost had tears in her eyes she was so touched and happy. She told us how lovely it was of us and that it was a complete surprise to her. Derek stood beside her as she opened the presents and she would ask him what he thought each one contained. When they were all opened she thanked us all again and told us how much the baby will appreciate them. We talked a little while, mostly about the baby, and then we all went for a ride in the launch."

And so ended the summer's big events in the Big House. It was time for the Harders to leave and everyone in Mackenzie was sorry to see them go. It had been a happy summer and it was hard to say goodbye, but at least for my parents there was another happy event to look forward to on the near horizon.

tea with the Hendersons at
the Big House

the Bavistocks and Mrs. Rucker
in front of their Missionary
Church

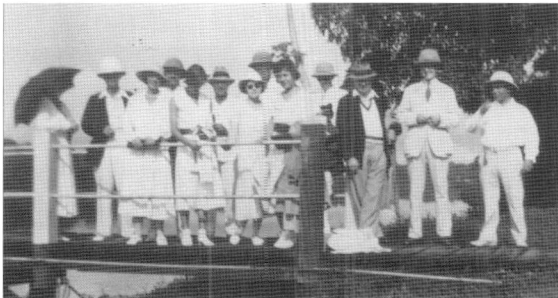

off on a picnic

top - friend, Ann Sutherland and Jos
bottom - Donald Sutherland, Mrs.
Sharpe, Derek in centre, with
Indian children at Kara-Kara Creek.

Mackenzie Office Staff 1934

(fr.row l. to r.) Mr. Hendra
(manager), Mr. Stevenson
Jos Whalley, Gil Wallwork.
(2nd row) Mr. Cruise,
Mr. Kerr, Mr. Sharpe

Harders and Watooka
community, 1934

Governor's visit
the Acting
Governor of
British Guiana
and his wife,
Sir and Lady
Douglas-Jones,
and their 18-year-
old daughter,
Marguerite

Guides lined
up for official
inspection

farewell party

1934 visit by Sir and Lady
Douglas-Jones, and their
18-year-old daughter,
Marguerite

The Coming of the Stork and the Clouds of War

There was a growing crisis in the little Mackenzie hospital by the fall of 1934. They needed a new doctor, and they needed one immediately. There had been a series of doctors since my mother arrived in the community. Several had been Italian, among them Dr. Giglioli, whose attractive French Canadian wife and small sons had been happy company for my mother before they had had to move to the coast so that the doctor could continue his important work in the eradication of malaria in the colony. An older practitioner, a Dr. Francis, had stood in while the Harders were there, but he went back to Georgetown when they left at the end of the summer. Since that time, the staff had been waiting anxiously for a medical replacement, but with no sign of one on the horizon.

By the beginning of September, Gladys was eight months pregnant and everyone in Watooka was getting anxious about the situation. Just when it seemed that the only thing to do was for Jos to take her down to the hospital in Georgetown, a new doctor appeared like a leprechaun out of the mists of Ireland. In the space of hours, the hospital was turned upside down with his rowdy brand of humour, and within days four brown babies had been born, including a set of twins, and everything was ready for the birth of the first white baby in Mackenzie.

I was born on the fifth of October, 1934. My mother always said that it was around four in the afternoon because she heard the whistle of the *R.H. Carr* coming in to dock across the river just as I arrived. It had not been an easy birth because no one had told her to diet and she had put on 40 pounds so the baby was quite heavy. But she was lucky that a new doctor had arrived in time to be there.

After it was all over, my mother fell into a deep, post-delivery sleep. She woke to find the new doctor standing by her bedside with a blanketed little bundle held lovingly in his arms. "Here, my dear," said her attending physician tenderly. "Here is your new baby." Gladys held out her arms eagerly to take her sleeping infant, and he placed the bundle carefully in her lap. Warmly wrapped inside the blanket was a tiny, six-month premature, Amerindian baby, as brown and wizened as a wrinkled prune. She screamed. "Thats not my baby! Take it away! Where's my baby? What have you done with my baby?"

I am truly surprised that she named me Patricia after this Irish scamp, but she was obviously under the spell of the fairies. My other name became Wendy, after that impossible motherly child in that unbelievable J.M. Barrie nightmare which I have always hated. If my grandmother grew up hating insects and snakes, I grew up hating fake, silly pirates, soppy Lost Boys, pouting Tinkerbells and posturing female Peter Pans pretending to be boys forever, but most of all little girls who acted like a mythical Mummy in the nursery and around kitchen stoves. Yet it was obviously the name in vogue in BG that year because when I got to Bishops School for Girls in Georgetown there were six of us called Wendy, all in the same class. The name, according to Andrew Birkin in *J.M. Barrie and the Lost Boys*, came from a corruption of 'My Friendy' which was given to Barrie by the daughter of W.E. Henly, Margaret Henly, who could not pronounce her 'r's'. With a surname like Whalley, the relatives in England all thought that Gladys must be crazy calling the child such an alliterative name. I think my mother had the romantic idea that I would be Wendy when I was little and living in Never Never Land, and Patricia when I grew up into the sophistication that she never had. Of course, it never happened. So much for the Irish.

Apparently I was not a total disappointment to my mother when the right baby was finally produced, even though I did not have her red hair as I was supposed to do, but my father did not make the right noises at all. He appeared at the bedside when she had the correct bundle in her arms and my mother held me up proudly for him to see. "Hmh," he said, and left to play cricket. I had been stupid enough to be born a girl, which disappointed my father greatly.

It was not long before another manufacturing defect was found in this new addition. My mother said anxiously: "There's something wrong with this child's eyes. Look, can you see how one eye is changing colour? They were both blue and now this one seems to be going brown. Do you think she is going blind in that eye?" There was nothing wrong with my eyes as far as seeing. I always said that they ran out of one or other eye colour in heaven so they gave me one of each. But the one-in-ten-thousand gene of different-coloured eyes made me different, which is not a fair start in life.

Looking at the old photographs, I see that my father seems to have relented a little about my not being a boy, judging from the proud smile on his face when we are together. The biggest smile of all is from my lovely black nurse, Maud, who looked after me every day from the time that I was born and became my second mother. So I must have pleased somebody. In all those Brownie box productions, all turned brown and sepia from the tropical heat and damp, I see a loved and loving child, smiling and happy, cleanly dressed and somewhat too well-fed, surrounded by oceans of stuffed toys. It is quite a different image from the one that my mother painted in her later account. Guiltily admitting in her long memoir that there was not very much about me and my younger sister in it, she set out to repair the damage. "Actually," she said, "their life from birth in the camp, until we left there to spend another two years on the Coast with a subsidiary of the company before going to Jamaica, was, by standards for children in temperate climes, rather underprivileged, certainly by mine, who as a child was able to whistle the dog and walk unmolested in woods and fields, alone!" Notice how there are only two words in this long sentence that actually apply to us ~ birth and underprivileged. "Too hot to even skip rope, jump hopscotch, even run about much. Just the daily swim at end of a rope, and a half hour outside in early a.m. and an hour before dark, supervised always by a nurse." There are four more sentences which seem to be talking about her children which she ends by bemoaning the fact that we never had the chapped red cheeks from the cold that she felt all children should have ("English children have such lovely rosy cheeks," she always sighed, looking pityingly and regretfully at our pale white faces, carefully kept out of the burning tropical sun) before she moves on in her narrative to applying rouge to her own cheeks and talking about my father's permanent tan. So I am glad the camera did not lie.

Life in Mackenzie continued much as it had before except that there was this new distraction in the house. My father went off to work each day on his bicycle and my mother had the baby to look after in the early morning and at night. The rest of the time I was Maud's responsibility, so my mother was free to go out in the corial and fish, or visit or play tennis or bridge, or write her letters home in which she no doubt reported that baby smiled burpily and said "mmmm" and "dddd," and crawled and walked and eventually talked, as everyone's brilliant first child usually does. If my subconscious or imagination gets very busy, I can feel myself always in somebody's arms, white or brown, and I can hear voices, the English ones of my parents, my father's laced with humour about something that has amused him, my mother's pitched just right, neither too high nor too low, and Maud's, low and slow and musical, with the Welsh-sounding lilt that is so characteristic of the whole of the British West Indies. Somehow we got through the hot, tropical days and all the wet and dry seasons of 1935. We got through the daily routine of "a half hour outside in early a.m. and an hour before dark, supervised always by a nurse," with the pram beaten soundly for possible sleeping snakes before each sortie, and the hot winter of 1935-36, which I think was when I had malaria and nearly died. "The staff on the whole didn't get much malaria as in some places in BG," my mother said, "thanks to one of our Italian doctors, Dr. Giglioli, who knew a lot about mosquitoes ~ DDT not in use then ~ and waged war on them. My elder child got it and had a malarial convulsion which can leave a child partly paralysed, but a kind coastal friend had briefed me, so I placed a tooth-brush handle between her teeth, yelled for hot water to put in a tin bath, and also for ice to put on her head, meanwhile laying her on the floor with loosened clothing. Her face was black - but gradually the color receded and she recovered."

In her memoirs, my mother claimed: "At first, Wendy the elder child was the only child in Watooka," but in fact this was not quite true because Derek Sharpe is there in all the early photographs, a nice-looking boy holding out his hand to a little girl with curly blonde hair who is rushing towards him with a big smile on her face. Or both of us in an inner tube, floating on the Demerara in the piranha-infested waters, laughing at the trustworthy parent who is taking this photograph. It was obviously a blow to me, as it was to the whole community, when the Sharpes decided to go back to England, because my very first memory is of Derek leaving on the Company launch. It's no more than a quick flashback, but it is as clear as yesterday. I am sitting on a bench on the noisy launch as it heads for the *R.H. Carr* and I am trailing my hand over the side feeling the splashing spray. Derek is lying on the opposite bench with his head on his mother's lap, and I can smell the bay rum that someone has used to put a wet handkerchief across his eyes and forehead. There is no explanation for the scene. I have no idea if he was ill and that was the reason for their departure, or he was just sad at leaving or had a headache. I can imagine that his parents felt that it was time for him to go to school and they were not keen on the colonial method of sending children away to boarding school. Whatever the reason, there is no doubt that I was sad that they were taking my only playmate away forever.

My only other early memory is one that must have had similar import, for in this snapshot in my mind I am standing next to my mother, at a level close to her knees, and we are both looking up at a tall man framed in a seemingly immense archway, the archway between the front verandah and the living room. The faces are anxious and the tone of the discussion is serious, but I cannot hear what they are saying. I never understood why I had this flashback until my mother explained that when I was two my father was seriously ill and she had had to call the doctor. Fortunately for us all, my father survived.

My father's long-anticipated next leave came up in the spring of 1936. My parents could not wait to get on the first boat to England, where my grandparents were anxiously waiting to see their first grandchild. In Georgetown, we boarded the *Costa Rica*, calling at Barbados again on the way north. On the ship, there was no baby cot or crib so I was tucked into a regular sleeping bunk, with planks in the side to make it safer. Unfortunately, as we progressed into the mid-Atlantic, we hit high seas, and I fell out, landing on my face. The captain insisted that my nose was not broken and that it was just a bruise and I would be fine, but by the time we arrived in England the bump had set and there was nothing anybody could do about it. It is never the big things that ruin one's life, it is always the small things, especially the accumulation of small things. A bump on a large English nose really does not sound very tragic in the grand scale of things, and I doubt if it made the slightest difference to a tot once the pain had stopped, but to a later teenager this was one of the Grand Tragedies of my life. Strike two.

But even that did not take away my parents' joy at going home. "Those leaves meant so much to us," my mother said, "arriving home pale and washed-out, our overcoats with holes and eaten by things. Sometimes we had a sweep-stake on board, the winner with the most holes. I used to surreptitiously leave mine in a shop after buying a new one. Then, my second need, a plate of real cream cakes! At home, my mother protested when I wanted nothing to eat but bread and butter ~ real sweet butter and crusty bread."

We arrived in England while the weather was still cool, and went immediately up north on the train to stay with my delighted grandparents. It was love at first sight. If I had stayed with them very long, I would have ended up as naughty as little Gwennie, but my mother was there to make sure that they did not spoil me beyond redemption. I can't remember any of it, but my mother told me of her anxieties. She, of course, was looking after me full-time for the first time since I was born, and this at a time when all my confident new stepping-out was going on. She found that she had to watch me every moment. Far from being free to do as I wanted, as my mother remembered her childhood, I had always to be restrained as there were so many new things for me to learn not to do in this new country. Not to put my hand in steaming water coming from a tap because, unlike Mackenzie, it ran hot. Not to get too close to the top of the stairs leaving the bedroom or I might fall down and hurt myself. Not to touch the roses in the garden, because of the thorns. Not to let go my mother's hand on the street or the cars would run me down. Not to run towards moving cars because I thought they were wonderful and no one had told me they were dangerous. Not to go too near to the fire. I had never seen an open fire so I was fascinated with the one my grandfather kept going in the grate, and I kept leaning nearer and nearer to look at the pictures in the flames. Afraid that I would fall in, my mother eventually felt that she had to put the end of my finger in the flame so that I would learn the painful way that fires were dangerous.

One night shortly after we arrived, it snowed while we slept. In the morning, my father picked me up and held me up at the window to see the beautiful white world outside. Desperate to show off the overnight miracle that had sprinkled some white stuff all on the ground, I raced into my grandparents' bedroom and bounced on their bed. "Granny, Granny, wake up, Granny," I cried excitedly. "Come and look at all the salt!"

There were things for everyone to learn about the differences and dangers in growing-up places. We had not been there very long when my grandfather took me for a walk over the fields. When we got home, my mother asked "Did you have a nice walk?" "Well, yes," he said, but his expression was puzzled. "But why does the child do the Goose Step every time she walks in the grass?" "Ah," my mother said. "She's not allowed to walk in long grass. She's afraid of the snakes."

The goose-step was disturbingly on people's minds that summer in England. Everywhere my parents went, from the Potteries in Staffordshire to the beaches at Rhyl in North Wales and the coves in North Devon, there were snatches of conversation like the ones that Philip Gibbs had heard the previous summer as Germany was rearming under Hitler. "I'm afraid it's beginning all over again," one retired army man said. "Germany has broken the bars of her cage. The tiger is loose again. Is Hitler mad, do you think?" Said a Yorkshire manufacturer: "It looks as though Europe were boiling up for another war. I don't see how we can keep out of it." "Aren't we going to have another fine war for the slaughter of our Youth?" said a doctor. A man in his garden said "I can't help thinking that Hitler is waiting to make trouble. Do you think there's a chance of his being at the back of Mussolini? Well, I wouldn't like to fight the Germans again!"

Mussolini's recent attack on Abyssinia and his brutal treatment of the Ethiopians had split the country into those who believed that England should support the League of Nations, that opposed Italy's actions, or leave well enough alone and stay out of it. Most people kept hoping that it would not come to war, that international justice would prevent the sacrifice. They were mortally afraid that this war would be worse than the last because of aerial bombing and poison gas. It was not an idle fear. As early as 1935, while the government line was one of appeasement and anti-war negotiation, behind the scenes officials were already discussing what to do in the event of air raids if the worst came to the worst and were talking about gas masks for everyone, including small children, to save them from poison gas. Eleven million people signed a door-to-door peace ballot in the hope that the League of Nations could prevent war. Was isolation possible for England and the Empire, leaving Europe to its madness? Some of the arguments resonated with the feelings to be associated with the United Nations over half a century later. "The League of Nations was supposed to be an instrument of peace. I used to think so. Now I'm convinced it's the most dangerous bit of bunk in the world. It would make every war a world war. It would drag us all into every petty dispute. Let them settle it themselves." Only one man was sure that the English people would utterly refuse to be dragged into another war for the sake of Abyssinia or the League of Nations.

Which, as it turned out, was quite true. Encouraged by the lack of support for hapless Ethiopia on the part of England and France, Hitler's armies invaded the Rhineland in March 1936, just before my family arrived in England. In his *Diaries and Letters of 1930-1939*, Harold Nicolson reported the reaction in Parliament: "Great excitement about Hitler's coup. House crowded. Eden makes his statement at 3.40. He reads it with his hands on the box. Very calm. Promises to help if France attacked, otherwise negotiation. General mood of the house is one of fear. Anything to keep out of war." All summer the arguments went on in Parliament and elsewhere about intervention or anti-intervention against Hitler's aggression. At the end of July, just before Parliament took a summer recess, the Spanish Civil War broke out, with the further feeling in England that Europe was going up in smoke. The newspapers were full of it all.

If it is true that an Englishman's home is his castle, then it is equally true that to the Englishman of my father's vintage his daily newspaper was his bible. He would as soon have thought of not reading the paper at breakfast as he would think of not cleaning his teeth or going through the daily ritual of shaving his face with a foaming bristle brush and skin-nicking straight razor. My father read the newspaper from front page to back. Anything that was important to England, whether it was stocks and shares, or war, or Royal gossip, or cricket scores, had to be read and considered in every detail. Ordinary Englishmen everywhere did the same, so no matter how dull and unimportant their jobs or their lives, no matter which side they were on in every presented argument, in one sense they all lived on a daily level of national importance.

On my parents' previous leave, the worry everywhere in England had been unemployment. This leave, it was the fear of war. There were, of course, no jobs for Jos to take. If war broke out, there would be plenty of jobs but at what price. He would be too old to sign up this time. Once they left, back in Mackenzie they would be cut off from everyone they loved that they had had to leave behind. There would be little to no mail in wartime, perhaps not even much in the way of newspapers, and they would be worrying all the time about how the friends and family were faring back at home. Who knew what the next four years would bring before Jos and Gladys could come back? Visits with relatives took on an edge that was shaped by something nameless that nobody wanted to mention. Fortunately, there were few boys in the next generation of the Whalley family of an age to go to war, but one of my father's nephews might be old enough if it dragged on. It did not bear thinking about.

Against the fears and desperate hopes for peace, my parents had nothing to do but make each moment count. With their little girl in tow, they went to see and hug everybody. While the popular new young king, Edward VIII, was beginning to worry court circles with his romance with Wallis Simpson, they walked the beaches and made beautiful magical castles in the sand. While Edward took his scandalous American lady friend on a luxury cruise in the Mediterranean and the English newspapers did everything they could to keep the news from the English people while American papers blazoned it to the world, my parents watched me pick daisies and my mother made them into daisy chains. While the Spanish Civil War broke out, they had a drink in the pub for England and watched a cricket match on a village green. They drank it all in, the little brick houses and the friendly people, the soft skies, the white sands and the cold grey water, the flowers everywhere and the ugly soot, the jerky trains and the green, green fields that were somehow a different green from the green under the tropical sun.

In the end, there was nothing for it but to return to British Guiana and hope that things in England would return to 'normal', that the war clouds would blow over and the economic situation would miraculously turn into a rainbow for the future, but it was not to be a normal time for many years to come. Later that year Edward VIII abdicated so that he could marry 'the woman he loved' and Hitler was eyeing Austria for his next conquest.

October 1934, Mackenzie Hospital

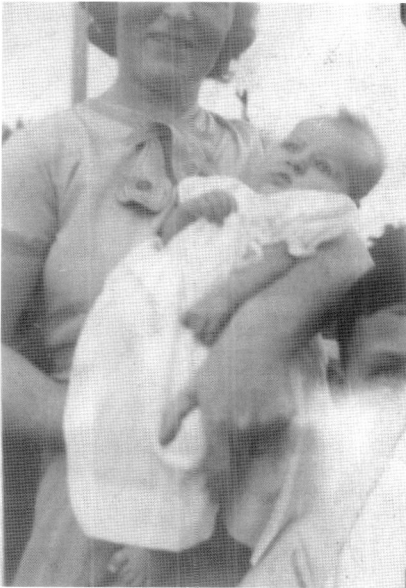

Wendy's christening

Miss Francis, Mrs. Stevenson,
Mrs. Francis, Mrs. Rucker,
and Mrs. Kerr. 1934.

with Maud

second house in Watooka

swimming at the stelling
with Derek

Gladys, Jos, Wendy on the *R.H. Carr*

holiday in England with grandparents.
1936.

the Sharpes leaving Mackenzie
ca. 1936.

Pre-War Changes

Slowly but surely, like the tide that came in over the Georgetown bar and flowed at times almost imperceptibly up the Demerara to the wharf at Cockatara, things began to change in Mackenzie in the years leading up to the war. For one thing, the world demand for bauxite began to recover, which brought a corresponding optimism back to the camp. For another, there were increases and changes in personnel that made all the difference.

New young staff began arriving with their families in 1937, among them Jock and Jessie Thompson and their son Ian from Scotland, who traveled out with the Beedell family. A Chief Engineer on many ships before looking for a shore job to be with his family, New Zealand-born John Beedell's acceptance letter from the bauxite company had arrived in England after he had already left on another voyage. His wife Ethel and their two small children were living in a crowded room full of suitcases when she visited the London office and they asked her if she would be willing to sail out in a few days, ahead of her husband. She said yes. With baby Nina on her lap and small Johnny at her side, she first met the Thompsons on the small boat that took them out to their ocean-going ship. She was amused to hear Jessie Thompson exclaim in horror: "Don't tell me that we're going all the way to South America in this!"

Wedding bells also made for changes in the camp. My parents' old friend and my godfather, Gil Wallwork, who had been a bachelor for so long, married an outgoing lass called Gertrude from his home town in Lancashire. The Clarks were newcomers who also were married in Mackenzie and I was Jeannette Clark's flower girl. Roy and Mary Hose were there before leaving for Malaya; Mary could be guaranteed to liven up any party. These were the last of the essentially British contingent. Jim Wright and Jack Batzold were the first Canadian staff members to come out in the mid-thirties and inject a different lifestyle into the colonial atmosphere, but it was to be 1938 before the real invasion from the Dominion descended on the camp and by 1942 changed it completely.

The big change for me with the new arrivals was that at long last there were other children to play with in Watooka. For about two years after Derek had left, the camp had consisted of all adults, and I was either left on my own to play or taken for walks by my nurse or on visits to other adults' houses with my mother. Fortunately for my parents, I seem to have found it easy to amuse myself. I was not very keen on dolls but I liked soft toys. I loved playing in sand and getting dirty. And I loved ants. Anywhere there were ants, there was something to watch. I loved to watch them under the house, at the base of the pillars, when they brought sand to make a bridge across the tar to be able to get up the columns and into the house. I am sure I often helped the 'fine ants' on their way, which could not have pleased my mother.

The other thing I loved was to 'help' the men who were working around the camp, when they would let me. This was a crew of Afro-Guianese from Cockatara whose job was regular maintenance. If they were working close by, they were kind enough to give this funny little white girl pieces of wood and nails and a hammer so that I could work alongside them. I loved to hear them laugh and joke with each other as they worked. My parents must have allowed me to venture further with them than ever I would be allowed to go alone for I can remember watching them one day when they were cleaning up the vegetation along the riverbank. They found a nest of water rats and thought they were doing me a favour by giving me a tiny sleeping baby. They said I could take the 'mouse' home. The little warm animal, soft and sweet, lay in the palm of my small hand, all curled up, and I could feel its heart thumping regularly as it continued to sleep. I carried it home carefully to show my mother, hoping with every step not to wake it up. She was coming down the outside front stairs, the ones that faced the river, when I got there, and I held up my cupped hand to show her my treasure. "It's a mouse," I said, in an awed whisper, patting its soft long hair. My mother screamed. "That's not a mouse, it's a RAT!" I couldn't wait to get it away from me, out in the long grass, and to this day I cannot hear the word 'rat' without a shudder.

With the arrival of the Thompson family in Mackenzie, at last I had a playmate who was my age. The photographs show Ian, later known as Scotty, as a jug-eared little boy with a wide smile and even more freckles than I had. They show the two of us in billy boots that seem to be huge for our size, with fraying hats and dirty clothes and an assortment of scruffy weapons for whatever game we were playing 'under the house'. Because of the light airy space created by the high columns, and because the space was concreted and relatively clean, under the house was the logical place for Mackenzie children to play outdoors. We could not play in the grass because of the snakes. We could not play in the wood piles because of the snakes. We could go on the road because there were still only two cars, one for the managing director when he came and one for the doctor, but it was hardly conducive for on-the-spot playing, unless we were happily engaged in catching tadpoles in the ditch. I think we liked lizards too but we played with them gently, watching their funny tongues going in and out and their beady eyes looking at us. But what older boy was it who came later who shocked us by making lizards walk a tightrope and then talked about cutting them up and cooking and eating them? I can't remember, unless it was Donald Sutherland the time he came to stay and he broke every stick of furniture in my dollhouse and then we had to spend all the rest of his time making or sticking everything back together with plasticine.

Those were the days when there was a daily trip to the stelling to go swimming. The mothers and children would congregate on the river shore. We could not go swimming on our own because the river was 36 feet deep and even for adults it was considered advisable to go in only when there were other people around. The children who could not swim had to be tied to a rope to prevent being swept downstream by the tide. Most of us learned to swim that way, harnessed to the rope by a canvas strip around our chests, dog-paddling to stay afloat. Little Nina Beedell nearly drowned in that contraption, however. She was so tiny, she slipped out of it and was only just grabbed in time. Even when we could swim, the river could be dangerous because of its depth and fast tidal current. It was here that I also nearly drowned. I was holding a piece of wood on a string and pretending that it was a boat. I crouched on the bottom step of the stelling to play the game of watching as the tide took my boat away until the string stopped it, then I would pull it back and let it go again. At some point, I dropped the string. Leaning out to grab it, I toppled over and fell in. There was no problem about my being able to swim, but that day I was wearing a little cotton dress and those huge billy boots. The boots filled up and apparently I sank like a stone. It was only the sound of the splash and my cry as I fell in that alerted the mothers, sitting just out of sight on the bank, that I was in trouble. Someone managed to dive in and get me to the surface in time. It was lucky that they could even see me in that brown river water. Lucky for me that day, that the 'Fair Maids' of the bottom mud did not get a new victim.

We never seemed to worry about the piranhas, although my mother reported that the adults used to splash the water about a lot in the hopes of frightening them away. We children had another confident and improbable belief. I remember that we told each other solemnly that we wouldn't feel it if we were bitten because a pirai's teeth were so sharp it would be a really clean cut. We never seemed to take it to a logical conclusion about the pain that would follow the clean cut.

We had some weird ideas about the snakes too. In our camp, we didn't play Cowboys and Indians, we played Snakes and Alligators. "If a snake chases you," we told each other knowledgeably, "you run straight, because the snake has to run crooked." This meant a practical demonstration, with one child running straight, pretending to be very frightened, and another running ominously behind, weaving all over the road. "But if an alligator chases you," we said darkly, "you run crooked, because when the alligator tries to run crooked it breaks its back." Fortunately for us, none of us was ever chased by a snake or an alligator to put our theories to an unexpected and unhappy conclusion.

One of my strangest memories of Mackenzie, connected with alligators, was when my mother took me with her to someone's house one night after supper. I have no idea why she took me, for this was very unusual in itself, or whose house it was. I only know that I was quite small and I sat on the floor with a colouring book while my mother and this woman sat in rattan chairs sipping tea. It was special for me to be out because I was never away from home after dark. Yet there we sat, with the soft voices of the chatting women and the teacups clinking in the saucers above me, while outside the beetles and moths were slamming themselves against the screened windows, and the tree frogs were barking, and all the other scary noises of the rainforest were coming in through the night air. There was something surreal about the scene, because this lady had bought lamps from a man who went upriver and brought back small alligators that he stuffed and made into light fixtures. Everywhere in that room, all around us, there were these stuffed alligators, reclining or standing or sitting, with a bare light bulb shining eerily out of each open jaw, as we sat serenely among them on that dark jungle night.

I think Evelyn Waugh met the same alligator salesman, whom my mother sent packing with a shudder whenever he came to the door in Mackenzie. No alligator lamps for her! Waugh said that he met an agreeable character in Georgetown called 'Professor' Piles who lived by selling stuffed alligators. He had a peculiar fascination over them and over snakes, and loved both species dearly. He used to go out to the creeks and call them. Although it went greatly against his sentiments to kill them, he had to live, he said. The 'Professor' told him a story which I think is an example of the kind of stories my nurse used to tell me, told with a believing heart in every impossible detail, which gave me nightmares that my mother could not understand. "Once," said Waugh, and he might just as well have said "Once upon a time," the 'Professor' had been put in prison at

Mazaruni, "and had secured release by the simple expedient of summoning every snake in the neighbourhood. Every morning when the warders came to his cell they found it full of assembled reptiles. They would accompany him at recreation and at work to the great detriment of good order and discipline, so that eventually the Governor was obliged to order his release." I can just see the white teeth flashing every time the 'Professor' laughed, eyes rolling with delight and slapping his thighs at his own cleverness as he happily told the author this bedtime fairy tale, so typical of the rich Guianese folklore that seemed to come directly from the heart of Africa.

The story that really got to us children in Mackenzie, which we must have heard from the servants because we certainly would not have heard it from our parents, was the one in the Georgetown newspaper that purported to be absolutely true because the newspaper never lied. It was about a three-year-old black girl who went missing from her village. She and her brother were dressed and ready for church, so their mother told the boy to look after his sister while she got ready. Somehow, the little girl wandered off. She was wearing a bright red dress with bright red shoes and a big red bow in her hair so she should have been easy to spot, but the whole village scoured the area for her without finding her. She seemed to have vanished without a trace. Then, two days later, some hunters came across a huge camoodie leaning against a tree by the river, bloated from a large feed. They killed it and cut it open. Inside were the undigested red shoes.

Strange that my mother thought we children had a boring childhood. It was only her life that was boring, for we children lived in another world, halfway between white and black, always the sheltered missy or young master of our too well brought-up white side, but never totally shielded from the wholeness of the other on the darker side. We never went into Cockatara. We never met black children our age. But the nurses who walked us and talked to us and rocked us to sleep in their warm brown arms did not live in the same world as our parents. They lived in a real world down the road, where people laughed out loud and danced and sang and yelled and screamed and slapped. When they met each other in the road, they talked to each other about every "blessed ting dat was new" and there were no holds barred for big ears not to hear. Of course, it was often puzzling ~ but what was "dis bad ting dat dat man did to dat woman ~ he na love she na?" ~ but what it did for us, or for those of us who were sensitive and aware, was that it brought us music and rhythm and mystery and romance on a deeper level than on the thin civilized ice on which our parents skated.

But at their level, life in Mackenzie went on. My mother was delighted with the company of the new young wives, bringing fresh ideas and more activities to share during the day. When the husbands came home from work, there were new partners for bridge in the evenings, and the parties at the clubhouse were much more fun. The company built a six-hole golf course for the community and my parents learned to play golf and took to the game immediately. Players had to be careful about retrieving their balls from the long grass at the side of the fairway because of the danger of snakes. She and Jessie Thompson had actually reached a green one day when their arrival suddenly woke a sleeping snake. "She did a sort of dance and I thought she had holed out," Gladys said, "but she had been bitten by a smallish snake, probably a fer-de-lance." My mother beat the reptile off with a golf club, then, following the usual procedure after a snake bite, ripped her skirt to make a tight tourniquet around her friend's leg and sucked the poison out of the wound. I remember Mrs. Thompson as a petite woman, which was lucky because there was no one else on the course and my mother was able to pick her up and carry her back to the clubhouse.

The noise of coming war got louder overseas, and war meant good times for bauxite because even the talk meant thinking of aluminum for future planes. At Alcan's head office in Montreal, the decision was made to increase staff in the Mackenzie operation and be ready to speed up production if and as needed. There would be no search for new staff in Britain this time round. "As soon as business began to pick up," my mother said, "the new staff was enlarged solely by Canadians, including a new Canadian Plant Manager and family, Leslie and Kay Parsons and their children, Jimmy and Barbara. Many of these were young college graduates, often just married, who both came together, also went on leave oftener than we, perhaps because it wasn't such a long and expensive trip." Some of the couples didn't like it and had their fares paid back home, which was galling to the Brits who had had to pay their own fares if they left before one year's service. "The Canadians soon made short work of those beds!" Gladys said. "Spring-filled mattresses yet, and happily for all, fridges. One lady moaned 'What, no lid on the toilet?' No electric stoves though!"

The best of these arrivals for me was the Bradley family. Jill was the same age as the older Barbara Parsons but Jackie was my age so now I had a girl to play with as well as Ian. Of course that meant a threesome, which does not always work, so sometimes it was Jackie and I, and sometimes it was Ian and I, and sometimes it was Jackie and Ian, with the third one left out making disconsolate circles in the dust with a restless shoe. Jackie and I often played with dolls because I seem to remember that she had a lot of them, but I only once played dolls with Ian. I had been sent a beautiful new one for my birthday, and for a change I actually enjoyed playing with it. It was Ian's turn to play with me and he liked the doll so much he asked if he could take it home. I said he could, and he carried it gently over to his house, hugging it happily, but his joy did not last very long. There was hell to pay when his Scottish father came home from work and found his wee lad playing wi' a dolly yet! "I'll not have any son o' mine playing wi' dolls!", Mr. Thompson roared. He took my beautiful doll under his house and smashed it to smithereens, and his son was forbidden to play with girls until he came to his senses. No one seemed to think it necessary to tell me they were sorry.

My favourite indoor activity was playing with my dollhouse. I or we could play with it for hours. We could play with it from any point of view, male or female. Ian could move the furniture around like a man, and listen to the radio, and be father to everyone in the miniature family. Jackie could pretend she was in the kitchen, or laying the table for supper, or all the other housewifely things she had learned from her mother that I had no interest in at all, but together, we moved small dollhouse people around as bossily as our parents, making them do our bidding and putting them to bed if they disobeyed. Happily, the dollhouse was not a completely furnished one, down to every adult detail, so it left a great deal to the imagination. I remember what I liked to do best was to make furniture out of plasticine, with immense pride in the less-than-perfect results.

I learned to knit by making a carpet for my dollhouse. At some point, my mother must have taken me with her to Georgetown, for it was on the way back on the steamer that I had my first knitting lesson. "We were allowed," my mother said, "my husband more rarely, to go to Georgetown on local leave, well worth the steamer trip each way to feel the cool trade wind on the coast. The pleasure of going into real shops! Though hardly any stocked dresses, the dressmakers there were so clever, and could copy a picture of one without a pattern, so, to the dressmakers I went, even though I did make some, and movies, black and white, the dentist, visit friends, and generally mess about freely without everyone knowing where you were, with whom, and what you did at all times." This may have been the trip when she took me to the hairdresser for a perm. She always regretted that I lost the golden curls I had when I was little, which soon turned into the straight dark hair that I had acquired from the Whalley side of the family. I can still remember that perm. I can remember the weight of the curlers and the heat that came from the huge electric beast to which I was attached. Above all I can remember the horrible smell of ammonia needed to set the curl. When they showed me the results in the mirror, I hated it but my mother beamed from ear to ear. I suppose I was lucky that they did not also mimic her auburn tresses. Instead she took me to my first movie, which was "I Married an Angel" with a red-haired heroine, played by Jeanette MacDonald.

On the steamer coming back, we sat in the little upper cabin above the open deck, and I wriggled uncomfortably on the leather seats that smelled of carbolic soap and got hot and sticky in the heat. It was a long day for a child but it was made memorable by the lady who shared the cabin with us that day. I remember that she was very elegant and she was knitting something long and interesting. It was Mrs. Charlie Rosa, the new doctor's wife, who sat serenely in the corner with a big grey cat purring beside her. She had extra needles and wool in her bag and she graciously taught me how to cast on a few stitches and wind the wool around and pull it through, a huge effort on my part that required frowning and grinding my teeth and making funny movements with my mouth and eyes. I knitted painfully all day ~ knit one, drop one ~ go back and pick up one, knit one ~ and by the time we arrived at Wismar I proudly had a tatty, bumpy square of wool about three inches wide and long to go on the dollhouse living-room floor.

One of the happiest results of having all these children in Mackenzie meant parties, for every birthday was celebrated with a party that every child attended. The person who was in her element about all this was Mrs. Kerr. As the oldest lady, she became like the grandmother that none of us had, for all of us had grandmothers only on the other side of the world. It was her self-appointed job to make the birthday cakes. She always made fruit cakes, several at a time, and she kept them in a cupboard closed securely against the cockroaches. Just to be sure, she added something to the cupboard to keep the cakes from being eaten. The special cake would arrive at the current party, duly iced, with candles for the birthday child to blow out with great puffs, sometimes with everyone joining in, making a wish for whatever was not already spread about the room in a lavish display of opened presents. Then the cake would be sliced into small pieces for every child to eat. The slices were not always eaten. There was always something that smelled and tasted a bit funny about Mrs. Kerr's cakes, although we did not know what it was at the time. Finally, when we moved to Georgetown when I was seven, I found that not all birthday cakes had to taste and smell of mothballs.

Gil & Gertrude Wallwork's wedding

Gil Wallwork,
Jimmy Wright

six-hole golf course

Wendy & Ian
with Gladys

Christmas Party, 1937
standing - Jimmy Wright, Gil Wallwork, Gladys & Jos Whalley, Jock Thompson.
sitting - Martha Wright, Jessie Thompson, Gertrude Wallwork, John & Ethel Beedell, Mary Hose.
children - Wendy, Ian, John, Nina, David.

A Teacher, a Bachelor, and a Romance

With the arrival of all the Canadians with their children, the need arose for a school in Watooka. Our first teacher, hired by Alcan in Montreal, was Jean Melville Tudhope from a small town in Ontario. She arrived in November, 1938, having come out from Canada on the *Lady Hawkins*, one of the CNR Lady Boats that made regular stops in Georgetown. She enjoyed her trip out, but, like my mother before her, nothing really prepared her for what she found on arrival. "It's hard to write now," she said in a letter to her sister on her last night on board, "surrounded as I am by smells, the smell of heat, the smell of the tropics, that peculiar something that pervades the atmosphere, the closer you are to the equator. It hits me full in the face, and finishes me temporarily for coherent thinking, writing ~ mayhap living." When they docked in Georgetown, she said "This place is weird, all horses, British West Indies, and markets. It smells too, of course, but the relief of being here overrides all that." She found the trip up the Demerara River rather an ordeal, travelling from 8.00 a.m. to 4.30 p.m. in the small cabin on the *R.H. Carr* with "the few whites sitting around like a Missionary Society meeting," but she thought the river was lovely, "very wide and the banks lined with jungle foliage. It looked all green and luscious ~ like lettuce, lovely, lovely lettuce."

Like my mother, her first impression of Watooka was quite favourable. She thought it was picturesque and charming with its one wide paved road. "On either side are the houses (numbering about 20), a clubhouse, and the hospital. The clubhouse is like one of our own golf clubs which adds grace and dignity to Mackenzie. Everyone has been most kind, firmly gay, in fact! The gang seems to pull together pretty well."

Until her new schoolroom was ready, the new teacher had a class consisting of the three oldest children in the camp, aged ten or over ~ Jimmy and Barbara Parsons, the son and daughter of the new Canadian manager, and Jill Bradley, whose father had also recently arrived as part of the Canadian contingent. Before long, she was also teaching Johnny Beedell, who was younger than the first three but older than four-year-old Jackie Bradley, Ian Thompson, and myself, who started soon afterwards in kindergarten. Of all of the children, Jimmy was the oldest and biggest of her charges and presented the greatest challenge. "A giant battle of wills is in progress," she wrote to her sister back at home in her first month of teaching, "one determined 12-year-old versus one sad, tired spinster. Much depends on the outcome so keep your fingers crossed. The other afternoon we (he and I) sat in silence from 3.30 to 5.30 until he finally gave in and wrote his punishment out, and I sat coldly, and gave no word of comfort. Result, at the moment I am ace high, on call all the time to see the new airplane etc., etc."

Jean Tudhope was quickly considered a great addition to the Mackenzie community. She was young, intelligent and attractive, she played bridge, she swam and danced, and she was fun to be with. Until her house, with one room to be used for the school, was ready for occupancy, she stayed with Archie and Minnie Kerr. She loved to listen to the conversations in the Kerrs' house and at the Club, with the infectious, rising sing-song Guianese lilt and the sentences that lacked an object. "Madam," she heard the Kerrs' maid Jordan say in one typical exchange, "Can you send fruit to Mrs. Thompson?" Mrs. Kerr, raising her voice to answering BG pitch, replied "No, I haven't got and can't send." Jordan tried again. "She says she hasn't got and she must have, missus," at which Mrs. Kerr weakened and gave her the fruit, saying "How can I give what I haven't got? Take, girl, and give!"

On her first Sunday, she and Mrs. Kerr went to the Presbyterian Church in Cockatara which the Thompsons also attended and where she would later teach Sunday School. There were only three pastel-clad whites present, in stark contrast to the rest of the congregation, brightly dressed in purple and scarlet. The Guianian minister prayed fervently for the Prince of Wales. She found that Mackenzie inhabitants were well-informed on international affairs and the disturbing news from overseas came up at every dinner and bridge game.

She was not long in Mackenzie before she saw her first snake. "There has been heavy rain and the snake was on the road. All snakes slither away from you except the Bushmaster, which is only in the jungle, of course. The only danger is that of stepping on one or riding over one on a bike, in which case the snake will strike." A week later she saw two more snakes, and the Manager's wife found a green parrot snake in her kitchen. "It had come in with the firewood. They are very dangerous. That is what scares me, the idea of my new house, all alone. Dear, dear, I expect to be in by Christmas. Coming home from a dance at the club the other night, Matt yelled 'Freeze' and lo ~ my huge foot was almost on a snake. He killed it and showed us its head. A spade-shaped head ... means danger. We examined its mouth, all very interesting." She had already heard the howling monkeys on her first Sunday, and on another of her early nights she thought she heard a baby crying, only to find the next morning that it was most likely a puma. Matt and Betty Waite were new arrivals in the camp and she and Betty quickly became the best of friends. "We ventured along the lorry road towards the jungle to-day, but our dreams of adventure were dissipated as beautiful, big, bright blue butterflies, and ants' nests on the trees were the sum total of our observations."

When it came time to get some things for her new house, Miss Tudhope took the river steamer back to Georgetown to go shopping. She bought several dress materials, a bicycle, electrical appliances, pots and pans, etc. while staying at a private hotel for "two dollars a day which included coffee at 7 a.m., breakfast at 11 a.m., tea at 4 p.m., and dinner at 8. And," she added, "inside the mosquito netting on my bed were 1001 mosquitoes, 1401 red ants, which bite like sin, and 4 large well-fed cockroaches. So I had three jolly nights. Added to that, the man next door snored and I mean snored. I woke up at 2 a.m. and before God, I thought there was a puma beside me."

When she got back to Mackenzie, the whole camp came down to meet the launch. "They all said how much they missed me, which made me purr of course. I now feel I will stay for a while." Although she hadn't moved in yet, her house was coming along. "My furniture is being moved into my house. It is done in cream and brown throughout with bathroom in white." She was also seeing and learning more of the wildlife in the camp but, like my mother in her early days, she was frustrated by the lack of information available. "You would love the birds here, I have never seen such colouring. But no one knows their names or species." Only one bird, the Kiskadee, actually told her its name, a bright yellow bird that she kept seeing around the camp, as big as a robin, that called "Qu'est ce qui dit" loudly all day long.

As Christmas drew nearer, she helped to decorate the tropical tree that had to make do as a Christmas tree at the Club, and made stars for the more familiar though tiny tree that fellow Canadian Betty Waite had brought with her which she was putting up at home. "Grimly she is leading it with lights, and firmly she has hung up a wreath and she dares anyone to make fun of it," she said. She decided to have a party for all the children in the camp, all 12 of them, which was a howling success, "though why dear teacher wasn't borne off on a stretcher, I'd never know. After Christmas, I am to have a kindergarten of three on Saturday morning." She was very homesick on Christmas Eve. "Christmas Eve was bad. Everyone walked up and down singing carols. So at midnight, I rose and joined the crowd. I entered right into the spirit of things and finished off the evening by wheeling the chief engineer (Canadian Jack Batzold) in a wheelbarrow. So now I think I will be on a boatie of sorts by New Year's."

As the only unmarried woman in Watooka, she now had a new problem on her hands. "Last Thursday, I noticed coy looks being directed at me, a bachelor has joined the ranks. I am a patient woman but I can't stand this!" The bachelor was Paul Fenton, a small dynamo of a man originally from Saint John, New Brunswick, who had been hired as personnel manager. "One of the most demanding jobs in Mackenzie," said Duncan Campbell, "fell under the title of personnel manager, which included most of the usual functions plus a score of other things, including construction and supervision of staff housing, running the bachelors' quarters, hospital, police, security, schooling, the company 'ration' or grocery store, recreation, to mention the main ones. For this relentless job Parsons found his candidate in Paul Fenton, who had arrived from Arvida in 1938 after working many years in construction, mainly on the Saguenay power projects. Fenton's first job was to rebuild and strengthen the old bridges on the bauxite railway, but he found many other bridges to build and mend in his new role. Most of the difficult staff problems, including housewives unhappy with housing or food supplies, fell on his shoulders." Later, Miss Tudhope was to describe him as "awfully nice, very good and an ardent Imperialist" but at the time his presence was just an embarassment.

Moving Day came just after Christmas. "I move to-morrow and there's to be no school for a couple of days, which is as well as, at the moment, the sight of a child is distasteful to me." On 30 December, she wrote: "The moving? Let us pass over that as lightly as possible. It has left a deep, jagged sear on the mind. Suffice it to say, I am now one of the landed gentry. Remember that bachelor? Well, this business is going to go too far. It's the damnedest nonsense, and believe me, I'm going to nip it in the bud soon, or go nuts. He is actually not bad, good sense of humour, but no one is going to be *arch* about him to *me*."

By 3 January 1939, Miss Tudhope was still finding life challenging in her new home, inundated as it was with workmen and children and one unhelpful maid. "Nemesis has certainly overtaken me in a big way. Here am I, surrounded by children, all of whom, thank God, have not the overwhelming energy of Jim. My impression at the moment is that my lovely new house is bulging with children ~ dear children. I have a staff of one…. At breakfast on her first day she appeared with a potato ricer and said to me, 'Ah mistress, must I squeeze oranges with this?' I have to remember to do no work. She is one of the belles hereabouts so I have little trouble getting any job done by any carpenter. I have just written my order for food. It takes a long time to become accustomed here to the things one can order and get. There is a vegetable of which I am very fond ~ ochroes. In fact it is a standing joke among the natives; they bring me huge baskets of them. Right now they are killing a chicken under the house. Cute. The 'chickens' are all three-year-olds who have been fighting for their lives since they were hatched. They have spurs two inches long and are about as succulent as shoe leather." School no sooner started the next day when two ladies came in to watch, followed by three electricians who immediately started hammering, and finally Gwen Bavistock, the missionary's daughter, now ten years old, appeared when the train from the mine returned from its first morning run.

January passed quickly for the new teacher in her busy surroundings. Notably, the new bachelor began to squire her to various community events and she no longer seemed to be protesting about it in her letters. Plans were being made for a masquerade party for them all in February. "Here I sit," she said, "when I should be writing for household goods, and sewing on a masquerade costume. I have aged 50 years and am going as a plain, black aged Granny." She still struggled with the workmen in her new home. "The house is full of carpenters all adept at standing around looking busy, but never getting anywhere. *Hurry* is a word with which our BG negroes are not acquainted. It took eight carpenters to put up my blackboard." She loved their sense of humour, and their unusual use of words, relishing the time she put her hand on some wet paint and a workman came over with a rag, saying "Ah, school teacher, let me cleanse you."

In school, she now had nine students, all different ages, and she was enjoying them. "The children are really fun. We are moving along at a good clip. Tonight I shall spend going over a few Bible stories. Jim is a demon for facts. He knows all the names of Abraham's children and is given to asking 'Miss Tudhope, where did all these people live?' I reply vaguely and smile sweetly and change the subject. Later, he appears with a Bible map. I take a deep breath, cross my fingers and fortunately find the right place... Today, with a great shock, I realized that I like the school hours best of all. Also, I believe I prefer Jim, the terror, to all the children. He is a hound for information, and keeps me on my toes ~ while I try to be a hound for discipline and make him toe the mark... He has a giant grasshopper named Walter. Now he is collecting nests made by mason wasps ~ or else he screams for me to come and watch an earth worm being borne off by ants... The kids here have grasshoppers 6" long. They bring them to school. We also have lovely green lizards 9" long."

By the end of January, Saturday kindergarten was "strenuous but flourishing" and Miss Tudhope had started giving music lessons at noon, amused to find herself wrestling with a piano six degrees from the equator. "Gosh, the rainy season is lovely, very wet, but cool. I shall have to get myself a blanket, I nearly froze the other night. How it pours! We went to the movies last night on our wheels, and when we got there – I wrung out my dress and hair." She was told to rub her luggage with shoe-polish to control the mildew problem. She was finding life very full, involved not only with school but with an adult French class and taking private Italian lessons from Mary Hose. "Undoubtedly, the method by means of which to keep northerners happy down here, is to fill their waking hours until no vestige of freedom remains."

On the last day of January, she wrote: "All the little children came to school today at 6.50 a.m., which I consider unholy, but all the dear little children love Auntie Jean, so that fixes things. They swarm around all day long. Each day finds me with mayhem in my heart, but so far I have not damaged any of them. Between the parties, the children, the house, the fights, the maid problem, the bills *and* the cockroaches I am not capable of registering a thought." She tried in letters to tell people how difficult life was without the things that everyone took for granted at home. "Can you imagine not being able to buy shoes, stockings, underarm deodorant, *good* meat or hairpins? To say nothing of tomatoes or lettuce or milk. Of course you can't, and even today I am bewildered myself. You find your clothes worn out, and you have no idea what is being worn, or how short or anything. My poor coat is all rolled up in a can, periodically I open 'er up and have a look. When I come home, I'll be in the same hat, shoes, etc. Isn't that strange?" Her greatest joy was receiving parcels from Canada with new clothes from Eaton's.

In February, Miss Tudhope gave a Valentine party at school. "The children have made their own Valentines, and wonderful is the result." She also enjoyed herself at the masquerade party at the Club and won third prize for her costume, but the "bachelor nonsense" was still continuing as some practical joker lassoed her and Paul together when they were dancing. They both "crashed to earth. Gosh, I was mad." She received a visit from the Jewish Commission one evening, flown in from Georgetown to ask questions about life and happiness in the tropics with a view to settling refugees in the country. She was unsure that this would be successful since they did not have an agricultural background. However, by then she had a new neighbour who had a great interest in agriculture as he had started the small farm in the community. Giving the opportunity for more eyebrows to be raised, Paul Fenton moved into the house next door, and they both planned gardens and went for bike rides together, as well as going out on the river in a corial. "I do not know what I would do without Paul," she wrote to her sister now, "he keeps me cheered, and best of all makes me laugh heartily all the time."

On 26 February, there were two comments in her letter home that had meaning in the Whalley household. "Wednesday, there was a stork tea for one of the girls. Thursday I went to Snow White with Paul." The stork tea would have to have been for my mother, who was expecting a second baby (unbeknownst to me) in April. *Snow White* was one of the first movies I ever saw. Comparing notes with John Beedell in later years, we both remembered being taken to see it and having nightmares afterwards because of the horrible witch in the frightening Disney scene. Not long after this, Miss Tudhope had a hard time with young Johnny when his parents went away and left her in charge. "That is more of a charge than you might guess as he has three maids baffled and the house in a continuous up-roar. He capped his exploits by climbing to the top of a scaffolding and throwing down the workmen's tools. Poor lad, he is just very lonely with no other children his own age. The servants are not allowed even to reproach the white children which creates a difficult situation for all of them."

By March, Miss Tudhope was looking forward to an Easter outing to get away from the kids. She was exhausted. Up at 6.00 a.m., she had to be ready to start teaching at 7.30 a.m. School was out from 11.00 a.m. until 12.30 p.m. when the children returned to read or play. She gave Barbara and Jill music lessons from 1.00 to 2.15 p.m., during which time she kept the rest all quiet (and "By God, I do too," she said) until regular lessons began again. Between 3.30 and 4.00 p.m., she had to try and get rid of them before her Italian lesson at 4.00 p.m. Her 'terror' was still keeping her nose to the grindstone. "I should be making sure I understand Fahrenheit and Centigrade as I teach it to Jim to-morrow. I simply must be sure of it as I made two mistakes in Arithmetic today which he spotted at once."

Easter was coming and she and Paul and the Mackays planned to go up the river in two corials. She and Paul had already been given permission to go up the nearby creek one Sunday as long as they were back before dark. "We saw a carrion crow so high that he was just a speck, and the sun shone through his wings. Do you know, the penalty for shooting one is six months in gaol. Also, there was a little green alligator on the bank. He jumped off and swam along beside us. Then there were innumerable gorgeously coloured birds. The creek got very narrow, about eight feet and very shallow, about two feet. It is very different, very eerie and altogether fascinating." It is interesting to note that what had been outrageous in my mother's day was now quite acceptable to people who were used to going canoeing back in Canada. It was all part of the change that was creeping into life in Mackenzie, with the newcomer Canadians slipping into lifestyles that were more akin to what was familiar to them rather than the more rigid colonial rules that my mother had had to adapt to on arrival.

That spring the Canadians planned a progressive dinner party. "Dispositions are having a spring slump here, so it should be a jolly little affair." She and Betty sat on the stelling every Saturday morning, reading letters and planning their part. One day they walked three miles up the mine railway track and back, to be greeted with the news that two tiger cats ("these are jaguars and Paul says they'd run from us") had been seen near where they were walking. Two months later, they were forbidden to walk up the trail alone because the workmen had killed an anaconda there. Wildlife seemed to be encroaching on the camp on all sides. One of the men had a sloth in a cage. Snakes began to turn up everywhere. In March, a big snake got away on the road, "a lovely green one about 1½" in diameter and three feet long." In April, Paul killed a big one, 2½" in diameter, on his back steps, and another resident was in swimming when a snake believed to be an anaconda came along in the water. Two small ones were also seen at the Club. One evening, Jean and Paul went walking up "William's trail" into the forest. "Paul kept flashing his light up and I protested frantically that I could step on a thousand snakes and not see them. Finally it dawned on me that it was *Boas* for which he was on the look out in the trees. Immediately my knees began to knock *badly*. Then we rounded a corner, a pair of eyes *gleamed* at me and I *screeched*. I was rebuked scornfully for being an *ass* but I was very frightened really."

By Easter, a tired teacher said the children came to school as subdued as rabbits because she had been giving them the devil all week, but she made up for it on Good Friday by giving them a happy party with all the trimmings. The progressive dinner on Easter Saturday was very successful and gay, although the Brits were amused that the Canadians were celebrating the glad news, of no interest to them, that chewing gum was suddenly available in Georgetown. On Sunday someone sent Easter eggs for all the kids. "There was one over, which they presented to me. They all screamed and clapped and loud cries of 'Miss T.' rang through the place. I was overcome and grew moist about the eyes." For Sunday School, she laboriously constructed a house supposed to be of the vintage of early Jerusalem, "this to give zest to Sunday School classes. Ian T. sings 'We are weak and He is long' which throws all and sundry into gales of bawdy laughter."

On Easter Monday, Jean Tudhope began her letter of resignation to the Company. Her teaching work for the year was nearing completion and she did not think that she wanted to come back again for another season. "I am writing tonight to Montreal to advise that they get a nice, new, strong, cheery teacher who *loves* children." It was a hard decision for her to make. "Had to bolster myself up to my resignation ~ it wasn't easy. Had a fine session with the big boss over my going home, my resignation, and several other little things. It lasted all evening and then when I got home I called him in the wee small hours and we went at it again. He was very kind about my work and wants me to think it over. But it's a weird life ~ for one school year fine, but for longer, not I."

She wondered if she would get her energy back when she got home. "I am so lethargic all the time, it makes me uneasy. Last night Paul and I took a picnic in a corial up the river. Tide and current were both against us ~ I had to paddle, too. The paddles are about 2 feet long and about 3 inches wide. It was magnificent ~ not a sign of life, not even a bug ~ cool and gorgeous, only while we were stopped, eating, the tide went down. In trying to push us off a tree, I fell in, and then went right off to sleep. Poor Paul had to do all the paddling himself."

They were to have one last adventure before she left for Canada. On Sunday 9 May, they left at 6.00 a.m., heading for an Amerindian village on the Savannah Lands. "It was the most interesting yet. The Watooka is a tiny creek, and the branches of the trees meet overhead. All the way we had to cut these down with a cutlass to get through. At spots along the creek there are wood-cutters' paths with a hut. These so called huts have only thatched roofs and no sides. Except at these paths it's wiser not to get out of the corial as it's swampy. Farther along are two Indian settlements, interesting because they make corials there, and we saw them in all stages of development. It's hard to describe an Indian settlement but one thing they all have is a community cassava squeezer. They all sleep in hammocks, of course. Alas, we stayed too long and had to come down the Creek after dark. The Creek is a series of hairpin turns with stumps sticking out here and there. The tide was going down which carried the corial at a good speed and made it very difficult to steer. I lay flat, according to instructions and all was well until a stump struck Paul and knocked him flying backward, cut his head and almost broke his neck. He paddled all hunched up from then on and when we reached Demerara he was exhausted and gasping. Caught hell for being out on the Creek after dark."

She was still holding school in mid-May. "Just now I am keeping the kids in on general principles. I am having a good time and my mind is peaceful and at rest for a change." Her peaceful mind was not to last because on 22 May, Paul Fenton asked her to marry him. Her reaction was to go into a confused tailspin. "Yes, he actually wants me to marry him. Think of it!" she wrote to her sister the next day. "Don't expect any coherent thinking, because I stopped thinking yesterday." A week later she was still in the throes of decision making. "Everything is too-too. I watch carefully as I walk along to see if I can get both feet on the ground at once! It's perfectly ridiculous to be so upset by having a normal decision to make." Trying to keep her mind off what to do, she took the children to see a boa that one of the men had in a cage at the Club. "It was just a baby one 7 feet long and perfectly beautiful. The owner was told to dispose of it which he did by letting it go out behind the camp and fairly close to the Tropical Farm. Next day, a calf was missing. Pleasant thought."

She still had not made up her mind about Paul on 11 June, a month from her sailing date on the S.S. *Cottica*. "And it's going to be hard to leave. Everyone has been very kind and flattering. No one knows about Paul and me. Every night there is a dinner or a party. So it goes on and on, *very* violent social life." She would be teaching school to the very end, closing with a party for the children on 6 July and leaving Mackenzie on the 10th. While she pondered her big decision, she was still facing disapproval about her leaving from the Company Manager. "He thinks I am a quitter," she said, "He'll get a shock if I come back and marry Paul." There was packing to be done, a school children's party and a Sunday School entertainment to organize, the last Saturday dances at the Club, dinners, luncheon ~ and in the end she finally said yes to Paul's proposal. "My luggage goes in a week ~ I'll be coming back all right ~ although I have to stop Paul from ordering wedding announcements, and he wants to tell everyone. He is coming to Georgetown with me on Monday and he is ordering and planning furniture. He's enjoying very much the odd bit of kidding over my departure. All that, of course, drives me mad."

In the brief time left, they talked about whether they should get married before she left for Canada. "This war threat has put the finishing touches on our plans. Everyone seems to think we're for it soon, and then there would be the question of whether I'd ever make the grade back again." In the end, however, they decided to wait until she got back later in the year. Her last letter from Mackenzie read: "We are not going to be married till the fall. I do not want the news made public here. My china, bike and accessories like cushions, I am just going to leave with Paul. What they suspect, I can only guess, but I just smile sweetly and look vague. We had our kindergarten closing and I got all sorts of presents and tears. Then the Sunday School concert took about ten years of what is left of my youth and I am squeezed dry ~ no emotions left to me. See you in Montreal."

The next time Jean Tudhope returned to Mackenzie, she would no longer be the spinster teacher. The war had started and she would have to fly part of the way. She and Paul were married in Georgetown in November. When they arrived in Mackenzie, the first thing she saw was a motorboat with a crowd of people in it, cheering. All the children were lined up with flowers at the stelling, and everyone in the camp came out to meet them. When she reached their house, Paul's old maid Johanna and her niece opened the door chanting, "Ah, welcome with joy and all prosperity," while scattering rosebuds. At night there was a big party for the newlyweds, with a wedding cake surrounded by gardenias. She was now Mrs. Paul Fenton, wife of a member of staff. There would be a new teacher in the fall, who stayed even less time than she did, and was not nearly as friendly or satisfactory, and left us without another teacher for months to come.

1938 Staff. Messrs. Kerr, Wallwork, Parsons (manager), Whalley, Fenton.

Jean Tudhope and class

Art Williams
Sea-Plane began trips to Mackenzie in
mid to late 1930s

1939 Masquerade party

Paradise

Around the time that Miss Tudhope resigned as schoolteacher in the spring of 1939, an important event was taking place at my house in Mackenzie, but no one felt that they should tell me. Instead, when I was four and a half years old, not knowing anything about this tremendous happening that would change my life, I was sent to Paradise. Paradise, British Guiana, that is, not the Paradise that all the rest of the world thinks of as a beautiful, heavenly place in the hereafter.

Like the opening scene of an old movie, I can picture myself being driven along a road in the back of a huge car. The place we are driving through seems to be just this one long dirt road, with deep ditches and little run-down wooden houses on stilts on the side of the road. The doors and windows of the houses are wide open, and going in or out of them are dozens of brown people ~ men, women, children, babies. Bustling chickens and skinny dogs are also running in and out of the houses. Everyone looks very cheerful but no one waves, taking the big car for granted. Everywhere we look is muddy, with big puddles from recent rain, and in every direction, everywhere in sight, there are pigs, pigs, and more pigs, anywhere there is a ditch or a puddle, rolling in the mud. At the top of the road is a wrought iron fence, with a closed iron entrance gate, very high and elaborate. Beyond the gate, in a sea of lush green shrubbery, I can just about see a large house, but no one comes to open the gate. We just sit there in this big dark car interior, in Paradise, in front of Uncle Peter's Pearly Gates.

For the longest time, I tried to figure out how I got there. The only Paradise I could find on the present-day map of Guyana is an Amerindian reservation up the Berbice River, and I was pretty sure that I did not go by boat or why the big car? Then I found another Paradise on an old, old map, on the coast near New Amsterdam. It was an old sugar plantation that had been manned by blacks instead of East Indians. Immediately what I remembered as a child made sense, for the layout was a typical plantation one, with the Big House and garden set back on its own, away from the workers' houses, and the people I had seen were Afro-Guianese rather than the Indo-Guianese more usually associated with the sugar estates I knew. It seems that Paradise, no longer producing sugar, was being used at that time by the British Guiana District Commission as its headquarters for the Berbice district. 'Uncle Peter' Niven was a District Commissioner and I had been sent to stay with him and his wife, 'Auntie Minnie', a district nurse who examined and treated out-patients in part of the big old estate house.

The District Commission was typical of the entire network of administration in the British Empire. Outside of the cities, a few chosen men usually had to take care of the problems of a large number of people in what could be a vast territory. In little British Guiana, the territories were reasonably manageable in size and population but were often inaccessible or difficult of access, which made the job challenging. As Charles Allen described the way it worked in Africa: "Classically, the District Officer did not order, he advised; he did not rule, he administered. In practice, of course, there were good DO's and bad DO's, just as there were good and bad chiefs, so that 'advice' could mean anything from unambiguous instruction through tactful intervention to feet up on the office table and a sigh of 'let them ask if they want to learn'. There were always some who believed that the 'best' district was the one that gave no trouble, was rarely heard of in headquarters and never in the Colonial Office or the House of Commons." I am sure that in our day in the colony, this was a 'best' district, but as an example of how the District Commissioners themselves varied, Evelyn Waugh seems to have met a particularly bad specimen of the breed on his travels up the Berbice River; my mother quite liked the one who accompanied them to Kaieteur Falls; and we heard nothing but good of the administration of Peter Niven. As a whole, the Commission was often criticized for being only interested in law and order, never in economic or social development, but of course there could be no development without a settled population. It is hard not to wonder whether the flourishing muddy pigs that I saw so plentifully in Paradise were part of a development project for the peaceful estate workers now that there was no employment with sugar cane.

I am not sure at what point my parents had met Peter and Minnie Niven but they had all become firm friends. A sign of this was that I did not call them by the customary titles of Mr. and Mrs. but by the more familiar honorary ones of Uncle and Aunt. It is possible that they were on the boat when we came back from England in 1936 and we just adopted each other. My father adored Auntie Minnie. She was a practical but birdlike little woman with a delightful, infectious laugh, who endeared herself to everyone. Uncle Peter was a quiet, self-effacing man with a droll smile who gave the impression of being wise and knowledgeable behind his modest demeanour and gentle, affectionate humour. Between them, these two embodied the best kind of administrators who went out from England to the colonies, devoted to the people they served and to each other, practical and sensible, and always kindness itself.

When the gates of Paradise on earth finally opened, I was warmly welcomed by these two wonderful people. I had no idea why I was there. I have no recollection of saying goodbye to my parents or of being upset that I had been banished to this place. I only remember that I was there for no apparent reason except that I had been invited and I had a big bedroom all to myself with no mosquito net. The garden of the house was beautiful and I was allowed to swim in the irrigation canal that ran through it. I remember the bathroom because there was a huge tiled floor in the area that acted as a shower and when I took off my bathing suit a small fish slithered down to the floor. Somehow, I had caught a fish in my suit when I was swimming. The only other thing that I can remember about staying there was that, every night after dinner, I went walking with Uncle Peter in a rough pasture behind the garden. It probably stuck in my mind because I was not normally allowed to walk in grass but here there was not the same problem with snakes. It was a grazing pasture for sheep, appropriate enough for Paradise but surely odd for tropical British Guiana. I know it was sheep because I had a job to do. My job was to help Uncle Peter collect sheep manure for his garden.

I have no idea how long I stayed with the Nivens. I only know that when I went home to Mackenzie from Paradise, it was April and I had a baby sister, which came as a complete and nasty surprise. It was my first betrayal. No marital infidelity could be more heart-rending than suddenly finding, without any preparation at all, that an adored and adoring father was now gazing in rapture at a total stranger, and worse, that this stranger, who was undoubtedly cute with her big brown eyes and curly hair and incredibly dainty features, had come to live with us out of nowhere and I would have to put up with the situation. The old brown photographs tell the story. All the easy confidence of the child who was the center of her parents' universe has shattered into a thousand pieces, replaced by a look of jealous uncertainty or hurt, stubborn, independent pride. Of course my parents had no idea that they might have helped the situation by making me feel that I had not been supplanted in their affections. They had not read all the books about child rearing. My father came from a big family where sibling rivalry was taken for granted as perfectly normal. I think he felt that if he teased me I would see the error of my ways. Instead, it made it worse. My mother, as always, was oblivious. So Margaret Jean came to stay with us and I had to share my bedroom with her. I don't remember poking her in the eye while saying "Nice baby" as older siblings have been known to do in the same situation, but I know that my resentment ran deep and dirty, and if I had not been basically a good child who knows what I might have done.

I am afraid I was a very unsatisfactory older sister. There was too much difference in our ages for us to be real companions and I was simply not motherly enough to adopt Margaret, whom we later called by the softer-sounding name of Margie, as 'my baby'. My dislike of playing with dolls meant that I was not in the least interested in dressing and undressing and changing the baby, even if my mother had let me, for she treated this baby as if she were a china doll. I was always told that she was 'fragile'. And I was painfully jealous all the time, for now the entire household ran around the needs of the baby. Even our nurse, Maud, no longer treated me as her special little girl. She doted on her new charge and bristled at me, "Me na love you, Miss Windy, if you na behave." So love that had been unconditional was now conditional. She still loved me and I still loved her but, as it was with my parents, it was not the same. Still, I loved to watch Maud walk home at night, wearing her prim white nurse's cap over her neat tight curls, her back ramrod straight, her big African hips swaying seductively, and a full milk bottle balanced on her head without any support from her hands and arms.

Not long after my sister was installed in our house, and possibly at least as an indirect result of this, I ran away from home. This came about because I had a cold and my mother said I could not go swimming the next day. I told her, as usual, that I would tell my grandparents how cruel she was to me. She paid no attention to this foolishness. She was changing the baby's diaper at the time and her attention was all wrapped up in getting the adorable infant ready for bed. I announced that I was running away. Again, she made no sign that she had heard me. So I packed a hatbox with my teddy bear and the clothes I thought I needed, which must have included night things and a swim suit because where I was going they would be sure to let me go swimming to-morrow. "I'm going," I announced defiantly. Still no answer. Through the kitchen I went and slammed the outside door. Down the narrow back stairs that led to the street, propelled by fury at what I perceived as unbelievable unfairness. At the bottom of the stairs, the night hit me like a slap. It was totally dark outside. I had never walked alone in the dark. The sounds of the jungle night descended. The tree frogs barked. There were no street lights, only a dim lamp from the Kerrs' house opposite and, across a vacant patch of community lawn, the brighter lights of the house next door where the Thompsons lived. I could not see if there were snakes in the road but I had been taught to fear them all my life and I was sure they were there, waiting to strike.

Remember I am only four and a half going on five years old. But I was mad enough and determined enough and scared enough to keep walking purposefully towards the light where Ian lived. Just before I reached the Thompsons' house, the thought of snakes underfoot got too much and I panicked. I broke into a terrified run. I raced up their stairs as if I were being chased by the Hounds of Hell. I pounded on their door and Mrs. Thompson opened it. She looked surprised to see me. "I've come to live with you!" I announced breathlessly. "Well," said Mrs. Thompson, not looking thrilled. "Come in." Ian was very excited at my arrival. We giggled and played together. I think we even had to get into pyjamas and get ready for bed as if I were going to stay. But by then I was beginning to get the idea that Mr. and Mrs. Thompson would be pretty strict parental figures. And then my parents came over. They didn't say anything, just went in to sit with the Thompsons and have a drink. We could hear a lot of laughter coming from the living room. Then I remember my father saying quietly "Time to go home, Wendy." "Five minutes more," I pleaded, and he nodded. Ian and I played a little longer. And then we went home. I seem to remember going home in pyjamas. I can't remember but I am sure that I did not go swimming the next day.

I am not surprised that my mother did not want me to go swimming with a cold. I seem to have been prone to lung problems and she had already had one bad session with me when I got bronchitis. Being so close to the Equator meant that the present doctor, who was not the mad Irishman, did not have much experience with bronchial treatment. He recommended the good old-fashioned mustard plaster. My mother duly smeared a warmed flannel cloth with her hot English mustard, made into a thick paste. She had no sooner put it on my chest than I started to scream. The doctor had barely got back to the hospital when he got an urgent call and had to come back post-haste. All the outer skin on my chest was raw and red and it all peeled off. I don't know what he tried as a remedy after that or maybe that cured everything.

That may have been the doctor (in all likelihood it was Dr. Charlie Rosa at that time but I can't be sure) who had to give the entire camp an injection for yellow fever. A man at the mine died, suspected of having the disease, so we were all lined up to get a preventative needle, adults and children alike. I can still see Ian's face, white and scared and trying to be brave, probably mirroring mine, as we waited to be stabbed, but no one else died, and we were immensely proud of our courage when it was all over. This may also have been the doctor who picked me up in the middle of the road where I lay bruised from a fall off a bicycle. The bike was my father's and it had been leaning against a pillar under the house. I must have been a little older, because I was tall enough to climb up onto it and set off happily. However, I was still barely able to reach the pedals and kept wobbling all over the road. Unfortunately for me, the doctor's car came along just as I reached the loop at the end of the road. I was afraid of being knocked down and had no idea how to get off the bike, so I fell off. I wasn't too badly hurt and neither was the bike, and he brought us both home safely.

Funny how one episode reminds you of another. I don't think I had to go and see the doctor when I fell off a platform I was using as a launching pad for flying. I had got tired of rigging up ways of making my dolls walk with strings, like puppets, in an effort to make them DO something, so I turned my attention to making wings for flight. I was quite sure that if I had these attachments of paper and string tied to my outstretched arms that I would soar like a bird. Needless to say, I didn't. But I know I had to go to the hospital for stitches on my lip because I fell off the doghouse under the Big House. Stupid as it sounds, this time it was not really my fault. By this time, all the children who were old enough not to have to go walking with their nurses, as my baby sister had to do the whole time we lived in Mackenzie, used to gather under the Big House in the afternoons to play together. We fell naturally into two groups, three or four 'big kids' and three 'small kids' As far as I remember, there was no adult supervision. Something was happening that particular afternoon and everyone had climbed on top of a rather large doghouse and I wanted to see what was happening. I think it was either Barbara Parsons or Jill Bradley who tried to lift me up but didn't quite make it and I fell. I bled very impressively. When it came time to have stitches, though, I made it very clear that I was not going to have the doctor sew up my lip with a needle. I made such a fuss that in the end he put a butterfly bandage over my mouth and I had to drink out of a straw and not eat solid food except in tiny bites until it had healed. I still have the scar to show for it.

It was under the Big House that we children had another event that was not to be forgotten easily. It was just after Christmas and I had been sent a big book from England. It was a beautiful book and I loved the pictures but I couldn't read the words. So I took it to the Big House at play time so that one of the big kids could read us a story. Afterwards, while they all got together and read it to each other, Jackie and Ian and I played ball. We weren't really listening to them when Jimmy Parsons, who was the one who usually got everyone into trouble, had a brilliant idea. It was getting late in the afternoon, almost time to go home, when the big kids put their heads together, laughing, and then came back over to us. "We want to tell you another story," they said, "a true one this time." So they told us about the Green Monster who lived under the Big House in the Hendersons' car. The Green Monster was a very terrible creature ~ just how terrible was described with relish ~ and he liked to kill and eat children. Just as we were shivering with fright, eyeing the car very carefully, one of the big kids screamed "He's coming! The Green Monster's coming! Run!" And how we ran. If Johnny Beedell, one of the big kids, had been there, he would have gone in the other direction from the rest of us. Down the only road in the camp the rest of us raced, too scared to look back over our shoulders, too full of the terrible descriptions in our heads, and too frightened for our lives. Jimmy and Barbara lived nearest to the Big House so they turned into their house first. Jackie was lucky; she and her big sister were next. That left Ian and me running our little hearts out, until he turned panting into his driveway and I had to run all the rest of the way on my own. That night, I lay in my bed under the mosquito net and shivered. When I finally fell asleep, I dreamed that I woke in the middle of the night to see a horrible green face staring at me through the window screen. The monster lifted a gun and shot me and I saw myself dead on the bed. I raised the house with my screams. In the next house, Ian was sick all night and further up the road Jackie too had bad nightmares. Needless to say, the big kids got a sound talking to the next day and the Green Monster, except the one that represented jealousy, was never seen again.

Jimmy, however, had other plans to entertain the children of Mackenzie. I was amazed to read that Zahra Freeth and her husband regularly went for walks on trails around the camp when they were there 20 years later. In our day, we were completely surrounded by virgin rainforest, made impenetrable with lianas and undergrowth, and there was nowhere to walk except along the railway track to the mine. It was Jimmy who planned the Great Explorers Trail-Blazing Adventure, when the children were to go into the bush with machetes and knives and hack their way through the rainforest to make a walking trail like the ones he knew in Canada. They were going to camp in the bush, I think, and make a real adventure of the whole thing. I doubt whether the big kids would even have wanted this little squirt to go along but I was very excited about it. This meant another confrontation with my mother, and this time my father also, both adamant that I was too young to go with them. "But I want to go!" I wailed. "At five years old? Going off into the bush alone, with all those snakes? Certainly not!" they said firmly. I stayed home feeling very sorry for myself but the great explorers did not last long in the bush. Johnny Beedell had to be carried home as an injured soldier and the trail did not go very far through the thick tropical vines and buttressed trees.

It must have been around this time that Ian and I had an adventure at the community farm. Some years earlier, an area had been cleared upriver from the camp, by bulldozing a flat portion and eliminating the natural drainage watercourses, to make the golf course, and now there was also a cattle farm which included a stable and field for horses. There were two horses and a donkey, I remember. One day, Ian and I set off to visit the stable. To get onto the field, we had to cross a man-made drainage ditch which we did by going down into it and up the other side. Halfway across the field, we heard a commotion and saw one of the horses coming out, followed by the donkey that had the horse's tail in a secure grip between his teeth. There were men around them both trying to get the donkey to loosen his hold. Suddenly, he let go and the horse bolted, straight across the field towards us. Terrified that we would be trampled under the galloping hoofs, Ian and I turned and fled, with the horse still apparently racing after us, and in our terror we leapt the ditch at the edge of the field. The horse, of course, was not chasing us at all. It came to the edge where the grass was longer, stood still, and having got away from the donkey's painful attention, began to graze. Feeling safe now, Ian and I looked in awe at the small depression that we had jumped over when we were pumped up with adrenaline. "That big thing was chasing us and we got away from it," we boasted. "And we jumped a ditch that was FIFTEEN feet across!"

There were a lot of ditches being jumped in terror in other parts of the world that year. The year that my sister was born was the year when Hitler's tanks rolled into Poland and World War II began.

Mrs. Kerr, Auntie Minnie holding Margie, Wendy, Ian Thompson.

Nina, John, and Mrs. Beedell with
Wendy and Gladys at the stelling

Minnie and Peter Niven

War: The Beginning Years

War in Europe meant the start of the long years of worry for colonial families isolated from their family and friends in England. The newfangled wireless, crackling with urgency, became a familiar tool for hearing the worst news daily. Letters from home came sporadically, all trying to be brave about the cutbacks, the blackouts, the gas masks, the air raid shelters, the sound of sirens and enemy planes, and the gearing up for battle everywhere. The worst of it for the folks abroad was not just the dangers that surrounded the people they loved but not being there to share it with them, to help in some way, to do something. Both my parents felt this keenly, especially my father, who had volunteered so readily for the first World War. Never did my mother's accounts of her daily life in Mackenzie seem less useless, less remote, to the recipients than the letters she wrote home from her comparative safety. Yet, ironically, the work in the bauxite camp had never been so useful, so close to what was needed, as now when the country they loved needed air power in the shape of planes built of aluminum.

Mackenzie had been gearing up for increased bauxite demand since the arrival of Mr. Parsons as the new manager in 1938. Duncan Campbell said: "Demba had only two open-cast mines in operation before World War II. By the start of 1939, with Arvida expanding and the war clouds gathering, it was essential to plan for much greater production. The site selected for development was Hope Mine on the opposite bank of the Demerara River. This mine had the advantage of a relatively thin overburden of sand and clay to be stripped off before the bauxite was exposed, and it could be connected with the existing railway by constructing a bridge across the river, a task of some magnitude. Large scale production of bauxite from Hope Mine began in January, 1940. In truth it could be called the mine which helped to win the war, because it provided the bulk of Demba's wartime production." It was calculated that from 1940 to 1944 inclusive, the Hope Mine supplied a total of 4,600,000 long tons of washed and dried ore, sufficient to extract 1.1 million tonnes of primary aluminum.

The magnitude of the bauxite contribution to the war effort can best be seen in the figures that show that almost all Canada's military aircraft built between 1940 and 1945, 16,000 of them, were built of aluminum supplied by Alcan. In Britain, 80 percent of the aluminum ingots used in manufacturing military aircraft during the war years came from Canada. The industry there expanded from 2,828 planes built in 1938 to 7,940 in 1939, 15,049 in 1940,

20,094 in 1941, and exceeded 23,000 per year thereafter until the peak year of 26,461 in 1944. These included 14,500 Hawker Hurricane and 20,000 Spitfire fighters and over 7,300 of the heavy Lancaster bombers.

To handle the additional ore from the Hope Mine in 1940, larger plant facilities were needed to crush, wash, dry, store, and load the bauxite for shipment. New staff were kept busy with all the expansion. Jack Batzold was in charge of most of the wartime extension in the plant and railway system. Paul Fenton was busier than ever building and rebuilding railway bridges, supervising and building staff housing, and running all the facilities such as the hospital, store, police, security, and schools. My father handled all the paperwork with the expanded shipping. Jock Thompson became production manager for the duration of the war.

Because of their late arrival from Scotland, the Thompsons' contract was similar to that of the Canadians, with only three years to wait to go on leave. Having arrived in 1937, in 1940 they were ready for their first leave, which coincided with my parents' four year wait since 1936. There was certainly no chance of going home on leave to Britain that year. By 1940, the war news was terrible. The fall of Poland in 1939 had been followed by the defeat of Denmark and Norway in the spring of 1940. By the beginning of May, the German tanks were rolling again, into Luxembourg, Belgium, and Holland, and the new Prime Minister of England, Winston Churchill, was telling his people that all he could promise them was "blood, toil, tears and sweat". By the middle of the month, having taken the Low Countries, the German armies had crossed into and were sweeping through France. It seemed as if nothing would stop Hitler's terrible race to conquer the continent, and fears were growing every day that England would be next.

Impossible as it now was to go to Europe, the United States had not yet entered the war, and her passenger ships were still running without interference from neutral Brazil to New York. The Thompsons and the Whalleys decided to go on holiday in North America together and booked passage on a large Grace Line ship that called in Trinidad en route. We went by freighter from Georgetown to Trinidad. Going around the arc of the West Indies on what was then a huge liner was the first time that I remember seeing clear sea water. The ship called at various islands on the way north. At one of them, a number of laughing boys came out in small rowboats to dive deep down in the turquoise water for the coins we threw overboard. We also stopped at a small island where everyone went ashore in rowboats to a white coral beach, completely deserted, where we could swim and pick up a huge conch shell to take back to the cabin to "listen to the waves."

Back on the ship, the wives and children had no problem relaxing and enjoying the luxury but the men walked the decks and found it difficult to let go. It was May, 1940, Belgium had surrendered or was on the point of surrendering to the Nazis, and the armies of France were collapsing before the tide of tanks and overhead bombing. It was Richard Hough, in his biography of the Churchills, *Winston and Clementine*, who said that the German armored columns swept forward as if on maneuvers. Little or no attempt was made to halt them. They just followed the roads, and when they ran short of fuel they simply filled up, like summer tourists, at the filling stations while the French troops handed over their arms. The tanks, if they had time, simply crushed their rifles on the road before moving on. "Our menfolk were very worried about the war news," my mother said, "not helped by arrogant Germans from South America on board who exulted on reading the ship's newspapers." My father, who worked with the captains of the bauxite freighters all the time and worried about their safety as well as that of their precious cargo, was furious at some of the loose talk on board about area shipping. When we reached New York, my mother said "These fellows were landed first, and we were almost last, and on being asked how long we wished to stay in the U.S. my husband replied, 'Long enough to get out of it.'" My parents and the Thompsons found it hard to understand how ordinary Americans, who could be so kind and friendly in every other way, could not be affected by the advancing war in Europe. "It was awful to stand in Times Square and watch the news moving on a building '250,000 GERMANS CIRCLING FOR THE KILL' and look around at unconcerned faces," my mother said. It would not be until Pearl Harbour that the people of the United States of America would realize that the principle of isolationism would not work in this global war.

Meanwhile, my parents and the Thompsons tried to make the best of their needed vacation and keep the worries about the war away from us children. We spent a week in New York that May while France was falling, and another on the way home in August. We went to the World's Fair where my father and I saw the Giant Panda bear that everyone was talking about. My mother missed it while she was taking my little sister to a rest-room for changing. They kept losing me at the Bronx Zoo because I fell in love with the sea lions but it was easy to keep tabs on the baby. She had not yet learned to walk, and saw the zoo on my father's shoulders. There was no crib for her at the hotel where we stayed so my mother filled a large drawer with pillows and tucked her in. They must have got a sitter for her one night because the Thompsons and my parents took Ian and me to Rockefeller Center to see the Rockettes. They had obviously decided it was a good idea to divide us, so both sets of parents sat in the middle, with Ian at one end and me at the other. Their plan backfired. Halfway through one of the Rockette numbers, Ian leaned forward in his seat. "I don't think much of this, Wendy, do you?" he shouted. "No," I yelled back. My mother always swore that the famous chorus line wavered.

My father and Mr. Thompson went out for a haircut as soon as they reached New York. "A propos of their tans, vowing to pay no more than 75 cents each, they were spotted by the barbers as being either from the Tropics or had wintered in Florida. They were fair game, so each was told (separately) after being showed white stuff on a fine-tooth comb that they had dandruff. They were given the works, hot oil treatment, etc. and came back hours later each sheepishly holding a bottle, each having been gouged $7.50!" The wives hooted. The white stuff was only coral sand.

From New York, we took the train to Montreal, where a friend took my mother and Mrs. Thompson to Ogilvy's, a venerable department store where she knew personally one of the sales ladies. While they were looking at dresses, Mrs. Thompson shocked the friend by telling the sales lady "No, that material won't do, the roaches would eat it!" Meanwhile, my father and Mr. Thompson paid their respects at Alcan's head office. It was interesting for the men to meet some of the people with whom they had been dealing from a distance. Coming from the equatorial heat, they found it chilly in Montreal, and they were wondering what to do next when "some angel in the office" recommended Knowlton Grove in the Eastern Townships. My mother had been afraid that we would all end up in a cabin in the Laurentians where she and Mrs. Thompson would have to cook and child-mind all summer. Instead, it was as if we had landed in a made-to-order heaven. "We were at the summer camp in Knowlton for two months," my mother reported happily, "staying in one of many bungalows scattered in the woods around the central building, where we got three good meals a day, the whole thing very reasonable and patronised mostly by Montrealers with children." The cabins were on a wooded hillside, with Brome Lake at our doorstep, and it was no walk at all to go down to the yacht club with its private beach on the other side of the road below. Our parents hired a nice local teenager named Jennie to look after the three of us. They joined the yacht club so that we children could swim there and took out summer memberships at Knowlton Golf Club for a daily four-some. The photographs show everyone having a wonderful time. Margie happily learned to walk with Jennie holding her hand. There is even a photograph of me looking at her lovingly. While Ian and I swam in water that was shallow and safe from pirai, and played with other kids, and picked juicy wild strawberries, and managed to behead every hay-scented and bracken fern in the county with the toy golf clubs we had been given, our parents spent every day on the beautiful golf course. They could not get over the pleasure of playing on real greens and fairways after the rough course at the camp, although on their first morning they had an instant reminder of where they usually played. On the very first green at Knowlton, they encountered a harmless grass snake, reminding them of the time when Mrs. Thompson had been bitten by the venomous snake in Mackenzie and my mother had saved her life.

All in all, that summer of 1940, the summer of the evacuation of Dunkirk, the summer when Winston Churchill thundered to his people "We shall defend our island, whatever the cost may be, we shall fight on the beaches, we shall fight on the landing grounds, we shall fight in the fields and in the streets, we shall fight in the hills, we shall never surrender," they were "halcyon days," my mother said, "marred only by listening to the war news while having tea (real cream!) in the clubhouse. My husband said at the end that he felt he could push over a house!" Any letters they received from England were censored so although they learned something of the heavy bombing from the Luftwaffe that began mid-July and continued all that August, they could not know what was going on about the preparations against possible invasion. Richard Hough described how people were put to work digging tank traps and filling millions of sandbags. Almost over-night, concrete pillboxes appeared all over the southern counties, barbed wire defenses and mine warning signs were put along the beaches, stout stakes and old vehicles were positioned in the fields to prohibit landings from the air, all road and railway station signs were removed, and the order came to immobilize cars when parked ~ all this was going on in England while we spent that happy sum-mer in Knowlton.

All too soon it was time for the reluctant return, with another week in Montreal of catching up with old friends like the Harders, and official briefing on the overall aluminum picture at head office for my father and Mr. Thomp-son. It is highly probable that they met our past Mackenzie manager again, Mr.

Hendra, and learned from him what had happened on his trip to Greenland that May. With the fall of Denmark in spring, the staff at Alcan had become increasingly worried as to whether the Nazis would stop the flow of cryolite, an essential mineral in the conversion of bauxite into aluminum, from the Danish colony to Canada. (Even we children knew about the importance of cryolite in the electrolysis process, because the company had put out a priceless booklet for children about the Bauxite twins, Billy and Betty Bauxite I think they were, who left Mackenzie and went up to Canada to meet their friend Chris Cryolite from Greenland, and they all held hands and became aluminum.) With this vital resource in peril, discussions ran long and heatedly between the company and the Canadian and American Governments about what to do about the situation. The Americans in particular did not want to have Canada taking over Greenland. Eventually, with cryolite supplies so desperately needed for the war effort, Canada took things into her own hands.

In May, about the time our families arrived in New York, the Hudson's Bay supply ship, the *Nascopie*, set sail from Nova Scotia carrying Canada's postmaster for the Arctic, two army majors, six RCMP officers (of which five were in mufti to disguise their official purpose), one government surgeon, one government botanist, Danish-born Erling Porsild who had just been appointed Canadian vice-consul to Greenland, and two men from Alcan, one of whom was H.J. Hendra, recently of Mackenzie. The ship also carried a cargo of food, clothing and medicine as a donation from Canada, and a cabin stocked with liquor from Alcan. On reaching the coast of Greenland, it was frustrating for the Canadians to be refused to land until the arrival of a new Canadian consul from Britain, Kenneth Kirkwood, who managed to get them ashore to see the Governor and eventually to sail back to Port Alfred in the Arvida area with a relief supply of around 1,500 tonnes of cryolite. Campbell said that subsequent negotiations made it possible for the supply to continue throughout the war years.

From Montreal, our families spent a last week in New York before taking another Grace Line ship, fully lit up, to Barbados. As we passed the Virgin Islands, my father and Mr. Thompson could not have avoided the grim knowledge that the German U-boats were already operating in the vicinity. They had just been reviewing the shipping situation in Montreal and they knew all too well from their end of the business that Sprostons had leased a private coaling station at St. Thomas as a storage and 'top up' area for bauxite. The shallow water over the Georgetown Bar and in the Demerara River, even when constantly dredged, meant that only small, shallow-draught boats (limited to 15 to 18 feet) or half-loaded larger vessels to a limit of 8,000 tonnes could be used to carry the bauxite away from the Mackenzie plant. By creating a small fleet of shallow Canadian lake vessels to run a shuttle service between Mackenzie and St. Thomas, the larger vessels could top up or load there for the journey north. In spite of being as far as 800 miles away from the mine, this trans-shipment system worked reasonably well from 1938 to 1940 but, as the U-boat threat in that area increased, Alcan was trying to find a safer location.

There had been little U-boat activity in the West Indies up to this time because the German command had been concentrating on the North Atlantic (where the sinkings had been so successful that the submarine crews christened it 'Happy Times') and Hitler's preparation for the invasion of Britain called 'Operation Sea Lion'. But in war, nothing was certain. Hitler had already relaxed the U-boat rules several times from his original permission to sink on sight and without warning any blacked-out ship off the coast of Britain or France, but they were still expected to rescue the torpedoed crews without endangering their submarines. By the end of May 1940, he was allowing them to sink any ship without warning, including unescorted neutrals and passenger ships, in British and French waters, and with no assurance of safety of anyone on board. With the new fueling location in the Virgin Islands, there was no knowing when the rule of 'British and French waters' might again be relaxed to include the coasts of the British and French Caribbean.

I am sure my father and Mr. Thompson would have done their best not to let their wives and children know of their fears for our safety as we passed the Virgin Islands without incident and went on to dock in Barbados. There we left the large, brightly lit, neutral ship to transfer to a small, blacked-out, English freighter for the rest of the journey. My mother did not elaborate on their feelings as we made that trip safely to Georgetown where we transferred to the river steamer for Mackenzie, but the darkened boat would have meant that the men's fears could no longer be concealed. She merely said of a trip that I can only imagine was one of constant, unspoken anxiety as the engine chugged through the dark waves, "I suppose we were lucky not to be torpedoed."

Soon after we got back to Mackenzie came the news of the Battle of Britain in the skies over England in the fall of 1940. It was the bombing that brought the war close to the English people. Too close. Night after night, wave after wave, before the Royal Air Force Fighter Command took back the skies on September

15, the Luftwaffe bombers came over the Channel and flew over England, dropping their exploding messages. My grandfather later told me that when the siren sounded or they heard the mosquito whine of the German planes overhead they would dive into their air raid shelter like frightened rabbits, never knowing if they or their house or all the houses around them would survive. The night that five hundred German bombers wiped out Coventry, just to the south of the Potteries, was one of the worst. In London, the bombing was ceaseless. My grandmother's niece living in South London was in a middle flat when the doodlebugs came. They hit and set on fire the flat above them and the flat below them and they just got out in time.

Much as the war reports constantly worried my parents, who were always looking for and at the same time fearing the light blue envelopes with the sticker that said they had been opened for security purposes, giving them news of friends and family, yet none of this affected us directly. It was only the U-boats that really brought the war home to British Guiana.

Knowlton, 1940

passport photo

Wendy & Ian with Walter Foster

KNOWLTON GROVE P.QUE BROME LAKE. QUE

Margie and Wendy

Bauxite and U-boats

I had always thought that my early years were spent in a quiet backwater place that was of marginal or no interest to the outside world, until I read the story of the U-boat years, filled with tragedy and drama, with the urgent need to get the bauxite out for the requirements of war, and with great sadness at the loss of lives and cargoes.

Although the war in distant Europe often touched our lives indirectly, it was the U-boats that seemed to come so close that we lived in constant dread of the unseen enemy that lurked in our coastal waters like a predatory shark. It would be decades after the war until we learned what it had been like for the young German submariners doing their enemy duty in the confines of those metal horrors and were able to read with some degree of sympathy about their underwater life in the hot tropics that was nothing short of hell, but during the war their merciless attacks on Allied shipping brought nothing but a bitterly horrified reaction from all ashore.

Even we children, who were sheltered from so many of the war-story horrors, could not avoid the sense of menace engendered by the U-boat dangers or the sadness of whispering adults when a tragedy occurred. The sinkings were particularly devastating when innocent passenger ships were involved. After one such attack, H.C. Collier, writing in the *Canada-West Indies Magazine* in February 1942, spoke for everyone when he said: "Shocked by the ruthlessness of this deed it is only natural that we should cry for vengeance on the cowardly Nazi rat who cold-bloodedly committed this murder without civilized consideration to women and children." The ship lost on that occasion was the *Lady Hawkins*, which was well known to the Canadians in the Mackenzie community for her role in transporting staff to and from her home port of Halifax. Her sinking was to bring sorrow and tragedy directly into the homes of the resident staff and call for an edict from head office that, from that time on, no company personnel or their families were to travel to or from the colony by sea.

The U-boat threat was slow in coming to the Caribbean area. It was not until the end of 1941 that the German *Unterseeboots* began to play a large part in the life of our isolated community and it was a bleak year for those in charge of shipping bauxite. The year began with Alcan and the American navy negotiating with Britain for a Trinidad base in the Chaguaramas area, Alcan for a trans-shipment station to replace the one in the Virgin Islands and the U.S. for a naval base to guard the oil interests in the Caribbean. Eventually, Duncan Campbell said this was resolved with the unique establishment of the bauxite shipping station being built inside the navy base, which was very satisfactory for the company because it provided the opportunity to form small convoys of bauxite carriers while in the protection of the base. However, it was not until May 1942 that this was completed so until that time the bauxite freighters out of Mackenzie still had to make the dangerous trip north to St. Thomas.

There were few losses in the spring of 1941, but as the summer went on, things began to get increasingly more serious. Although not yet in the war, the United States was actively assisting the North Atlantic convoys to get through with fewer U-boat losses, so the German admiral Donitz began to send his U-boats further afield to pick off lone merchant ships. The U-boat targets in the Caribbean were not only bauxite, they were also oil tankers carrying badly needed Caribbean oil for Canada and Britain, giving a double reason for the increase in U-boat activity.

By late summer, the problem of shipping had worsened dramatically. Campbell looked at all the reports and stated: "In the early months the situation was virtually hopeless as so much bauxite was held at the mines through the near total failure of assigned ships to report in to load. In September six ships were nominated to lift bauxite in Guyana, but only one reported. In October, other scheduled arrivals failed to show. In November 'the first of scores of bauxite carriers was lost'." The losses included two former US Navy colliers, the S.S. *Proteus* and S.S. *Nereus* that made the run from St. Thomas to Portland, Maine. Both departed with full cargoes of bauxite, 23 November and 10 December respectively. "Neither ship was heard from again ~ not a trace of raft, float, body or boat was found." Sadly, three of the lost were young engineers returning from Alcan assignments in the Caribbean.

The last staff and family members in Mackenzie to leave the country by ship were John and Ethel Beedell and daughter Nina. They had been living in Mackenzie ever since Mr. Beedell had joined his wife and family after his last ship assignment as Chief Engineer in 1937. Now, with their son already in school in Canada, he was being transferred to the Forge or North Plant, the new Alcan expansion project in Kingston, Ontario, for making aluminum propellor blades and other parts for aircraft.

The Beedells left for Georgetown on the *R.H. Carr* in the fall of 1941 and my mother was very sad to see them go. My father, with his constant communication with the captains of the bauxite vessels, was worried sick. By this time, the harbour in Georgetown bore little resemblance to the place where Evelyn Waugh and my mother had landed some 12 to 15 years earlier. Henri Charriere, the man known as 'Papillon,' who arrived in Georgetown in 1941 on his last escape from the infamous Devil's Island prison in French Guiana, described the scene: "The mouth of the Demerara river was very carefully watched and guarded by nests of machine guns, torpedo-tubes and heavy artillery. [In the harbour] A great many merchant ships, launches and men-of-war. Guns in turrets, standing on the banks of the river. What with these and all the others aboard the naval vessels, it was a positive arsenal. It was war time. The war had been going on for two years, Georgetown, the capital of British Guiana, was an important port on the Demerara river, and it was in the war up to its neck ~ involved a hundred per cent. I found it very queer indeed, this feeling of a town under arms."

In the office of the subsidiary company of Sprostons, the Beedells heard a radio message from 'Lord Haw Haw' that there were 23 boats in Georgetown Harbour loaded and ready to leave. This was the name used by William Joyce to broadcast German propaganda that was intended to demoralize the Allies with news that would shock or alarm them. Alarm the Beedells it certainly did, for they realized that the news would certainly go out to every U-boat in the area, but the family felt that there was nothing for it but to board their ship for the trip north and pray that they would get to a safe shore at the other end. Before they left, a man in the Georgetown office took them home for a meal with his family. John Beedell wondered aloud who had given the Germans the information about the ships in the harbour. "It certainly wasn't me!" their host joked. After the Beedells arrived in Canada, they were shocked to learn that their host *was* the person who had been passing on the information to the enemy. He had been arrested shortly after they sailed.

The *Lady Hawkins*, on which they boarded, was a Canadian National Steamship, one of the five 'Lady Boats' named for wives of British admirals with a West Indian connection. The ships had originally sailed out of Halifax on expensive, luxury cruises to the Caribbean and British Guiana in the 1930s. In their spanking white trim, the Lady Boats had given first-class passenger service as well as doing the double duty of carrying and delivering important cargoes to and from the further ports. Vessels of the line that took the eastern Caribbean run sailed all year round from Halifax, calling at Bermuda and various islands en route south. Georgetown was the final southern destination, but it was not a favourite for the ship's crews. "Georgetown was a hot sticky place which made for an uncomfortable three days' stay rarely anticipated with enthusiasm," said Felicity Hanington in her description of the Lady Boats in the book of the same name. "Indicative of the officers' attitudes was a written order from the Company forbidding them to make derogatory remarks about the place to passengers; for it had far-reaching effects that might interfere with the business." Business included not only human service but collecting a cargo of sugar from Bookers and perhaps giving the ship a good clean and white paint job in the three days while returning passengers were staying ashore in local hotels.

When the war started, the spanking white Lady Boats were transformed to drab grey and their duties became more utilitarian. One of them, the *Lady Somers*, was the first merchant ship to be converted to an armed cruiser and go to war, where she was soon sunk off the coast of France. The *Lady Hawkins*, along with others of the line, continued to travel West Indian waters carrying passengers and cargo, but it was an anxious trip northwards for all aboard that fall of 1941 as the ship called at several islands and did the usual Bermuda-Boston run en route, with everyone all too conscious of the ever-present threat of potential U-boat attack. Nina Beedell remembers the blackout curtains which plunged their cabin into total darkness, and said that her father never slept at night. Having worked on board so many ships in the past, he stayed up with the Captain as they anxiously scanned the ocean for submarines. They were lucky enough to land in Halifax as scheduled, but it was to be the last safe journey for this Lady Boat and her passengers and crew.

After Pearl Harbour when the United States entered the war officially, by the end of 1941 and the beginning of 1942 the Nazi submarines began to patrol the Eastern Seaboard. "It became extremely difficult to move ships safely to the Caribbean without providing escorts," said Hanington. "It was felt however that the ships must be kept moving, and those whose speed provided them with an additional measure of security were ordered to sail independently on routes which had not yet proven dangerous." The lone 4-inch B.L. Low Angle Gun and naval gunlayer with which the Lady Boats were equipped, with a guncrew chosen from members of the regular crew, was not enough to protect the *Lady Hawkins* on her next trip south, with tragic consequences for the staff in Mackenzie. John Beedell's replacement and another man flew to BG ahead of their families, who followed them out by sea. The men made it but not the wives. Campbell said "In January 1942, the C.N.R passenger vessel Lady Hawkins was torpedoed off Cape

Hatteras with the loss of 250 lives, including the four wives en route to join their Alcan husbands in Guyana." The fate of the passengers was described in painful detail in *The Lady Boats: The Life and Times of Canada's West Indies Merchant Fleet* by Felicity Hanington assisted by Percy A. Kelly. The ship went down in the early hours of the morning and only one lifeboat, so crammed with people that they had to stand and take turns while some were able to sleep sitting up, made it to safety. Two lifeboats got away from the ship but were never seen again while in the one remaining Chief Officer Kelly said in his official report that he had to give the agonizing order to pull away from the people left in the water around the sinking vessel because they already had 76 people on board a 30-foot lifeboat that was made to take 63. He said, "The cries of the people in the water rang in my ears for years."

The tragedies of war were now reaching Mackenzie directly, and the headaches with the bauxite shipping continued to escalate. The problems with the U-boats in 1941 had occurred mainly outside of the arc of the Caribbean area, but as long-range submarines were built, it became possible for the Germans to send them further afield. It was at the beginning of 1942 when the first serious U-boat forays to the Caribbean and the West Indies began. Clay Blair, with access to post-war German records, was able to detail the activities in *Hitler's U-Boat War*. On 20 and 25 January, five Type IXC U-boats, called the Neuland (New Land) group, were despatched from the coast of France by Admiral Donitz to the Trinidad and Venezuela area with the specific mission to prevent the flow of oil and bauxite from South America to North America. At one-engine speed, it took them three weeks or more to reach their destination. They all launched their attacks on the same day, 16 February, when the moon was new. One of the submarines, U-129, captained by Nikolaus Clausen, specifically patrolled the area south-east of Trinidad in the open Atlantic to intercept the bauxite traffic. In four days, 20-23 February, he torpedoed and sank four freighters. He then cruised south along the coast to British and Dutch Guiana to interdict the bauxite traffic at the source, but was defeated by the shallow waters of the 100-mile wide continental shelf and an emergency hold or diversion of shipping. Returning to the Trinidad area, in seven days, 28 February to 6 March, Clausen sank three more freighters. In total, because the U.S. naval base had not been completed at Chaguaramas, the Neuland U-boats had a heyday with commercial shipping and by the time they left for home they had delivered "a jarring and psychological wallop in the Caribbean". They had sunk 24 ships and probably damaged eight, of which 17 were tankers but the rest were likely bauxite carriers. Some of the attacked freighters may have been the long-awaited British ships sent out in February to help the bauxite shipping crisis. Of these, Campbell said 17 had set sail for British Guiana and only three or four arrived.

Further groups of U-boats were sent out in April to various areas in the New World ~ U.S. east coast, Bahamas, Gulf of Mexico and the inner Caribbean, the West Indies and Brazil ~ with varying degrees of success. The four VII-type boats in the Gulf of Mexico and Caribbean area had disappointing results by German reckoning. At sea for about 70 days, these boats sank 11 ships, an average of 2.2 ships per boat per patrol, which was small compensation for the extreme hardships the crews endured from the terrible tropical heat and humidity and the chronic shortages of food and fresh water.

But the 13 long-range IX-types that left France that April shattered all existing records. Including sailing vessels, they sank 95 ships (26 tankers) in about 76 days out, losing only one boat. One of the sailing vessels was the *Florence M. Douglas* which had three live pigs on board. The submarine crew killed and ate two of them but adopted the third as a mascot which they presented to their flotilla commander on return to France. Another vessel was Brazilian and encouraged the movement of that government towards eventually declaring war on Germany.

Just how close the U-boats came to Georgetown is illustrated in a story by Henri Charriere. He had met a Frenchman in Georgetown who had been on board a Canadian ship carrying bauxite that had been torpedoed in the mouth of the river. "He stood drinks all round. As a survivor he'd been given a sum of money on account of the sinking. Almost the whole of the crew had been drowned. He'd been lucky enough to be able to get into a lifeboat. He told us the German submarine surfaced and spoke to them. It had asked them how many ships were still in the port, waiting to sail with cargoes of bauxite. When they said they didn't know, the man who had been questioning them laughed. 'Yesterday I was in such-and-such a cinema in Georgetown,' he said. 'Look at this half of the ticket.' And it seems he opened his coat and said, 'This suit comes from Georgetown.' Unbelievers said it was just bluff, but Faussard would have it that it was so, and I've no doubt he was telling the truth. He said the submarine even told them what ship was going to come and pick them up: and indeed that very ship did save their lives."

The terrible toll at sea was depressing and frustrating for those involved in bauxite shipping. A map of the U-boat slaughter between January and July 1942 shows an incredible cluster of sinkings around Georgetown and Port of Spain, Trinidad, and continues around the arc of the West Indies and up the U.S. coast, with a loss of 2 1/2 million tons of shipping in independent attacks for very light losses. In May 1942, when the trans-shipment station for bauxite was completed and the U.S. naval base at Chaguaramas was fully operational, there were sighs of relief in Mackenzie that the shipping problems would ease. But according to Campbell, the submarine situation concerning bauxite was at its worst in the spring and summer of 1942. In June, there were almost daily ship disappearances. The company shipping group, Saguenay Terminals Limited, alone lost 25 laden ships and 117 crewmen in 1942. "For a considerable period, when naval ships were too scarce to offer much protection from the submarines, the bauxite freighters were dispatched out of Trinidad, St. Thomas or Guyana towards North American ports, particularly Portland, Maine, but subject to the captain's judgement to run into any haven on the seaboard. This presented a huge guessing game for Alcan's traffic department, which was forced to disperse up to 200 men to various ports ~ New Orleans, Norfolk, Newport News, New York or Portland ~ to receive cargoes wherever they might happen to arrive and arrange their movement by rail to Arvida. Some anxiety was lifted in 1942, after America had entered the war, and at least one convoy per week was dispatched from Charaguaramas with U.S. Navy protection." Campbell does not mention whether Canada participated in the convoys guarding the bauxite freighters although at least one had been committed for escorting oil tankers from Trinidad to Halifax.

Commander Tony German (*The Sea at our Gates: The History of the Canadian Navy*) said that when the Canadian escort service was started along the eastern seaboard in 1942, from Halifax to Boston and later Florida, merchant ships sailed with escorts by day and sheltered in anchorages at night. They called it the Bucket Brigade. Sinkings slowed. This left the Caribbean naked, allowing for Donitz's 'milch cow' submarines to do their work. Commander German reckoned that some 500 ships were torpedoed in the six months leading up to June 1942, and 121 in June after that. Once the convoy system was in place, however, with the Canadians interlocking with the Americans, in the first three months of 1943, 1400 ships sailed through the Caribbean and up the east coast and only 11 were lost.

To protect the vital oil supply from the Caribbean, the Canadian navy pulled eight Corvettes from the Atlantic run and started Trinidad-Halifax tanker convoys in May 1942. Six more Corvettes went later. "The Canadian convoys came through without a single loss," said German. The story of additional vessels used as Canadian escorts is one of desperation and ingenuity. "Luxury yachts were extracted from the U.S. by devious means. Some fishing vessels were requisitioned. Mostly, their crews donned uniforms. The dockyard fitted a gun if it was available, they hoisted the White Ensign, and they were in the navy. Some of the yachts, though quite unsuitable, were used as A/S escorts."

Of these unusual convoy vessels that ended up in the Caribbean, one in particular had an interesting history that relates to the bauxite industry. She was a luxury yacht owned by a Mrs. Hardcastle in New York. On her maiden voyage in 1928, around the time that my father arrived in Mackenzie, she sailed from New York with a number of stockbrokers on board, heading for British Guiana. She went up the Demerara River to Mackenzie to allow her passengers to inspect the bauxite mining and ore-washing operation. Then she sailed through the Caribbean and the Panama Canal to the Galapagos Islands and back before going up the east coast to Canada and Arvida, where they toured the new aluminum refinery before returning to New York. This was the year that Alcoa and Alcan were divided and these stockbrokers were interested to see the Canadian side of the operation for themselves. When World War II started, that yacht was one of the ones that was bought by the Canadian Government by someone posing as a private individual. He sailed her to Halifax where she was immediately gutted and transformed into the HMCS *Ark*. She did convoy duty in the West Indies throughout the war without seeing action. After the war, for a time she was used as a training vessel until she was bought by the New Brunswick government and refitted again as the *Grand Manan III* ferry. Many people on the island remember her for the way she rolled in heavy seas and how she hoisted only nine cars on board at a time, and they still talk about the day the crew accidentally dropped one car in the drink. To complete the circle of our story, when the ferry rounded the last piece of land to come in to the wharf at North Head, Grand Manan, she passed the summer home of Milton Gregg, who represented Canada in Georgetown when British Guiana became Guyana, when the bauxite industry was nationalized and Mackenzie changed its name to Linden. But that time was still long years ahead.

There is a final and interesting postscript about the U-boat, U-66, that downed the *Lady Hawkins*. Related by Michael Gannon in *Operation Drumbeat*, it is surely one of the most extraordinary stories of the U-boat war. U-66 was captained by Richard Zapp when the fatality occurred. After many successes in Atlantic waters, Zapp left to become commander of the 3rd Flotilla at La Rochelle in France where he defended the U-boat base up to the end of the war in May 1945. His boat, however, after sinking 33 ships and damaging four others in total, met its end a year earlier. It could not have happened without the breaking of the Nazi Enigma code. Commanded by Gerhard Seehausen, on the moonlit night of 5 May 1944, U-66 was forced to surface off the Cape Verde Islands and radio Berlin that it needed to refuel. Complaining that the mid-Atlantic was worse than the Bay of Biscay for stalking Allied naval destroyers and carriers, Seehausen gave his usual position information. In no time, the message was picked up and decoded and relayed to the destroyer USS *Buckley*, which raced to the spot on the morning of 6 May. With torpedoes and gunfire from the surfaced U-boat and firing from the evading destroyer, the captain of the *Buckley* made the risky decision to ram U-66. A surprising event followed the encounter. The crew of the crippled submarine streamed out of the conning tower and forward hatch and up into the fo'c's'le of the destroyer prepared for hand-to-hand combat! Five Germans were overpowered and taken below before Captain Abel reversed his ship's engines and his gun crews fired furiously into the sub, which then proceeded to add to his astonishment by ramming his ship, shearing off her starboard shaft and propeller and causing widespread damage. With this final blaze of glory, U-66 went down for the last time. The *Buckley* recovered 36 prisoners, including four officers, before making it safely back to the New York Navy Shipyard on her port screw with her own crew unharmed.

162

Bauxite production for the war effort

Bauxite plant, Mackenzie

the Mine
Akyma

Trewern Mine

Last Days in Mackenzie

Aside from the U-boat tragedies and anxieties that had so affected our small community, and before the size and pace of Mackenzie changed completely with the pressures of the outside war in 1942, life for our families in Watooka remained much the same in the early years of the war. Yet there were undercurrents and hints that all was not entirely smooth sailing, a portent of things to come.

When we got back from our idyllic summer in Canada in the fall of 1940, Ian Thompson and I were ready to join Jackie Bradley in real school instead of kindergarten. Yet, try as hard as I have to remember, I have absolutely no recollection of a new teacher coming to replace our beloved Miss Tudhope. She was now Mrs. Paul Fenton and had moved into Paul's small house next door to the school after she was married. In her letters home, she mentioned a new teacher arriving, but who it was who taught us the alphabet and the tools for reading, and whether we ever met the immortal 'Dick and Jane' of first primers in North America, is an unsolved mystery in my life. By the following year, I seem to remember someone saying that another new teacher had come to teach us, but she hated Mackenzie and was gone by Christmas, leaving us with no school for some time.

In the gap without a teacher, I was ready and desperate to read, anything and everything I could find. There was not much in the way of books in our house. My mother said the silverfish or the cockroaches ate all the pages of every book she took out there. But she did have one readable copy of *Wind in the Willows* which I read, slowly and painfully, from cover to cover, not relating to a word of it. For a first reader, it was tough going, with smallish print and a lot of new words for a child to learn, but it was in the essence that it was a problem. It was so hard for me to imagine the tiny English river, so tame and pretty with its willow-laced edges and its talking animals of whom I had never heard, when the only river I knew was alive with piranhas, and alligators up hidden creeks, and it was wide and tannin-stained brown and overhung with dense tropical greenery and totally undomesticated.

Looking back, I realize that we do not absorb what we just read, only what we can read and truly understand, and this book, like so many of the English children's classics ~ *Alice's Adventures in Wonderland*, *The Water-Babies*, *The World of Christopher Robin* and *Winnie the Pooh*, even the hated *Peter Pan* ~ had no base for me to begin to understand. The lack of knowing our parents' England was a general problem for colonial children. Outwardly, unless we had been unable to resist the lovely local lilt of where we were living, we might have had imposed English accents like our parents, and we might have displayed the English attitudes that were dinned into us, consciously or unconsciously, by our English parents, but unlike them we had no English roots that went deep down into the soil of our knowing. We lived on guesswork and second-hand information, so that all the books we read were double fiction. Unfortunately, in the smaller colonies like British Guiana, there were no local books that told us things that were rooted in what we could see and understand around us, and no one told us that this was really home because it was where we were living, so we ended up being strangers both in the land that our parents called 'Home' and in the land that should have been ours for the sharing. For a child like me, who was a true 'mudhead', the term used for anyone born in BG, I had as much right to be Guianese as anyone born of the six nations who had all come from somewhere else, even with my alien white skin and overlord political inheritance. Yet I was never allowed to think of myself as Guianese because I was considered to be a little English child who eventually would go home where I really belonged. The end result of this was the feeling that I belonged nowhere.

Living in Mackenzie brought another confusing dimension to the problem of belonging. It brought teachers from Canada who did not reinforce, even second-hand, the English assumptions and feelings of my parents. When more and more new Canadian staff and families arrived, they brought more and more strange ideas with them, which meant an adjustment not only for us English-oriented children but for our parents. What stands out for me most, in my induction into Canadian tradition, was my first Hallowe'en, which was equally strange for my mother and father. For them, that time of year in England was celebrated with the effigy-burning fires and fireworks of November the Fifth to commemorate the capture of the traitor Guy Fawkes before he managed to blow up the British Houses of Parliament. Celebrating All Hallows Eve instead, the night when all the dark Underworld forces prowled the universe before they were banished by the coming of All Saints' Day on 1 November, meant that, for the first time in Watooka, we non-Canadian children had our initial acquaintance with hobgoblins and things that went bump in the night. We were also, magically, allowed to do something that had never happened before. We were not only allowed but expected, on that night, to go outside after dark.

Dressing up was not new to us. We had had a children's fancy-dress birthday party at the Bradleys' before this, when I was Heidi with long fake braids and

Jackie was a wonderful Chinese lady with a black wig and silk robes, but this time we all had to be scary and dress accordingly. My mother, whose heart may not have been in all this Hallowe'en business, dressed me up as a ghost. Standing unhappily in the bedroom being covered in a white bedsheet with holes cut out for eyes and a slit for a mouth, I complained bitterly that I couldn't breathe. After a few necessary adjustments, twitching impatiently, I joined the other ghostly and witchy children in an exciting trek along the black road (presumably someone had been out beforehand to clear off any snakes) to the Canadian houses where we certainly stopped at the Fentons' ("On Hallowe'en the children came to Shell Out, just like home and they are a scream") and perhaps it was at the Parsons' house where we all went inside and partook of a weird drink called Coca-Cola and ate strange orange sweets that we were supposed to call candy. It was very hot and uncomfortable under the sheet, even on a cool tropic night, and it was hard to drink through the engulfing linen without acquiring a lipstick of liquid, but we managed to survive amid the grins of the adults who seemed to enjoy it all far more than we did.

Our old teacher, Jean Fenton, had had to make some adjustments to her lifestyle in Mackenzie after her marriage, when, with no children to teach, she suddenly had long daytime hours on her hands. Although she was happy to hide under the house where she and Paul had created an attractive outdoor sanctuary, she finally joined in some of the ladies' activities she had been glad to have an excuse to avoid in the past. She decided to play golf and sent to Canada for a set of clubs ("I know there are several old lots at home and they would be perfect for me to whizz in and out of sand traps") which arrived with an Entry Tax of nine dollars to pay. In her letters, her game is often mentioned as she struggled with mixed results, but she did say that she was enjoying her good pals on the course. These must have included my mother and Mrs. Thompson for there was one occasion when she mentioned that one of her pals was bitten by a snake and on another she called my mother by name. It was not one of her brightest days. "Thursday, I started out to play golf, alone," she said. "First one of the girls joined me, and then Paul came along. All this time, my game grew steadily worse. Finally one of the lads joined us, and I went haywire. I fanned until I was breathless and sobbing. They all stood politely watching. Gladys stood beside. Sez I: 'Gladys, move, I hit Eric the other day and he was standing just where you are.' She didn't and I hit her, then they all moved in a hurry! Oh, it's awful. I simply cannot play very well alone – but let anyone appear, and I am beside myself!" In time her game improved although for a while after this incident she was somewhat cautious. "I think I am too dangerous, when I play games," she mourned. "Having hit Gladys and Eric with golf balls, and, having to all appearances, thrown a club at Paddy, I have not played lately."

In her letters home from 1939 to 1940, she commented that she would no longer be able to send photographs to her family in Canada. "I find that no snaps are allowed out of the colony now, war time regulation. Apparently, even my smiling countenance against a background of trees is included in the forbidden list." At first it seemed that life in Mackenzie went on as usual, interrupted with anxious comments as to how the war was going. It was not long before her letters arrived in Canada opened and marked by the official Censor. In April 1940, she wrote: "We are all feeling low over the war news. We just don't talk about the war among ourselves in the colony but Paul and I are horrified at the way the Nazis are whipping along. Several of us gather each night to listen to the news together. Zinduven, the head painter, comes to hear." Reflecting on the mood of the times, she said "It's impossible to beat the British West Indian when it comes to unquestioning loyalty to Britain."

The Fentons were having their house enlarged that spring and the mess was indescribable. "They started work on the house proper on Thursday, and the banging is beyond description, but I don't mind. Only this morning it poured rain and of course the roof leaked where they are joining it. And lo! a tidal wave swept through the house, so I am sitting here with rugs up and curtains and chairs soaking wet. I went to the kitchen to quiet my nerves with a little snack and found all the electric power off, so our week's supply of meat lay putrefying in the Frig. Rage filled me so I flung it on the stove and cooked it all. I usually don't look at the cheaper cuts at all, as they have dear little bits of hide on them. But, as it cooked one piece of steak drew me like a magnet, so at 9.30 a.m. I ate a large portion covered with green tomato pickle. It was very tough but I sucked it happily." Two weeks later, she wrote: "The renovation is still in process, but we have the worst behind us! We dwelt among falling timbers and crashes all week. Our stove was spirited away, and I brewed us little bits of food in the living-room on our hot plate, witch style on the floor, with painters and carpenters all around me and wet paint. Then we had bat trouble and had to have the attic de-batted. That nearly ruined me. I went out to the kitchen which was a series of planks to walk on, with no walls, and a hideous smell of bat pervading the atmosphere. Next step was no lights, like Lucy Gray, we wandered in the darkness with naught but a candle to light our way. Now, I am crouched here with our worldly goods piled high around me, and cockroaches gambolling hither and yon. Carpenters are hammering contentedly on all sides of me and in the new bathroom the great unmentionable is overflowing happily. Wish you could hear the conversations of the painters. Zindaven, the foreman, cries at intervals 'Pull, man pull on that brush. What wrong, Man?' Follows a long tirade on war, Hitler and Mussolini." Earlier, she had heard the workmen working on a garden and one of the men was late. Said the foreman: "Wheah you ben, man?" The workman, who had just come from church, said: "Boy, I ben wid Jesus." "Boy," retorted the foreman, "Jesus right here wid us. Git aftah dat shovel!"

One night in August 1940, while the Thompsons and Whalleys were still away on leave in Canada, she was startled awake by a nasty accident. "Have just been rudely wakened from a lovely sleep. About 20 minutes ago the most blood-curdling cries for help rang through the night. A corial, with two men, upset and one man was drowned, and the other was taken to hospital. So Paul is away with the police. It is incredible how quickly one can drown. Perhaps there was a peri around. Anyway, it gives me the creeps."

Domestically, she was still struggling with everything that seemed to go wrong with too much frequency. The washerwoman, who was slow and surly, drove her crazy and she tried to fire her but the result was tears and weeping so she continued to keep her on, but it was not a happy arrangement. In the kitchen, she still had Paul's old servant and theirs was an up-and-down relationship as they tried in vain to understand each other. One morning Jean looked around the kitchen and asked "Why didn't that garbage go with the collector this morning, Johanna?" Surprised, Johanna answered "Madam, this is today's garbage, nice and fresh, he took away yesterday's garbage." She decided to teach Johanna what she considered the proper way to wash dishes. "Her method is to put all in the sink and splash, looking out the window the while. She is very cross with me and I am being very firm. I found her cooking steak with a nail in it to make it tender the other day. Also I discovered that she puts the meat in a sunbeam for two hours before cooking it. She has a deep distrust of the Frigidaire and would prefer it quite empty always, with the food on a shelf nearby. However, on the credit side, she just made some marvellous guava jelly. Ah me—" One day, she mentioned that Johanna was in deep disgrace because she had let ants and cockroaches into the fridge, which had to be defrosted every other day in the heat and humidity.

170

She was constantly plagued by the armies of ants and the ever-present cockroaches. She house-cleaned the cupboards searching for cockroaches but "This morning when I washed my face (still half asleep) there was a huge cockroach on the wash cloth. How I hate them." As if this was not enough, she said "This is evidently 'Ant Time' in Demerara! And it doesn't help out the everlasting domestic troubles. Did I tell you I had purchased some deadly poison and I dole it out and try to lure the ants to partake of it and everyone is horrified at my even having it. I care not for that, though. Tuesday, I golfed and trod on a nest of red ants which ended my golf and disposition. Our red ants are real man eaters and I wept with pain and rage. It's a case of survival of the fittest between me and the ants. I hear that it's mostly my imagination but it's not!! My pants, slips, shoes and socks are always full of them and I scratch steadily. Have lured a giant spider (2" across the beam) into the dry closet to fetch out ants. However, one ant sting will fell even that monster!" By Hallowe'en: "I have lost in the war against Ants and now I just try to get out of their way. They have their favourite treks and I would not for the world interfere. I only hope they don't decide to move the dining room table. I suppose I told you about the spider -- a stout fellow of good proportions I put in with the Ants. Alas, the next day the ants carried off its battered carcass. Last night in the middle of dinner a clutch of ants appeared in Indian File, bearing the still struggling body of a huge cockroach with the foreman riding in style upon the victim!" She was always amazed by what the ants could do. "Last night we killed a cockroach at 10 p.m. and left it where it lay. This morning the ants had carried it right up the wall, easily 8' -- wonderful speed really. I have just flitted all of them: 5 foremen, 6 scouts and 150 workers. Good-night."

Wartime problems with food supply began to filter into the camp in 1940. "Am making marmalade a la B.G. in wartime out of one grapefruit and some colony [brown] sugar," she said as August ended. "This week I went frugal again and decided that Johanna should bake our bread and ordered no bread from the store. Imagine my horror to discover no flour at the store. And of course I could get no bread as I hadn't ordered it. They just smile and say 'None at all, Mistress!' " Duncan Campbell said that since Mackenzie was entirely dependent on imported commodities, when the returning bauxite ships were torpedoed, the food supplies dwindled too. At one point butter was rationed to two ounces per person, and cigarettes to ten per adult, per week. When Mackenzie ran out of flour completely for a period, Paul Fenton ground up the local corn intended for the chickens and rationed it to the housewives, who weren't very pleased.

On 24 September 1940, the Fentons heard about the children in southern England being evacuated due to the bombing raids: "Have just heard the news. We listen to all short wave broadcasts avidly. Heard the King and were so sorrowful about the children. I think the mothers very brave." To answer her family's questions about how the camp got the news, she wrote that "we hear the B.B.C. news at 12.15 noon (rebroadcast from Georgetown), and English news at 7 p.m., Lowell Thomas at 8 and the 11 o'clock later. There isn't much use our subscribing to the daily papers from town, as there are only three mail deliveries a week. I wish we could all get together and talk about the war. I belong to Britain's silent column here and we never mention it. Though, true to form, I find the English members of our group are cheerful and bright, while their people are under fire in England. We are making a cook book for the Red Cross. At our last dance we raised nearly $200 for our Bomber fund." As Christmas approached, she said: "Things are so different with the war that the parties are becoming few and far between. We'll have to gather up some pals to celebrate with us in our little nest... Paul has bought a [live] turkey (15 lbs supposedly) which I will lead into the doctor's office and weigh as I suspect I am being overcharged or undercharged or something. Then we will buy a little grain to fatten up the victim." They had a bad day when she got a spell of homesickness and Paul was brooding because he was not in khaki, when "a school of cockroaches came swinging along so we had to spring into action. It's been hellishly hot and I have little energy but I got out our box of Christmas decorations ~ contents: one dead cockroach, two ends of red candle, so I gave up feeling Noelish." She decided she would try her hand at making stuffed giraffe toys for the younger children for Christmas, and have a go at making sunsuits for the 3-4 year olds and aprons for the older girls. Her spirits rose in December when a box of presents, including new clothes, arrived for her from home and some of the ship's officers from one of the bauxite boats turned up with 30 lbs of spare-ribs so they had a marvellous feast. Johanna was very impressed by the spare-ribs, awed by the 'beautiful fat', having only seen meat from the lean Guianese cattle.

Despite the restrictions, yuletide celebrations in Mackenzie that year were "very merry and a lot of fun! One very young newcomer constituted himself the spirit of Christmas and followed me around all night blessing me and saying: 'I bring you a special blessing as the only child in a family of 12.' Later at another party, he didn't recognize me at all, until after his first cocktail had been consumed. Then I immediately became his dearest friend again... The Parsons had a lovely party and we all sang and sang, all the Walt Disney songs. The children and I were the loudest and strongest... Forgot whether I told you that I got mixed up in a game of Nuts and May at the school closing and found myself 'pulling Jim away'. However in two years, Jim has grown a lot and besides he had on sneakers... With all the children looking on, Jim hoisted me clear off the floor ~ so my prestige is gone!"

Christmas was not the end of the parties in the community, for in January 1941 they received an official visit from the Governor and his wife, the first for many years. "Their Excellencies were charming," said Jean, "and the reception and accompanying parties were lovely. A very delightful interlude all round." It certainly made a change from her new pursuits in a different field because she was helping her husband when he was put in charge of the dairy at the Mackenzie Farm, which was now supplying the entire community with milk. "I've been up to my neck in Dairy Cattle with Paul since he has taken over. I have been reading and learning about feed with him. He has just sold the Bull. The Bull, I may say has been the chief source of amusement at all functions lately. The Bull, it seems, is no good. Anyway, after selling the animal, the problem immediately arose of how to remove it. Paul was off in a flash with rope and stuff and soon, sure enough, along the road came quite a cortege. There were eight men in front of the Bull, and eight behind, with Paul behind them again. It's simply colossal and took some managing to get away. It's a Holstein, not a Creole ~ the Creole cows and bulls have a sort of dewlap in front. The last stage of the Bull episode was a wondrous steak which was presented to Paul. I brooded over and then ate a great deal of it. It was gorgeous. Then the new Bull butted his keeper ~ started the Bull conversation all over again!" Finally, she reported that Bull Number Two was fair ~ "only just fair, I hear ~ but we're getting such dandy milk at the farm now, we may get a sterilizer for it."

It was entirely thanks to Paul Fenton that the farm was doing so well. He was in constant touch with the Director of the Botanical Gardens in Georgetown, so their garden at home fared much better than the one my mother had tried in her earliest days. "The day after we were married we called on him in town. He and Paul had a touching conversation (about two hours long) on manure. They are blood brothers and send each other shoots of things all the time. Poor Paul, I try and take over the garden now that he is so busy and every day, I break my finger nails to bits pulling out the hose and greater love hath no woman than this!"

The Fentons went on leave in the spring of 1941, the spring that was to mark the last year of our family stay in Mackenzie. By now, the camp was beginning to change rapidly. "I struggle to keep up with events," Jean said, "but they happen too fast for me. Amazing things happen every day ~ new people float in and out. I gasp and by the time I get around to asking them here, they have gone." New staff members kept arriving from Canada, some with wives and children, and the hospital was kept busy with new babies, two of whom were born on the same day which put the doctor and nurses in a frenzy. "They were mostly young college graduates," my mother said, and with their arrival the whole camp soon changed character completely. No longer interested at all in maintaining a British colonial status quo, no longer willing to put up with all the inconveniences with which my mother and even Jean Fenton had struggled with all those years, these were young Canadian professionals with Canadian ideas and expectations. Even in wartime, they expected Mackenzie to be like a Canadian company town. New houses had to be built to accommodate them. Eventually, 50 new houses and some bachelor quarters were needed in Watooka to house the incoming staff, which grew to 70 after we left and before the war ended.

By now, a new mine had been opened across the river from Akyma and a bridge had had to be built to connect the original railway with the new location. The Hope Mine was in full production by January 1940 and bauxite was pouring out. Gil Walwork was in charge of the mines as the wartime pressure mounted to fever pitch. Soon they would expand again and work day and night with a new diesel locomotive to carry more and more ore to expanded plant facilities for washing, crushing drying, and loading onto whatever ships were able to escape the U-boat blockage.

By Christmas 1941, the first December after Pearl Harbour when the States had finally entered the war, we children had apples as well as oranges in our Christmas stockings. The apples came from the U.S. Air Force base at Atkinson Field, situated about halfway between Mackenzie and Georgetown, that Demba had helped to build. Campbell stressed that the base was needed urgently for the staging and refuelling of planes being flown for the United States, via Belem in Brazil, across the Atlantic to Africa and to the war zone along the Mediterranean. It was impossible for the U.S. Forces to provide sufficient heavy equipment to construct the base until Demba loaned a large complement of bulldozers, floating them down the Demerara to Atkinson on barges. Demba also supplied operators and mechanics to accomplish the heavy grading of the airfield. This allied cooperation received hearty appreciation. In our day, there was no road to get to the base from Mackenzie but we knew they were there because from time to time we were buzzed by young pilots flying much too low over our tinny rooftops. Eventually, inevitably, one young pilot got too careless and his plane had a closer than intended encounter with a large tree in the rainforest canopy. A lot of "I told you so" comments went around the camp when that happened, and after that the pilots displayed more decorum in their overhead patrols.

That was the Christmas when the Watooka children rehearsed and put on the Bethlehem story for an audience of parents in the Big House. It was staged in the large drawing room, with all of us children standing just inside the archway from the hall. The room had been completely cleared of its usual furniture except for one big couch in the right hand corner by the window, which apparently had been too large and heavy to move. All the parents, looking proud and expectant, plus interested adults, which was probably at least half the rest of the Watooka community, were seated on straight dining-room chairs in front of us. Appropriately, as the oldest and the Manager's children, Jimmy and Barbara Parsons were Joseph and Mary, but I am unsure about the rest of our roles. I seem to remember having to suffer being a shepherd in a scratchy outfit of sackcloth because we didn't have enough boys in the camp. In fact, I can only think of Jimmy, Ian, and a little fellow called David Wallwork, who was born a year or two before my sister, but the photos show other small boys who are new arrivals so maybe after all I was draped in that bed sheet again as an angel. I do remember that my baby sister, who was not yet three years old, and another tiny girl, whose name I have forgotten, were the littlest angels. They looked truly angelic standing there as we awkwardly laid the doll-baby in a bed of straw and trebled carols about the magical birth in the stable. Halfway through the performance, in the middle of 'Away in a Manger', the little angels got bored with the whole thing. With a roar of laughter from the audience and a look of utter disgust from an older sister, Margie and friend took off for the couch, and bounced and giggled and had a wonderful time as we struggled for a dignified ending to our Christmas miracle.

That was our last Christmas in Mackenzie. By the spring of 1942, my mother was the last of the original wives from the 1920s, and she looked in envy at the young women who came out via Miami in smart, suitable lightweight clothes that had been bought while they waited for an available plane. By comparison, she was a tired old veteran, much as she had viewed the older wives on her arrival 13 years earlier. She missed Ethel Beedell and her old friend Minnie Kerr. By now, Archie Kerr had retired and they had moved to Georgetown. But it would not be long before she saw them again because my mother's 'prison sentence' in Mackenzie was nearly at an end. My father would soon be transferred to Sprostons to handle the shipping papers from the Georgetown end. My mother always proudly told her daughters that after we left he was replaced by eight men, making us think that he was a mathematical genius of mythic proportions. It was true that he was good at figures, and fast, for he used to annoy his juniors later in the non-adding machine age by adding columns rapidly in his head from left to right while they were still adding up from right to left at a slower pace, but of course the reason he was replaced by so many people was because of the general expansion. By the time we left, it was the end of the old Mackenzie that we knew, which would never be the same again.

Nina Beedell, David Wallwork and Margaret Whalley behind friend.

Hallowe'en costumes, 1940

The Sea Wall Years

Moving from Mackenzie to Georgetown in 1942 was like moving to another continent. Where Mackenzie was closed in by the high green walls of the rainforest and restricted to a small number of familiar people, Georgetown was wide open to the sea and sand and sky, with an ocean of strangers, all shapes and colours and nations of origin. For the first time, we could actually classify ourselves as 'colonials'. Mackenzie had been an isolated company town with its own rules, which could have been anywhere except that it was set against the accidental backdrop of a colony. In Georgetown, on the other hand, the subsidiary company of Sprostons where my father now worked was only a small part of the greater life of the capital of the colony which flowed all around us. For my mother, to be back in a larger world of shops and activities, away from the scrutiny of her every action in Mackenzie's tight white community, Georgetown spelled freedom, and until she outgrew it again, she revelled in it. For us children, accustomed to knowing everyone around us, and exactly what to expect and what was expected of us, it was all a bit bewildering.

We were lucky, however, that we were able to stay with the Kerrs, now retired from Mackenzie, until we found a house to rent. It was an 'old people's' house where we were staying, full of the kind of furniture that meant that my sister and I had to mind our manners and not knock things over, but Mrs. Kerr was as kind and sweet as she had always been. Mr. Kerr still called me 'Wendy-moo' after a popular song that went, at least when sung in BG, 'When de moon comes over de mountains', and entertained us girls, as he always did, with dancing false teeth that captured our horrified fascination. They had beautiful china in that house with strange exotic birds in the design, which, for reasons known only to himself and Whalley tradition, my father called 'kyootas'. And they had a wonderful garden that has been my idea of a secret garden ever since, with masses of shrubs and shell pathways that wound around tortuously so that every turn came as a surprise. It was a perfect place for Margie and me to play hide and seek.

After some searching of their own, my parents found us a house on Duke Street, which was in an old and fashionable district that had been named Kingston after a popular British officer when the colony was captured in 1781. All the other districts in Georgetown except this one retained the names of the original plantations ~ wonderful names like Werk-en-rust and Stabroek and Wortmanville, Le Repentir and La Penitence and Plantation Thomas ~ that had flourished there under the different national governments, Dutch, French, and English, that had all laid claim to the land, until in the end the sugar cane fields were replaced by a rigid grid of arrow-straight streets and stinking drainage canals. In time, the canals were cleaned up or diverted and covered over as the town grew. Kingston, where we moved, was a very small part of the whole, less than half a mile square, while the city spread east and south of us for a couple of miles or more. Our residential district, said to have been the best in Georgetown since the early 19th century, was situated in the extreme northwest corner, bounded on the west by the wharves of the Demerara River, on the north by the Sea Wall and the North Atlantic Ocean, on the east by the military barracks and parade ground, and on the south by the Cummings Canal and the Railway Station.

All the rest of my life, I thought I knew Georgetown, but in fact I did not know it at all. It was, after all, a port in wartime and the streets at night in the business areas were full of sailors and military men, all out looking for a good time. As Henri Charriere described the scene: "The town was crammed with people. Whites, blacks, Indians, Chinese, soldiers and sailors in uniform, and a great many merchant marine sailors. Great numbers of bars, restaurants, pubs and night-clubs; and their glare lit up the streets as though it was midday." We children were sometimes taken by day to the 'Brown Betty', an ice cream parlour recently opened and run by Mrs. Giglioli, the Mackenzie doctor's French Canadian wife whom my mother knew so well, and treated to huge sundaes and banana splits such as we had never seen before, but we were never taken out after dark to see what Georgetown looked like at night. In fact, except for a few forays to the Botanic Gardens where my sister and I would feed handfuls of pulled grass to the manatees, and one outing to the racecourse where someone accidentally lit a fire under the stand on which we were sitting and we all had to climb down in haste, except for going to school in the next district south of the railway station in the last year we were there, the only Georgetown that I really knew was Kingston.

The house we rented was typical of all the others in the district, a large, old, wooden, white-painted Dutch colonial residence with tall slatted shutters to keep out the rain. High columns underneath, like the ones under the bungalows in Mackenzie, added to a sense of airiness. For a garden city, our property did not exactly do its part, however. Everywhere around the house was green except for the front lawn that my mother desperately wanted to look like England. The long weedy grass along the side of Duke Street flourished. The long weedy grass behind the house flourished. But the front 'lawn' that the gardener did his best to water and make good for her always looked dry and sad. Beside the path to the house were two flowerbeds that also did not flower because they contained the wrong plants. It seemed that my mother never learned to stop trying to anglicize the world.

Behind the house, it was not a garden but a yard. The only vegetation that I remember apart from the grass was a group of three banana trees that they said never had fruit because they were all male. Part of the house itself stretched backwards on one side, forming an L, with rooms going back from the kitchen that were used for doing the laundry, and there was the sewing room where the seamstress came every week and worked to make the dance dresses for my mother to wear to club parties and the cotton dresses for us girls that my mother insisted were both the same, except that my sister's were always pink for a girl and mine were still a subconscious blue for the boy they had always wanted. I think there may even have been a room there for Maud, our nurse who had come with us from Mackenzie, and I know there was a bathroom because a skunk-like animal called a 'uwarie', a kind of opossum, got in behind the wall and died there and the smell was awful.

At the very back of the property, by the fence, there were living quarters for the black servants and their families, consisting of perhaps three or four small houses. I never saw inside them because we children were forbidden to go down there. Whatever her grown-up reasons were for stopping us, my mother told us it was because they needed their privacy. Sometimes I saw the adults sitting on their porches rocking and talking, or the women out in front making 'fou fou', a vegetable dish prepared by pounding plantain in a huge wooden mortar with a giant wooden pestle. I don't remember seeing any children or hearing any babies cry, although there must have been children there, but neither from the back buildings nor in the house did I hear angry voices at a level that would frighten a child except once when there was a man yelling down there and everyone screamed to get into the action and then the police were called and peace was restored. Of course we children were kept in the dark about what had caused the fight. Often there was laughter and music floating up from the back and we desperately wanted to go down and join in, as we did when we heard gaiety in the kitchen, but we were firmly showed back to the part of the house where we belonged. We all kept our distance from each other so that life went on in our separate worlds.

As in Mackenzie, 'under the house' was where we children played. There was no one my sister's age when we moved there (she had just turned three) but there was a nice girl next door who was my age and we quickly became buddies. Our parents enjoyed each other's company so we soon settled into a comfortable neighbourly existence. Barbara had an older sister Anne who sometimes joined us under the house. With the enormous difference in ages, our 'play' usually consisted of all of us girls climbing into the big string hammock and giggling in unison about nothing.

Our play changed somewhat when we got animals. We started with a black cat called Roddy, a handsome Persian, who was deaf and dumb. The only noise I ever heard him make was a strange 'Erk' when I accidentally trod on his tail. Roddy fancied himself as a hunter but he was singularly unsuccessful at it. He would see some birds ahead on the path and he would plod purposefully towards them. You could almost see them wait for him, hearing his every step, until just at the last moment they would break out into raucous bird laughter and take off. Sometimes they even flew back and pecked him to complete his humiliation. Roddy sometimes curled up with us on the hammock but he was not very comfortable with our unstable hilarity.

Then we got Ginger. My mother was cycling home in the rain one night when she heard a faint meow coming from a deep puddle and there in the middle of it, drenched and frightened, with two huge woebegone eyes, was the sorriest tabby kitten you ever saw. So home Ginger came to be dried and warmed and fed. The only trouble was, she was always sickly, and when she became a cat and got pregnant, she produced three kittens and then crept away to die, leaving us with three funny little orphans to raise. For the first time, the doll feeding bottles came into play for we would fill them with milk and then we could each sit with a kitten on our lap and watch it suck eagerly at the nipple. That was not hard to teach them, but the hard part came later. We had no idea how much a mother cat teaches her kittens until we tried to discipline naughty little charges and teach them how to clean themselves and how to eat solids. They were very happy with sardines but not at all fond of porridge so the idea of giving them a piece of fish in the middle of their dish in the hope that they would eat their way into it back-fired with a vengeance as they waded in for the part they wanted. With no mother to teach them how to lick their paws, they just thudded around everywhere afterwards, leaving a messy porridge trail behind them. We spent hours with those kittens, dressing them up in dolls' clothes and taking them for walks in the doll carriage. They may not have been very good as kittens but they were immensely cooperative as playthings. We got rid of them to other homes eventually but I am afraid they would not have been the best of pets because of their lack of proper training.

Our final pet was Spot, a mongrel of very indifferent parentage. How boring of us to name him Spot! So ordinary, so plebian! So appropriate! But Spot came to us in grand style. My parents had been to a garden party at the Bishop's Palace and my mother happened to mention that we would like to have a dog. A short time later, an enormous, imposing limousine, flying a very official government flag, drew up at our door on Duke Street. The smart liveried chauffeur bowed to my mother. Would she be interested in a stray dog from His Excellency, the Governor of British Guiana? Well, given the circumstances, who could refuse? The chauffeur opened the back door and brought out a cushion on which lay a skinny, sickly dog, looking miserable. My mother took the dog, cushion and all, the chauffeur saluted and hopped back into the limousine and pulled grandly away. My mother came into the house in a fury. "A pi-dog!" she hissed, referring to its mongrel ancestry. "He's had the gall to send us a pi-dog covered in ticks and mange!" Goodness knows where His Excellency had found the animal. He was a mess. He was covered from head to toe in sores and his hair was matted and dirty. Into a bath our new dog went for an indignant rub-down with carbolic soap that was followed with a good coverage of disinfectant. Spot took a while to start looking like a real dog but he turned into a good pet for the short time we had him. He didn't want to join us in the hammock but he liked to stand underneath and bark his head off, which added to the general excitement.

I remembered the street we lived on as wide and handsome, with many tall trees along its borders. Size, however, is the most unreliable of all our childhood memories. Apparently, everything shrinks as we get older, so I doubt that it was as wide as I remembered it. I also recollect that in front of our house, hanging over the edge of the pavement, was a magnificent buckbean tree. When it was in fruit, it rained the small hard scarlet beans that were so cherished for stringing into attractive necklaces. Hordes of little black boys would appear at harvest time to pick them for their mothers. We too tried picking them to make holes in them for necklaces but they were hard and shiny and extremely difficult to pierce so we eventually gave up in disgust.

Little black boys looking for buck beans were not the only people who came to the house on Duke Street. Sometimes there were peddlers of an unusual sort. These were the men who came from French Guiana selling butterfly brooches. They were ex-convicts from Devil's Island who had served their time behind bars but were forced to remain in the colony for another year before going home to France. To make some money, they made silver jewelry inlaid with pieces of wings from the beautiful blue morpho butterfly and they were allowed to come to British Guiana to sell it. I still have one that my mother bought depicting Kaieteur Falls. Charriere, the man known as 'Papillon', met many convicts from French Guiana living in Georgetown at that time, ones that had either got bored with the 'doublage' sentence after being released and moved away to try and make a living elsewhere, or a few like himself who had made their escape from the terrible prison. Since France had fallen under Nazi occupation, they had no trouble being accepted to stay in British Guiana, although the authorities kept a wary eye on them. They had a difficult time surviving in Georgetown economically. Most of them ended up living on handouts and scams. One man worked out a trick of using the names of French sailors who were reported to have died on a torpedoed ship; he would go to a mason's yard and photograph a tomb with the name of the man and his ship painted on it, and then go door to door at the 'rich English houses' and say they ought to do something for a monument to this Frenchman who had died for England. He had done very well out of it until a Breton who had been reported lost turned up alive and the jig was up. Another man Charriere met captured butterflies and sold them as a collection. The pair worked out a scam to create a phony hermaphrodite butterfly for a client who offered to pay them $500 for one, a ploy that worked initially but ended up in court when the trick was discovered.

Duke Street was not very far from the sea, and every free afternoon when I was not at school, I remember that my sister and I were taken for a walk to the Sea Wall, with Maud, our nurse, pushing Margie in a stroller until she was old enough to walk there on her own. Georgetown would not have existed without the Sea Wall, both as a necessary barricade against the tides and as a place to walk and socialize. Every brown nurse in stiff white uniform that worked within walking distance of the Sea Wall took her charges there in the afternoon. It was an easy walk along the high promenade, cooled by the onshore breeze from the sea, strolling along this masterpiece of man's invention against the tide, and for the nurses there was the double joy of sitting on the benches and laughing and gossiping with each other while their charges happily played on the muddy sands.

We always followed the same route to the Sea Wall. Barbara Good from next door often came with us as we started up Duke Street, because her mother was a nurse who was seldom home in the day. Occasionally, somewhat aloofly,

Anne came too, but abandoned us as soon as she found her older friends on the promenade. Going up towards the sea, we turned left on Young Street, which was much wider than Duke Street. It was one of those avenues with a small canal that ran along one side or down the middle, and it was grand and open and lined with flamboyant trees with their brilliant red blossoms in season. On one occasion as we walked along Young Street when the blossoms were out, I remember seeing a white-haired lady sitting on a stool on the grass verge in front of an easel. She was Mrs. Monty White, a noted water-colour artist, putting the scarlet glory of the trees on paper.

At the corner of High Street, where we turned right, we sometimes picked up my best friend, Betty Jean Raatgever, on our way. As far as I was concerned, Betty Jean was the most beautiful girl in the world. She was also the nicest. She lived in a house that was much bigger than ours, in a family that demonstrated three national origins. Her father was half Portuguese and half Dutch, and her mother was Afro-Guianese. The offspring from this union could not have been more unlike each other. Only Betty Jean's older brother and sister, with their capuccino-coloured skin and dark eyes, looked Portuguese like their father. Her little sister was completely black like her mother, with tight curly hair and a cute smile. Betty Jean was a throw-back to her white Dutch grandmother and looked like no one else with her fair skin and hazel eyes. Her grandmother lived nearby and spoiled her but her lovely nature was not altered. I worshipped her and was terribly flattered that she called me a friend.

From the corner of Young and High Streets, it was a short walk up to the Sea Wall. We did not usually follow the road all the way to the old Dutch fort, anglicized to William Frederick but originally Willem Frederik, but cut up a path that led directly to the wall. If we had gone to the end by the fort, the Sea Wall ended in a hook going out towards the sea parallel to the Demerara. Below the wall on the sea side at that end, it was mainly rocks and was the only place where the sea really seemed to come in and pound and foam when the tide was high. Turning to the right, however, walking on the top of the wall that was wide enough to be a promenade, the rocks on our left slowly disappeared and became wide muddy sands at low tide, contained between low accessory walls that stretched out towards the sea like spider legs from the main retaining wall. At high tide, the sea came up close to the Wall and we were not allowed to swim because of the undertow. But at low tide, the mud-sands and shallow sea were ours to conquer.

When we got to the Sea Wall at low tide, my little sister stayed back with Maud, sitting with all the other babies and toddlers and nurses on the benches at the back of the promenade, while Barbara and Betty Jean and I scrambled down the stone steps to the sand level and set about the serious business of play. Like Rabindranath Tagore's 'Children of the World', in his poem in the *Gitanjali*, we revelled in the sea and shore. We waded out in the warm brown water and went wave 'swimming', which was light-years away from swimming in the deep Demerara. We built sandcastles. We mapped out dream house plans, in which we made up the furniture that would go inside each room, and entertained like our mothers with delicious sand cakes. We wrote messages on the sand. Anne was old enough to be sweet on a boy called Trevor so we wrote 'AG loves TE' and 'TE loves AG' all over everywhere and Anne would come along behind us and furiously rub out our Valentines. We played hopscotch. We collected shells. We threw stones at Portuguese man-o-war jellyfish that had been stranded on the beach, stepping back in fear of being stung from the interior spray as they burst like balloons.

Easter was the season of kite-flying at the Sea Wall. I remember that our kites were not very glamorous because we made them at home from two crossed sticks over which we glued tissue-paper. We spent hours decorating the tissue-paper so that ours would be the best kite of all. We added a string tail at the bottom, along which we tied pieces of rag, and a long roll of string which we tied to the center where the two sticks met. The other end of the string was carefully rolled onto a stick that we held in our hands. Then off to the Sea Wall we went to fly our kites in the wind joyfully, running along the sand to get them aloft, each secretly certain that ours was the most beautiful of all the bright kites that filled the sky around us. Now and then, an older boy, or a man, would come along with something more sophisticated than ours, a box kite perhaps that soared way, way higher than ours and dipped and dived breathtakingly, and we would be awed at what this fantastic thing could do, and then next day we might be a little less eager to take our own kite with us and in a few more days we lost interest and were ready for something new.

Most of the time, our activities were completely self-absorbing, but now and then they involved other people. Once there was great excitement on that beach because some swimmers had killed a stranded swordfish in the shallow water and they brought it in and dragged it up on the sand and butchered it immediately. I remember someone holding up the 'sword' as a triumphant trophy while others eagerly took home some of the flesh to cook, and we girls watched in disgust as eager little black boys ran around waving slimy pieces of fish guts that looked like large intestine.

And once, once only that I remember, we joined in a huge sandball fight with every child on the beach. Because the sand was muddy, it stayed together better than regular sand, so there were occasional small friendly versions of sandball fights. But nothing like this one. I don't remember who started it, or how or why, but it was probably one small group of boys who threw sandballs at someone, it might even have been us, and in no time at all we all joined in, every size, colour, nationality, sex or whatever, with no definition of who was on what side except which gang was nearest. It blossomed into two large sides, with each multicultural army sheltering behind a seaward wall and creating huge piles of sand weapons to throw at the other. We called out rude names to each other and then we threw our weapons and then we made a whole lot more. Then someone on one side leapt over his wall and the rest of his gang streamed over it towards the enemy, who retreated to the next wall with everyone screaming like the little savages we were. Safely behind the next barricade, we started all over again to stockpile. Sand flew everywhere, and it was lucky that no one got blinded by it. No one stopped us. It was a perfectly splendid battle. There might be a grand war going on in Europe but nothing like this had ever been seen or would ever be seen again on Georgetown's Sea Wall sand beach. It was the kind of battle of which history is made. When it was over, it was perfect. There were no conquerors or conquered, no wounded soldiers, no dead. Just a bunch of tired, happy, rainbow kids who had had the best afternoon ever. Going home with our nurse, walking decorously like proper little English children, covered in the tell-tale sand that would make our mothers exclaim at us when we got home, we were very proud of our disgraceful conduct.

Going home at the end of the afternoon, we sometimes saw a long flock of scarlet ibises trailing across the sky in an easterly direction. The military bandstand was situated on the Sea Wall east of where we usually played and at weekends the brass band was there in all its glory. The children and the nurses might have the Sea Wall to themselves in the week but at weekends all of Georgetown was out there enjoying the sea breezes and the jolly music.

We always took the eastern route past the bandstand when we were going home, walking down Camp Road where couples lying under the bridge were doing peculiar hugging things that our nurse seemed loath to explain to us. We would go past the military base on the way. If it was very late afternoon, the soldiers would be outside in the Parade Ground doing the Last Post. We would stop and watch them standing smartly at attention while the bugler played that awful, soul-searing lament, which was joined by one of the bystanders. This was a small, insignificant, apparently stray dog that was always there. When the first thrilling notes sounded, the little dog would throw back his head and howl in unison until it was over. Then he would put his tail between his legs and slink westwards, while we too went home to Duke Street.

Wendy, Barbara and Anne Good, Margie

Betty Jean Raatgever

Sugar Cane and Mosquitoes

When my mother tired of Georgetown, there was one place where she always wanted to go. Ogle Sugar Estate, owned by Bookers, a large Guianese company that produced sugar, molasses, and rum, was situated about five miles to the east of town and managed by her old shipboard friend, Jim Sutherland. He and his hospitable wife Ann always made a visit to the estate a warm and welcoming experience.

"My first stay at Ogle was after an appendix in town," my mother said. "I was conveyed there by Jim's chauffeur from the hospital, feeling every bump of the red burnt-earth road." On arrival, the convalescent was given a relaxing hot bath in a galvanized iron tub that had a backrest, a real treat for her after the unheated showers in Mackenzie. The hot water had to be carried upstairs from the kitchen, but there was no shortage of people to carry it as the house was grandly staffed. "The servants were mostly black," she said, "counting those in the kitchen, the two maids, the nurse and chauffeur, but the two butlers were East Indian, very neat in white suits." There was also a groom, sundry gardeners, and a crotchety elderly woman who cleaned the brasses. She did not mention the East Indian 'egg man', who regularly came up to Georgetown to bring us eggs from the estate. His fascination was that he had whiskers coming out of his ears, long straight ones that made him look like a cat when viewed from the rear.

When they knew that we were going out to visit them, the Sutherlands sent their chauffeur, Watson, into town to collect us. Watson was almost as fascinating as the egg man because he had a glass eye that didn't blink. He had lost an eye from getting a splinter in it when he was chopping wood. No one seemed to think that it was remarkable to have a chauffeur, albeit a very nice one, who had only one good eye.

If it was only our family traveling to Ogle, I sat quietly inside the car with my sister and parents, but if the Sutherland family came into town on errands before picking us up, their son Donald and I would be ordered to sit outside in the rumble seat, a joyous open ride where we could shout and laugh in the wind without adult disapproval. I always looked forward to seeing Donald, two years older than me, with a slight tinge of reservation, because he was a boy and I never quite knew what to expect. Whatever it was, it was likely to be something that would shock me. As the only son of the manager, he was used to thinking up daring things to do and getting away with them.

To get to Ogle, we drove out of Georgetown on the Public Road, running parallel with the Sea Wall along the edge of the coastal plain. The road continued with the same name for the 57 miles along the coast to Rossignol. I do not remember buses rattling along it named 'Clark Gable' or 'Claudette Colbert', like the ones mentioned by Edgar Mittelholzer in *Corentyne Thunder*, but I do remember it as the strangest road in the world. To the left was the flat mud ocean that had become somehow unreal, half hidden behind the scrub of mangrove bushes and the low retaining seawall which continued for about 20 miles out of the city, much further than our destination. To the right was wet marsh land, sometimes reclaimed for cultivation in geometric rice paddies going back to the higher, flat savannah. Skinny cows attended by white cattle egrets and the occasional sheep grazed in patches. The road itself was raised to avoid being flooded, with drainage ditches on either side, so that the general impression was of driving along on a dusty red ribbon stretched above a watery world where nothing was certain. The scenery was not pretty in any sense, just wide and flat and open, with the horizon visible in every direction under the great upturned bowl of the sky. Even for a child it gave a feeling of being ten feet tall. Michael Swan in *British Guiana: The Land of Six Peoples* mentioned "the huge sky, intensely blue and hung with the ever-present cumulus. They are East Anglian skies," he said, "Constable skies, made more vivid, on sunlit days, by the tropical clarity of the air." Along the way, there were East Indian women and children fishing with seine nets in the drainage canals or picking the muddy bottom for shrimps for curry.

The strong Afro-Guianese men who cut the cane on the estate when it was ripe came from the village of Ogle outside the estate. Said Swan: "The villages found where the road crosses the planted area are the prettiest on the coast, for the shacks that appear so squalid on the open land gain some beauty from the setting of palms and the huge flapping leaves of plantains and bananas." These villages had originally been settled by the freed slaves who had worked on the old sugar plantations that stretched all along the coast. Sugar cane cultivation was especially hard on coastal Guiana because labour was needed not only to tend the cane itself but to build and repair the walls that kept out the sea, to dig the canals that drained the low swampy land, and to build and maintain a back-dam to stop the interior waters from flooding the area under cultivation. It has been estimated that for every square mile of back-breaking cultivated land in that area, a total of about 65 miles of drainage canals were needed. For this reason, the Dutch settlers had early imported slaves from West Africa. By the time slavery was abolished in 1807, there were 100,000 black slaves in the colony. When emancipation was complete in 1838, they deserted the plantations in droves. In order to be able to continue, starting in the 1840s the sugar planters began to bring in indentured laborers, from several countries but mainly India, who could return to their own countries when their term had been served. By 1917 when the arrangement ended, 240,000 Indian laborers had migrated to British Guiana. My mother remembered the last boats that were set up to take them back to India but she said most of the ones on the estates opted to stay. All the cane workers at Ogle, except the black men from the village who did the final cutting, were East Indian.

Each estate was laid out in a long rectangle stretching back from the sea. To reach Ogle Sugar Estate, the car turned inland from the village, up a narrow road that crossed the railway track and passed the cane fields on the left and the small joined houses of the workers on the right, beyond which stood the tall chimney of the factory where the sugar was processed. The road divided before the end, with one branch turning to the factory and the other turning left over the canal towards the manager's beautiful house and garden.

In our day, the old Plantation-style house at Ogle was a magnificent three storeys high. The top floor was for family and visitor bedrooms, the middle floor a general living area for the family, and the ground floor for kitchen and estate staff and storage facilities. Visitors entered by climbing a wide curving outside staircase at the front facing the garden to reach the second floor level. I remember a large hall with a wide inside staircase leading up to the bedrooms, and on the landing was a small table with one of those weighted Japanese dolls that wobbled when the table was tilted. The living room was large and comfortable, rather like a country inn in England, and I seem to remember a dining table that could seat a great many people for dinner. Covered with sheets, it made a great hideaway place for us children to play. Mr. Sutherland had an office on the factory side of the building at the middle floor level, reached from the outside by a straight, narrow staircase, and there was also an estate office where my mother said she used to go on pay-days "and watch the lovely East Indian girls and women get their pay for field work, planting rice, etc, their arms encased in heavy silver bracelets, even ear, nose and toe studs, and lovely necklaces."

The system of pay on the estate was an elaborate one, made complicated by the many types of labour. There was no question that working in the cane fields in any season was hard work, all done by hand in the baking sun and humid mud. When the canes were tall, no breeze could drift through to relieve the heat and humidity. Even before starting, the labourers often had a long walk to the area where they would be working. Donald Sutherland does not think they had any children working at Ogle, but Matthew French Young, who worked for Bookers from 1929 to 1935 at an estate on the west side of the Demerara River, said his youngest workers, called the Creole gang, were children who left home at 7.30 a.m. to walk two or three miles to their work, were on their feet the whole day in the sun and rain, then had to walk back home in the late afternoon. They did much of the carrying, either in gallon buckets carried on their arm, or on wooden trays balanced on their heads. The older boys or young men worked in a gang that cleared out the drainage ditches or canals. The all-women weeding gang had a number of jobs which included hauling cane trash from the roots and drains and rolling it between the rows of young canes, weeding young or high canes, and cleaning half of the cross canal at the beginning and end of the work. When Young was promoted to the cane-cutting and punt-loading gangs, his duties included burning the fields to be cut the following day before working out what had to be done. The canes had to be cut down to the root. The tops were lopped off for planting in renewed fields and the remaining cut stalks bundled, carried to the cross canal bed, and loaded onto punts for transport. In the cane-cutting season, the overseer got little sleep. "I have been known to leave my house at 7.00 a.m. and spend the entire day in the back dam," he said, "only to return home at dawn the following day to get a bath and a cup of coffee and return to the fields once again."

There was little sleep for anyone when the cane was harvested, with the factory grinding and steaming all day and night. At Ogle, a crane usually lifted the cane out of the transport punts onto a belt that carried it into the factory where revolving blades cut it into chips to be crushed by a series of rollers. The resultant fiber (bagasse) was taken away to be used as furnace fuel, while the juice was purified by adding milk of lime and boiling the mixture until most of the impurities settled at the bottom in a sludge that was removed for use as field fertilizer. Finally, the pure juice was boiled and evaporated in a huge vat to form the familiar brown sugar crystals and thick molasses syrup, separated by a centrifuge system. The molasses was piped off to the distillery in another part of the factory where it was mixed with water, fermented, and distilled into that finest of all rums, Demerara rum.

The sugar crystals were conveyed on a belt to go out to the transport department. On one of our visits to Ogle, the factory was going full tilt and Donald took me to watch what was happening. I remember leaning over the steaming vat of boiling syrup, but best of all Mr. Sutherland stopped the belt coming down with the sugar crystals and allowed us to scoop out the sweet brown treat with both hands. We had to eat it by bringing our full hands up to our mouths. When our mound of sugar was finished, we had the pleasure of licking the sticky crystals off our palms and fingers. Dentists everywhere are allowed to shudder.

Pay-day for the labourers on the estate meant having a big stack of coins on hand in the office because the workers distrusted paper money. Donald told me that he and his mother were once the subject of a kidnapping attempt because of this practice. Mrs. Sutherland used to go into Georgetown with the chauffeur every Saturday to do the shopping, and before she left town she would stop to pick up the wage money that was waiting for them at Barclays Bank. A Portuguese man in town had noted this arrangement and planned to kidnap her and her young son and steal the money, but someone found out about it ahead of time and he was arrested.

Mrs. Sutherland was a large, imposing woman who carried herself with immense dignity. She was always kind and gracious, but I found her booming voice and imperious manner rather overwhelming when I was a child so I was not surprised to hear that on one of my mother's visits when she and Mrs. Sutherland had been alone in the house, a group of striking workers had gathered angrily outside and her hostess had gone out to the top of the stairs and ordered them to go home ~ and they had immediately dispersed. This was in the depression years when wages, low as they were, had had to be cut for the estates to survive. Not all strikes on the sugar estates were so peaceful in later years. Jim Sutherland was at dinner on an estate in the Corentyne when an engineer sitting two seats over from him was shot in the back through the open window. But in general, it was only after we left British Guiana that the disagreements began to get violent, as in the riots of 1948, with the stress of an increasing population and the belief of men like Cheddi Jagan that much of the ills of the colony arose from the unfair practices of 'King Sugar'.

Back in our day, outside of harvest time, a sugar estate manager's life was usually fairly leisurely. Alec Waugh in *The Sugar Islands* said it began at sunrise with a light first breakfast of coffee, fruit and toast. At 7.30, it was roll-call, then supervisory work around the estate, talking to his overseers and gossiping a bit with his labourers until the Guianese 'breakfast' at 11.00 a.m. After the late breakfast, he would have time to read the paper and mail and perhaps doze until 2.00 p.m. when it was back to work. After tea at 4.30, he would work in the office on accounts, reports, and correspondence until sunset when it was time for rum punch or swizzle, visits at home or out, 8.30 dinner, and then early bed. Although diluted and later strictly forbidden, something of the old Plantation spirit still lingered at Ogle in those earlier days. My mother talked of the overseers arriving on mules or on horseback after being out in the fields, "all looked so attractive when arriving en masse for breakfast, clad in topees, white jackets, breeches and boots, carrying a whip and fly-swatter." Something in me cringes at the thought of that kind of equipment, but the swatter was mostly used by then for insects and the whip for a stubborn mule. Young said he had a singularly vicious first mule to ride when he worked for Bookers, and the mosquitoes in the rainy season would devour you alive and the sand flies in the dry season bit and stung every part that was exposed.

On her visits to Ogle, my mother remembered the mosquitoes at night as being unbearable. "Sometimes one had to encase one's legs in pillow cases if not possessing mosquito boots, also if wise, sit on a cushion as they bit through the cane seats of the dining chairs, through one's thin clothes. We were surrounded by cane and rice fields, often flooded, also drainage canals, ideal breeding places." My mother had been very conscious of mosquitoes from the time she arrived in Georgetown, and later when she had to cope with my malarial convulsion as a baby after Dr. Giglioli had left the bauxite company to begin working on the problem of malaria on the sugar estates of S. Davson and Company in Berbice. My mother always claimed that he single-handedly wiped out malaria in British Guiana.

Dr. Giglioli's initial study expanded to all the sugar estates and continued through the war years and beyond. The biggest problem was that the cultivated coast, where most of the people lived and where the country's most important crops of sugar cane and rice were grown, had become a prime breeding ground for *Anopheles darlingi*, the malaria-carrying mosquito that was normally found in the sheltered forests of the interior. The problem was man-made, due to the stagnant water behind the sea defences and in the irrigation ditches and flooded fields. "The canals have no grade so that water is practically motionless," Dr.

Giglioli stated in his official reports, "particularly in the blind ends of the cross canals, which are well sheltered by the tall, overhanging cane. The water level is more or less constant, and aquatic vegetation abounds." In addition to irrigation canals, the estates used a technique, peculiar to British Guiana, of flooding the cane fields after four years cultivation and leaving them to lie fallow under water for a year. Abundant aquatic weeds, rainwater, and heavy filtering clays reduced the acid, peaty water from its source and improved the sugar cane yield, but unfortunately produced ideal mosquito breeding sites.

A chance happening in August 1944 gave Dr. Giglioli his tool to control the malaria problem. Three prominent research scientists were stranded in Trinidad and decided to pay an overnight visit to British Guiana. In conversation at Government House, the effective use of DDT in the Burma campaign was mentioned. Although the use of this synthetic insecticide was strictly on the war secrets list and no technical information had been released, it was felt that this might be the answer to British Guiana's difficult malarialogical problem, and through the good offices of the research scientists a limited quantity was released to British Guiana and the first experiments began. After the war it was used intensively by Dr. Giglioli's group in and around the coastal housing and as far upriver as Mackenzie. Said Raymond Smith later in *British Guiana*: "It is a common fallacy in discussions of British Guiana to state that the rapid increase in population is due to the eradication of malaria following the very successful campaign carried out after the war. While this contribution was a notable contribution to the health of the country the population 'explosion' must be attributed to improvements in health and sanitation which began long before, in the 1920s and 1930s."

I have two special memories involving the canals around Ogle Sugar Estate. One memory is of the small clean canal that irrigated the garden, where we children used to go swimming. Donald had a dinghy and we took my little sister out on it, and generally just had a great time mucking about in the water. One day, there was a sudden shout from one of the gardeners for us all to get out quickly. A very large alligator had just appeared at the other end of the canal, heading in our direction.

The other memorable event began with one of Donald's great ideas. He was always having ideas which seemed particularly exciting to me because there was usually an attached element of danger. This time it was a Sunday morning and the factory was not working because it was not cane harvest season. No one would be there checking machines or doing maintenance work so Donald thought it would be fun to go exploring. The only problem was that my sister wanted to come with us. No matter how much we protested to our parents that this was not a suitable expedition for a small person, we were ordered to take her wherever we were going. Sighing, we set off at speed while she trailed after us crying that we were going too fast. When we got to the factory, she was terrified of the dark inside. It was not long before we brought back a tearful Margie and unceremoniously dumped her in the living room with the adults and said she had to stay because "she didn't like it." Back we went to the dark factory. Donald had found a white candle for us to light our way inside. It was scary standing there in the vast, dark, echoing space, with the light of the sky just a small hole a long way up high above us, surrounded by all the big crushing machines, silent and menacing, but I at least felt deliciously daring and important. We wandered around in the huge shed-like structure, and we climbed up and looked down into the cold, empty vat and dripped candle wax down into it, and then, feeling satisfactorily wicked, we made our way back to the house.

That afternoon, we all went for a picnic in grand style. We travelled by punt, hauled by mules, along a wide canal back through the estate to a clearing beside the Lamaha creek. It was the same trip on which the Sutherlands took the Governor and his wife when they toured the estate. The adults sat on cane chairs, with Margie being given special attention on someone's knees while Donald and I, disgraced, stood at the back and looked at the passing canefields, some with the cane so high that it was like a bamboo archway, one with a clearing where a group of brown boys were standing and bathing with no clothes on. They waved gaily to us as we passed and the adults turned their heads not to look. No one paid much attention to us until one of the adults said "What are you children chewing?" "Nothing," we said, looking guiltily at each other. Of course, it had been another of Donald's great ideas. Just before we left the house, he had thought it would be fun if we took some wax from the candle that we had used at the factory and chewed it as gum. It had a sort of nothing taste to it, if I remember, a bit sooty perhaps, definitely nothing to write home about but I don't think it would have done us any harm. They made us spit it out into the canal. When we arrived at our picnic area, the servants were there ahead of us. It was a very elegant picnic, with tablecloths and cutlery and china and glassware. My mother said: "We swam in the 'Lama', it being quite clean there, and ate roasted freshly-dug sweet cassava, delectable with butter. I was astounded to see a bunch of porpoises sporting around in the creek that must have got in and been trapped when the kokers were open to the sea."

The last time I remember seeing Donald in British Guiana was when the Sutherlands had been up in Georgetown for some festivity. It must have been just before he went away to school in England or before we left the colony. Although the timing doesn't make sense, I seem to remember that it was around the Christmas or New Year season but it could not have been one of the wild New Year's Eve celebrations such as Evelyn Waugh had witnessed or the ball that my mother and father had attended more than once when they came up from Mackenzie to stay at Ogle. These events usually went on all night. "Once a year in Georgetown was held the Bachelors and Benedicts Ball," my mother said. "Always compulsory Fancy Dress, so much so that the Governor was denied entry until he discarded his dinner-jacket for a dressing-gown and Sherlock Holmes pipe. This dance went on till nearly dawn, and on going back to the Estate if still dark we had to weave between red-eyed alligators stretched out on the road between the drainage ditches. Once, some of the chaps in our party, feeling no pain whatever, jumped into the alligator-infested trench on a bet, fully clothed in evening dress."

This present occasion had to do with something that ended in the early evening, when we children had not yet gone to bed, or I had been allowed to stay up a little later than usual because we had company from Ogle. I do remember that it was night. Perhaps everyone knew that this would be our last time together, for before the Sutherlands went home, our parents insisted that eleven-year-old Donald and nine-year-old Wendy should kiss each other goodbye before we parted. "Go on," they said. "You're friends. Give a kiss!" Very reluctantly, we did as we were told, quickly, to get it over and done with. Our parents beamed. I suppose because they were such good friends, they cherished some romantic idea about their children's possible future, but we were not impressed by this embarassing behaviour. Surreptitiously, when they were not looking, we both wiped off the offensive exchange with the back of our hands and then avoided each other self-consciously. The candle wax was better.

Donald and Wendy on
canal at Ogle

Ann, Donald and Jim Sutherland at
Ogle Sugar Estate

Ogle Sugar Estate

Dr. Giglioli

Sutherlands and Nivens in garden

When the World Fell Apart

The two years that our family spent on the coast, our last in British Guiana, were happy ones overall. However, from a child's point of view, it was a period in my life when my parents suddenly seemed to become rather remote. Unlike Mackenzie where I knew where they were all the time, in Georgetown when they left the house they disappeared. I never knew where they went, unless they were going to Ogle to see the Sutherlands. I never saw the inside of my father's office, or went shopping with my mother in Stabroek Market, although my sister did, traveling in a child's seat on the back of her bicycle. I never saw inside the club where my parents went all the time. I remember my mother coming in at night to tuck us children in and kiss us goodnight and she smelled and looked beautiful as she wafted in and out of our bedroom but we never saw the place where she and my father were going or met half the people that they knew. If adults came to the house for dinner, we were quickly banished upstairs to be cared for by our nurse, so if laughter floated up the stairs as they drank their rum swizzles, we did not share in their conviviality. Somehow, they had left us for a more important world, and it was one that we were not supposed to share.

With our parents so much absent, and without the loving support of our substitute family in the Mackenzie community, for the first time in my life my world became an uncertain place. We still had Maud but I was a big girl now and she spent more time with my little sister than she did with me. My first experience in a new school in Georgetown did nothing to make me feel more secure. I was seven years old, that most sensitive of all ages, when I was sent to Miss Wishart's private elementary school for nice little girls and boys. Since it was the middle of term, I was the only new child and painfully aware of it as all the rest of the children knew each other and had made their own friends. It was still a one-room school, but much bigger than the one I knew in Mackenzie, with about 30 students instead of 12. In class, we all sat together in well-behaved rows and did our lessons as Miss Wishart dictated, but at recess there was no supervision when we went outside and the boys could bear it no longer. Around the yard they ran, rough-housing with each other and showing off and teasing the girls to let off steam. There were two outside toilets in one corner of the school yard, one for the boys and one for the girls, but it was more than our life was worth to use them. It was here that I learned "Oh dear, what can the matter be, two old ladies locked in the lavatory," which we sang with a sense of naughtiness when the boys started it because it was a rude song. It had to be rude, because it mentioned lavatory, and we were just at the age when toilets had tremendous sexual significance.

It was not long after I started at Miss Wishart's that one of the boys thought that the new girl's alliterative name was funny and the rest took up the chant. "Wendy Whalley is a dolly," they chanted hatefully as I walked miserably around the yard with the girls. "Wendy Whalley is a dolly, Wendy Whalley is a dolly, Wendy Whalley is a dolly." When the girls thought it was funny to impress the boys, they all joined in. I had been teased often by my father but never like this. I could not bear it. I walked out of the playground, out of the school, up the road to Duke Street, and home to my mother. I did not cry. I just had a cold hard feeling at the pit of my stomach that would not go away. When I got home, my mother was having her usual nap, and she was never at her best when she was awakened out of a sound sleep. When I walked into her bedroom, she was furious, whether it was at me for waking her up and inconveniencing her, or for leaving the school, or for the fact that the school had allowed it to happen, I never knew. I only know that she marched me back to the school immediately, walking quickly and angrily down the white-hot road, without speaking. I cannot remember what she said to Miss Wishart or what Miss Wishart said to her or to me or to the school. I remember that we walked into the large room where Miss Wishart was standing at the blackboard with the whole school sitting at their desks, all deathly silent, all looking at me, and I wanted to die. After that, no one teased me, but I hated my name forever.

It is interesting to note that in British Guiana's most famous novel of the day, a man was murdered for teasing someone about his name. *Corentyne Thunder*, Edgar Mittelholzer's classic tale of British Guiana, was published the year before we went to Georgetown. It tells the tale of an old, frail East Indian, a cow minder who had been an indentured labourer on a sugar estate but now lived in a tiny mud house with his two daughters. Apart from what it says about mixed race marriages and the hard life on the savannah for Ramgolall and his family, one of its themes follows the trials of Jannee, the rice and vegetable grower, who had been into town to sell vegetables on his donkey cart when he met his rival, Harry Lall Boorharry, who proceeded to humiliate him in public. "Jannee-pannee-chimpanzee!" the overseer chanted hatefully, "Monkey-face Jannee! Boom, boom! Hup, hup, holoy!" To make matters worse, the urchins by the roadside gathered around and followed the cart, picking up the refrain. "Jannee-pannee-chimpanzee! Monkey-face Jannee! Hup, holoy! Hup, hup, holoy!" After this episode, Jannee was a changed man. He was silent and brooding at home and took to going back to town at night with his cutlass hidden under his loose shirt. One dark night he found Boorharry on the road and killed him. There are dire consequences for those who tease the wrong person.

For me, the delightful consequence of the teasing was that Betty Jean became my best friend and Barbara, the girl next door, my next best friend, and suddenly the world was a better place again. Barbara and I would set off for school together, walking the few blocks south of Duke Street, and sometimes Betty Jean would join us on the way to school but always walked with us on the way home. Every day, we passed a stall where they sold big, round, violently colored, locally made candy. There was one that I particularly liked that was neon pink and another that was a sickly green. My mother shuddered when she saw them and forbade me to buy 'those vulgar sweets' but we girls sometimes bought them secretly when we went past. They were so big that they filled our cheeks and took a long time to finish, so we had to time our arrival at home or school for when we no longer looked like chipmunks preparing for winter.

I wonder what we learned of importance at Miss Wishart's little school. I only remember weaving mats with strips of coloured paper, and music, which we seemed to do every day. We had a percussion band and everyone played an instrument. We all started on the triangle and then graduated to instruments with more challenge. I never got past the tambourine, which I was playing when my sister was old enough to come to school and play the triangle when she turned four. I remember that she came for the term at the end of the year when we put on a stage production for the parents. My sister was a carrot in a chorus of little vegetables, and I was the Queen of Hearts in the court scene from "Alice in Wonderland" and had a great time ordering everyone's heads off.

This stage experience obviously went to our heads because from then on there was nothing that Margie and I liked better than to put on concerts at home. We would practice for hours. Since I could read and write, I would print the programme. Neither of us could carry a tune so we mercifully did not sing in our concerts. I recited, my sister danced around trailing a scarf, I told unfunny jokes, my sister danced around trailing a scarf, that sort of thing. Of course we invited our parents and all the servants to these painful performances. We set up chairs for them in the living room while we created a stage in the archway into the dining room. With much scraping of chairs, our audience would settle themselves down politely but not with any great air of excitement. To do them credit, they managed to laugh and clap quite satisfactorily as expected, but there were no cries for encores at the end and, suddenly, cook had to make dinner and my father had work to do and my mother had to see to something important, so the performers would curtsey prettily or clumsily depending on which performer did the act, and with much scraping of returning chairs and significant looks at each other, the audience dissolved with relief.

Although there was a big gap in our ages, once my little sister turned four we were able to play together more often. She had always joined us on the hammock under the house and we played with the kittens for hours but now she could also join us on the sands at the Sea Wall. She followed me everywhere, happy for me to take the lead, because now I realize that she really had no friends of her own. My passion at that time was paper dolls. I loved cutting them out and dressing them with the cut-out clothes with tags that had to be bent back. It was hard work for a little girl to play with something so fragile so Margie often co-loured while I cut. Sometimes I coloured too, for what I loved best was to design my own clothes for the dolls, the more elegant the better, and these I did on lined paper coloured with wax crayons. The results were ghastly but in my mind they were the peak of perfection and ready for the Paris spring collection. I am very proud of my parents for managing to say they were beautiful, or at the very least, as with all our efforts, they were "very nice, dear" with an air of badly disguised indifference. I also wrote my first short story in this period, of which I was equally proud, but I haven't the faintest idea what it was all about, and I have an adult suspicion that it was not exactly spellbinding.

It was while we were at Miss Wishart's that Barbara and I joined the Brownies. It was an uplifting experience to be a fairy or an elf or whatever fantasy group was mine, but it was a difficult one because we were set a daily challenge. Every day, we were supposed to do a Good Deed, which we had to report back to Brown Owl. The problem was that, in my house, no one wanted me to do any Good Deeds. "Go and play now, dear," my mother would say dismissively if I asked her if there was anything I could do for her. The servants' refrain was even firmer. "Out of me way, Miss Windy," the maid would say, or "Out of me kitchen, Miss Windy," said the cook. So there was nothing for it but to invent the Good Deeds that I would have liked to have done if anyone had given me a chance. I lost track of how many old ladies I helped across the road on the way to school until the burden of lying got too much for me and I dropped out of hold-ing hands around a toadstool.

When we graduated from Miss Wishart's, Barbara, Betty Jean and I went to Bishops High School for Girls. It was not a particularly large high school but I remember being awed by its size and the number of students there seemed to be. Of what I learned, I remember nothing except the caterpillar that we collected and fed on the leaves of the plant from which we took it. In due course, it spun a cocoon and hung on a silken thread, and we waited with bated breath for the day when it would become a beautiful butterfly. The event miraculously occurred while we were in the classroom, and we all excitedly watched it emerge. After an interesting struggle while we all crowded around it, the "butterfly" became an inconspicuously dull brown moth, not worth looking at, and we returned to our seats in disgust. It should have taught us a lesson that in life we must not expect the beautiful and amazing to come out of every chrysalis and that every creature is wonderful in its own way but I am not sure that I learned the lesson. We must have had a good science teacher, however, because even if I remember nothing of the History and Geography of Guiana, or the English books we must have read, I have no trouble at all in remembering the row of jam jars on the window sill that contained the bean seeds that we had planted with wet blotting paper.

I only lasted two terms at Bishops High School before it was time for my family to leave the colony, but sometime in the first term or earlier, two awful things happened that deeply affected our lives. Both events were connected to U-boats.

The first tragedy concerned the older girl next door, whose best friend was a lovely girl whom everyone liked. The friend's father decided that he wanted to leave Georgetown and take his family to South Africa. He wanted to go by ship. All his friends pleaded with him not to risk it, to go by air where it was safe from U-boat attack, but he was adamant. Anne was desolate at her friend's leaving but turned to stone when we got the next news. The ship that carried them was only one night out of Georgetown when it was torpedoed while everyone was asleep. It was sunk with no survivors. Once again the war had come home to us but this time it struck us children hard for this was someone we knew and loved, someone our age or only a little older, and we had nightmares imagining her or ourselves lying in bed when the water closed in overhead. Luckily for us, we did not know the details of the sinking of the *Lady Hawkins* or we would have had worse nightmares. "The passengers never knew what happened," was the story they told us. "The ship just sank like a stone, with everyone asleep."

Up to then, the war had not affected us greatly in Georgetown. There had been small things, like the fact that my mother tried to tell us that the mashed yam we were eating was mashed potato, which we knew it wasn't, because the boat bringing potatoes had been sunk, or the hard cassava bread that we were eating was good bread, which it wasn't, because the boat bringing wheat had also gone down. We had all watched the great military march out of the capital by the soldiers up the road, in training in case the Germans launched a direct attack on the bauxite supply. We had cheered them on with enthusiasm, all the young brown soldiers in their smart pressed uniforms, marching away in the brilliant heat, and found them sad and funny when they limped home in straggling lines of hot, foot-weary men some days later, leaving us with a singular lack of confidence that Georgetown would be saved if the enemy attacked.

Of course, there was always the American Air Force, now firmly established at the base at Atkinson Field. We had stood on the beach and looked up with excitement when the first American blimp went over, an unbelievably huge balloon of a thing with a basket of people underneath, looking for U-boats in that soupy sea. The blimps were used mainly for escort, reconnaissance, and rescue purposes. It was against U.S. Navy orders to attack a U-boat because it was such a huge target, easily hit by submarine flak guns, but it was effective for a combined effort with aircraft to harass and bomb their target. The U-boats were much easier to spot a little further out in the ocean and in the clear Caribbean than in the muddy waters around the Guianese coast. We did not know it then but the air defence and convoy system was so effective that the tide was turning for the underwater craft, but they were still there in our minds if not in actuality. We sometimes stood on the beach or the Sea Wall and looked out over the Atlantic and wondered if there were U-boats out there that day, right at that moment, somewhere under the water where we could not see them, dark and dangerous, and we shivered as we thought of it, but they were unreal shadows that had not come home to us until now. We were not to know that there was another U-boat out there that would save my sister's life.

That afternoon, Maud, Margie and I had gone alone to the Sea Wall. My sister usually walked with Maud holding her hand. Sometimes she walked between us, swinging her arms and expecting us to swing her, giggling. When we got there, for some reason, we were not holding hands, and our nurse was walking on the inside of the promenade, Margie was on the outside, and I was in the middle. It was to be a terrible mistake. In the distance, I saw my friend Betty Jean and ran to meet her. My sister, who followed everywhere I went, ran after me but, in one awful moment when no one could reach her in time, she slipped and fell over the side of the Sea Wall on to the rocks below. She fell on her head, and she would have been killed instantly except that there had been a U-boat sinking recently with a lot of straw packaging. The straw had been swept in by the tide and was piled up thickly close to the wall, breaking her fall and cushioning her from the hard rocks beneath.

Beyond my memory of seeing Betty Jean and running towards her, I remember nothing except Maud sitting on the bench at the back of the Sea Wall holding a little inert form in her arms and rocking her. I remember the love with which she held her little charge and her grief that this had happened to the child that she had loved since she was born. I also remember her fear that she would be blamed. I remember we stayed there all afternoon, with Maud too afraid to go home, too afraid to get the help my sister needed, for she had concussion and should have been seen to at once. To make matters worse, when we did get home, my parents were staying at Ogle overnight and would not be home until the next day. All that night, Maud stayed in our room with us, rocking my sister and crying. Still she did not call Ogle or call the doctor.

When my mother came home the next day, she went berserk. She fired Maud on the spot, Maud, who had been with us forever. I could not imagine a world without Maud, and suddenly, without even saying goodbye, she simply disappeared. My mother screamed at me that I was to blame for not looking after my sister. With Maud gone and questions hovering in the air as to whether Margie would recover and whether she would ever be normal again, a dark cloud of blame and worry fell over our household. The servants crept around, subdued, and there was no more laughter coming out from the kitchen. My father and I were silent in the face of our worrying and my mother's overwrought anger. She blamed Maud, she blamed me, she blamed herself, she blamed the country. The doctor said that with care Margie would get better, that the signs were good that all would be well, but meanwhile we would have to be very careful with her.

My mother put her to bed. In my guilt over what had happened, that I should have been holding her hand, that it might have been my fault that I had not been able to catch her before she fell off the wall even though I had not seen her, because we shared the same room, I put myself to bed too, to keep her company. It was the second mistake. Margie was content to just lie in bed. I was perfectly well and soon got bored. Before long, I had a great idea to entertain us.

I moved the stool over from the dressing table and set it between the beds. "Lets pretend these are our ships and we're pirates and walk the plank," I suggested. I have had some dumb ideas in my life but this has to have been the dumbest. We walked the plank several times, giggling as we fell into the bed on the other side, and then, on one journey over, my sister fell again. She hit the floor with enough noise to bring my mother running. Margie didn't cry. She just lay there, soundless, and my mother screamed at me "You've killed her!"

I don't remember anything after that, except that I was sent away to stay with the Nivens. Dear Auntie Minnie and Uncle Peter. Auntie Minnie hugged me hard. Uncle Peter patted the top of my head. They both assured me that my sister would get well again, that I was not to worry, that all would be well. In their house, all was well. They had moved from Paradise to Vreed-en-hoop, across the Demerara River from Georgetown and I remember that I wanted to stay with them forever. To distract me, they gave me a fishing rod to catch fish for the cat. In the canal at the bottom of the garden, I caught a fish, all right. I caught a big catfish that absolutely terrified me. When I landed it, a big fellow with whiskers, it moved around on the ground making a terrible noise and I raced back to the house in fright. I think Uncle Peter came out and made short work of it and the cat had a good meal that night but somehow I had lost any interest in going fishing.

When I went home from the Nivens, my sister was getting much better and she greeted me with a happy smile. My father gave me a big warm hug and even my mother was friendly to me again, although for a while I treated her warily. But the dynamics of the house had changed. No longer was there a nurse to look after us children and walk with us to the Sea Wall. No longer was I a big girl who could be trusted to look after a little sister. My mother trusted no one but herself to look after Margie, who had somehow become a princess in my absence. She had always been treated as if she were fragile and special but now the whole household deferred to her and treated her as if she would fall apart if we looked at her twice. It was very bad for both of us, for I was eaten up with jealousy when she sat on my father's lap, or climbed up to be on it when I was already sitting there, for she had become spoiled by the attention and did everything she could to remain at center stage. She was better at it than I was because she used charm. She had grown into a very pretty little girl, with curly hair and big brown eyes and an enchanting smile. With the added attraction of outer frailty, she held everyone in the palm of her hand. There was nothing that I could do to recapture my position of truly loved older child. If I was good, I was invisible. If I complained, I was the horrid older sister. If I was silent and hurt, I was moody and a spoilsport. With Maud gone, there was no one I could turn to for comfort and understanding, for my mother was too wrapped up in her fears about my sister, and my father, because he took it for granted, did not realize how much I desperately needed to be reassured that I was still the loved and basically good child that I had always been.

Before this happened, I think it characterized our personalities when adults asked that silly question that usually elicited equally silly answers about what we wanted to be when we grew up. Full of unrealistic ambition, I was sure that I would grow up to be a daring explorer and travel all over the world, but my sister smiled sweetly and said cleverly that when she grew up she was going to marry a famous film producer and he was going to make her a famous film star. In the mirror of my mother's newly critical eyes, it seemed that what I wanted in life was stupid. Perhaps what was wrong with me was that I had none of the attributes of becoming a film star like my pretty sister. Perhaps I was just ugly, and useless. Perhaps nothing would ever be right in the world again. As I languished, my sister flourished, but the world was not as fragile as I was. In a very short time, the world that had been turned upside down simply righted itself. My sister needed me to be her producer so that she could star in our imaginary plays and I needed her trust that I was the greatest explorer of all time. As she got better, my mother's fears relaxed, and peace descended for the last time on Duke Street.

Margie was nearly five and I was nine and a half in the spring of 1944 when my father's four-year term with the company was over for the last time. This time there would be no overseas leave, only a transfer to Jamaica. Before we left, we went back to Mackenzie to say goodbye to the people we knew there. Mackenzie had changed almost beyond recognition in those two short war years, with the huge need for bauxite production and expansion of the mines and plant, and what seemed like an incredible explosion of new staff and families. I looked around everywhere in amazement in our brief visit. Was this really Watooka? What had happened to the Mackenzie I thought I knew? It was as if it were Brigadoon, real for a day and vanished forever. There were new houses everywhere, and lots of new people, and children I didn't know jumping and shrieking and laughing in a new aqua swimming pool smelling of chlorine. Everything, everyone I knew had changed. Even the ones with whom I had been closest, my old best friends like Ian and Jackie, were different. We hardly knew each other, and we no longer had anything in common. We were strangers, and so was Macken-zie. It was time to move on.

Back in Georgetown, my mother began to pack. She sold what she could that was heavy and large because we were going to fly to Jamaica. She set aside a few of the smaller heavy things she valued, to go by ship, knowing in her heart of hearts that they could very easily end up at the bottom of the sea. All our toys had to go to be sold or distributed elsewhere except for what we could take in two small rectangular baskets, about a foot long and eight inches wide and four inches high, one for each of us, which we were allowed to carry on the plane. We gave away the cat and dog. I got my first passport because we did not know how long we would have to stay in Trinidad waiting for the next plane and whether we could all travel together. In wartime, seats were at a premium, so the plan was that if only one seat came up, my father would go ahead and we would follow but if two seats came up, I would go ahead with my father and my mother and sister would follow. As it turned out, after three weeks wait in Port of Spain, four seats became available and we all travelled together.

When we boarded the plane for Trinidad, there were blackout curtains at all the windows and it was dark inside as we took our seats. My sister and I sat on one side of the aisle, my parents on the other. In front of us was a couple that my parents seemed to know but they were strangers to us girls. As the plane took off, these people found a corner of their curtain that they could lift up, so they were the only ones on the whole plane who got a last look at wartime Georgetown as we flew over the town and out across the muddy sea.

Watching them peering out of the hole below the curtain, I was scandal-ized. Rigid with suspicion, I turned to my sister. "They're SPIES!" I whispered. But there was no one to pay any attention to my foolishness. My parents were sit-ting very close together and I had never seen them look so happy. My father was happy because he was looking forward to the change of job responsibilities. My mother was happy because, after all those years of putting up with all the things she had had to put up with, with all the miserable waiting time of wanting to go somewhere, anywhere, anywhere but here, she was finally leaving That Awful Place, and this time it was for good.

final curtain-call

POSTSCRIPT

When I was young and in my prime
I lived in Demerara,
The river tidal, wide and deep,
To the shelf at Cockatara.

Far from cane and ricefield green
Where morning trade winds blow,
Far from evening breezes dying
After sunset's fiery glow.

By jungle bound and mangrove side
Of brown-stained Demerara
Far from the coast I did abide
And saw Tumatamara.

By shimmering day and cool of night
I fished the tidal water
In corial small not without fright
Of fabled fair maid's daughter.

I climbed to mighty Kaieteur,
The Essequibo traveled,
Baboons at dawn I heard their call,
The vocal sound unparall'd.

I glimpsed the top of Mount Roraima
From the sharp and green savannah,
Oh I have seen o'er all the land
From Berbice to Morhanna.

Written by my mother, Gladys Hilda Whalley,
and found with her memoirs after she died.

The pundits are always telling us that we cannot go back. Yet 61 years after I left Guyana at the age of nine, on a steaming morning in February 2005 I landed at Cheddi Jagan Airport in Timerhi with a group of friends. The Customs Officer, polite and smiling, took a second look at my passport and reached out instantly to shake my hand. "Welcome, welcome," he said warmly. "What took you so long to come back home?" With those words began the healing of a wound that I did not know I had carried to old age, an unrealized hurt buried deep inside long ago, that came from being suddenly and totally separated from everything I had known and loved and understood in the country of my birth.

Before coming back to this country, dimly sensing that something was unresolved in the fabric of my life, I had begun to collect pieces of my childhood -- my mother's memoirs, a friend's diary, old photographs and letters and newspaper clippings, books, paintings, objects -- anything that supported the memories that I hugged close to my heart for reasons that I could not explain even to myself. Part of the explanation for this jealous guardianship of an unimportant past was having no one to share it with since my mother died, for my sister was too young to remember and my father passed away when we were in our teens. So the time we had spent there was frozen in memory, and I was the only one who seemed to have kept the key. It was as if we had packed a suitcase marked 'British Guiana, 1928-1944', wrapping everything carefully in the newspapers of the day, and then we had taken it with us, move after move, and there it had sat, unopened, waiting to be unlocked and examined. Meanwhile, everything we had left behind stood still. Houses, places, did not change, children did not grow up, people did not alter, move, or die. It was all waiting for me to find it again.

After my mother had gone, I began to put the pieces together, at first for myself, and then for family and friends. When the fragments began to link and shape themselves into the possibility of a real book, I decided on a collage of memories, mine and others, together with all the information I could find that gave a picture of the time when my family lived in what was then colonial British Guiana. Our story, from our unfashionable white perspective, goes back to a time of relative innocence. In the isolated bauxite mining camp up the Demerara River where we lived, there were few amenities and even fewer amusements in our segregated enclave. We children were happy enough, and the adults made do with courage and humour while living for the breaks that took them home on leave to Britain or Canada, but it was still a very small world in which people tried to do their best, however outdated, naive, or politically incorrect their views might seem to be today. None of this world greatly interests present-day republican Guyana that naturally wishes to forget everything to do with the period of British Empire rule, yet it seems to me that the people and the times are still a valid part of the past that formed modern Guyanese society and as such they deserve to be remembered with some understanding of why they behaved the way they did.

When the second draft of my book had been completed, an amazing chance turned up for me to go back and see for myself how the country had changed. It was both exciting and unnerving, a test for the validity of what I remembered. How would I feel when I went back? Would the sight of what we found destroy the happy memories forever? I owe a great debt to the friends who had the interest and faith to accompany me and the people in Guyana who helped me to see it all again with love.

The Guyana of today is as complicated and uncomplicated as the old British Guiana of my childhood. The multicultural society left behind after the colonial whites departed struggles with deprivation, floods, and disease, with economic uncertainty and viability, and with agricultural monoculture and the need to develop resources while conserving natural attractions. So many Guyanese themselves have packed up and left the country that it is estimated that there are more of them living in London, New York and Toronto than are left behind in Guyana. The majority of visitors are all Guyanese coming home to see their families. During our stay, someone at our hotel commented that after a while some of the emigrants think they can come back to live. "They homesick, they buy a house, but then soon, soon, they sell up and leave again. Life here is very hard."

Certainly, heavily populated coastal Guyana now suffers greatly from lack of care and resources. Poverty and subsistence living are noticeable everywhere in the built-up areas around the capital of Georgetown. The city itself, once the pride of the Caribbean, is in dire need of rejuvenation. While it is true that when we were there we saw evidence of the recent devastating floods on the east coast, this could not entirely explain the unhealthy, long-standing rubbish we could not help seeing in streets and canals and along the Georgetown Sea Wall where it had not been inundated. It was still possible to see pockets of well-tended private oases behind guarded street walls, but the magnificent Botanical Gardens of the past were now only marginally cared for, and the general impression of the whole city was one of untidiness and neglect. Similarly, the immaculate mining town of Mackenzie, now called Linden, suffers from the decline in bauxite production and interests. 'Nice up Guyana' was a command we saw on a sign on the road to the Airport, and we felt that much could be done to restore overall health and well-being by the employment of dedicated workers to clean up and recycle the waste as a boost to local morale and to build up, like Barbados, a much needed tourist trade.

Guyana needs and deserves more foreign tourists to bolster its uncertain economy. It is sad that the country has received such unfair publicity, if any at all, from trade promoters who consistently ignore the beauty and emphasize the apparent dangers of the place. Of course, the city of Georgetown is not without crime, some of it no doubt directed at rich outsiders, but some of the nicest people in the world still live in this country and it seemed to us to be no more perilous for the wary tourist here than in a great many destinations around the globe where people continue to flock in droves.

One of the biggest joys of the return to my original homeland was to discover a Guyana beyond the confines of my childhood. The whole of the interior, stretching back to Amazonian Brazil, is beautiful and unspoiled. For the discriminating eco-tourist, there is much that is wondrous. Flying over the pristine rainforest is like looking down on a gigantic broccoli garden, and the Canadian-built walkway at Iwokrama at the top of those enormous trees is a chance of a lifetime to experience life in the tropical canopy. Birding in many areas is equally as rewarding as in much-praised Costa Rica, and there is always a chance of seeing jaguars and wild otters and caiman, as well as the howling monkeys that my mother saw up close so long ago. The spectacular regal waterlilies that she once admired in Georgetown grow wild in remote ponds at Karanambu where one can sit and watch the huge buds slowly open into perfect flower as dusk becomes nightfall. Kaieteur Falls, the tallest uninterrupted waterfall in the world where my mother once stood in wonder after a long trek overland and now easily reached by air, spills down from the hills and plateaus of the Guiana Highlands, while beyond lies the open Rupununi savannah country with the old ranches of the cattle-raising era and the thatched mud houses of the Makushis and Wapisianas. This is real El Dorado country, just waiting to be discovered, developed and protected.

Revisiting the places I remembered from so long ago was to realize the distance that Guyana and I had traveled separately over the years, but it was also an affirmation of what had made my childhood special. As the first white baby born in the Watooka Hospital in Mackenzie, during our short and recent stay it was a privilege for me to be able to go back to the maternity ward and speak to the present-day nursing staff. The welcome everywhere brought my soul home to my starting point. The spirit of kindness and gentleness, which I so much remembered while I was growing up, was still there in every place we visited. I came away from my birthplace whole and happy, my Guiana childhood complete.

Wendy Dathan, Ottawa.
March 2006.

Wendy at Kaieteur Falls

ACKNOWLEDGEMENTS

This book was inspired by the unpublished memoirs given to me and my sister by our mother, Gladys Hilda Whalley, who lived in Guyana from 1929 to 1944. In themselves, her notes were sketchy and disorganized, but her observations were acute and valid for the period. I have enjoyed piecing them together in some kind of order, backed with information from many unpublished and published sources as credited.

I would especially like to thank Carolyn Harder for allowing me to use extensive excerpts from the personal diary she kept in Mackenzie in the summer of 1934, which added so much to the book and without which encouragement I do not think I would have started. I also owe a huge debt of gratitude to Dr. Brock Fenton, Chairman of the Biology Dept. at Western University, who kindly sent and allowed me to use the delightful letters written by his mother, Jean Tudhope Fenton, to her sister in Canada, which provided another voice and invaluable insight into the later years in the camp.

I am also delighted to acknowledge the help received from the late Mrs. Ethel Beecell, her son John and daughter Nina, for their contributions to Mackenzie memories; Donald Sutherland for helping me straighten out my memories of Ogle Sugar Estate; the late Louis Wolfers for his help with background material for England in the nineteen thirties; Philip Mossman for his contributions to the *Lady Hawkins* chapter; my cousins in England, Don Mackinnon, Christine Rush, John Whalley, Martin Whalley and our beloved late Margaret Alcoe, for their help with family background; and my traveling companions to modern Guyana, Mary Howson, Arlette and Fred Parkinson, and Geoff Webster. In that last category, I would like to thank the Georgetown staff of Wilderness Adventures for working so hard to ensure that I could see again all the places of my childhood, and the Honourable Sam Hinds, Prime Minister of Guyana, for graciously giving us time for a short visit between important engagements.

In general, I have searched for information from or as close as possible to the period when my family lived in what was then British Guiana, and I am enormously grateful for the understanding these sources have given me into the land of my birth. I would like to thank the librarians in the Grand Manan, Westmount, and Ottawa systems for their help in finding this information. In addition, I am indebted to Messrs. John Power and Tom Daley for their assistance in locating useful information in the Foreign and Commonwealth Library in London, England.

I have wanted to write this book for many years and I do not think that I would have been able to do it without the help and encouragement of my much-loved family and friends, but particularly my son John who nursed me through numerous episodes of computer despair, Joan Barberis, Erleen Christensen, Anneke Gichuru, and Elizabeth Schenk who read the manuscript in earlier stages and gave me needed support, and Mary Marsh who kindly gave me a roof over my head in Ottawa while I worked on the final draft. Above all, I would like to thank my editor, Ryan Bergen, for his wise advice on how to improve the manuscript before it could be published; the Muller-Wille family for their generous support, especially Ragnar who honed his mapping skills on their combined project on Inuit place names in Northern Quebec; Sarah Robinson for her artistic work on the faded old photographs; and my wonderful publisher, Judy Isherwood, whose enthusiastic belief in what I had written made it all possible.

Published Sources:

Allen, Charles, ed. *Plain Tales from the British Raj: Images of British India in the Twentieth Century*. London: Andre Deutsch, 1975.

---. *Tales from the Dark Continent: Images of British colonial Africa in the Twentieth Century*. London: Andre Deutsch, 1979.

---. *Tales from the South China Seas: Images of the British in South-East Asia in the Twentieth Century*. London: Futura Publications, 1984.

Aluminium Panorama, Montreal: Aluminium Limited, 1953.

Attenborough, David. *Zoo Quest to Guiana*. London: Pan Books, 1958.

Baudot, Marcel, Henri Bernard, Hendrik Brugmans, Michael R.D. Foot, Hans-Adolf Jacobsen, eds. *The Historical Encyclopedia of World War II*. Translated by Jesse Dilson with additional material by Alvin D. Coox and Thomas R.H. Havens. New York: Facts on File, 1980.

Beebe, William. *Adventuring with Beebe: Selections from the writings of William Beebe, Director Emeritus, Dept. of Tropical Research, New York Zoological Society*. Toronto: Little, Brown and Company, 1955.

---. *Edge of the Jungle*. New York: Duell, Sloan and Pearce, 1950.

Bennett, Arnold. *Anna of the Five Towns*. Toronto: Bell and Cockburn, 1906.

---. *Clayhanger*. Toronto: W. Briggs, [191-].

---. *The Old Wives' Tale*. London: Chapman and Hall, 1908.

Birkin, Andrew. *J.M. Barrie and the Lost Boys*. London: Constable and Company, 1970.

216

Blair, Clay. *Hitler's U-Boat War: The Hunters Vol. I.* New York: Random House, 1998

—. *Hitler's U-Boat War: The Hunted Vol. II.* New York: Random House, 2000

Bond, James. *Birds of the West Indies: A guide to the species of birds that inhabit the Greater Antilles, Lesser Antilles and Bahama Islands.* London: Collins Clear-Type Press, 1974.

Bradbury, Malcolm. *Evelyn Waugh.* London: Oliver and Boyd, 1964.

Brown, C. Barrington. "The Discoverer of the Kaieteur Fall". *The Geographical Journal* Nov. 1932. [No. 3540. From the Foreign Office and Commonwealth Office Library, London.]

Campbell, Duncan C. *Global Mission: The Story of Alcan, Vol I to 1950.* [Don Mills, ON], Ontario Publishing Company, 1985.

Charriere, Henri. *Papillon.* Translated from the French by Patrick O'Brian. Bungay, Suffolk: Book Club Associates, 1975.

Churchill, Winston S. *The Second World War.* Vols. I-IV. Boston: Houghton Mifflin, 1949-1953.

Cruickshank, J. Graham. "A Trip to the Kaietuk Fall, British Guiana." *Empire Review* Jan. 1931. [No. 10572A. Foreign and Commonwealth Office Library, London]

Cummings, Leslie P. *Geography of Guyana.* London: Collins Clear-Type Press, 1965.

Daly, Vere T. *A Short History of the Guyanese People.* Kitty, Guyana: Vere T. Daly (printed by Daily Chronicle in Georgetown), 1966.

Davie, Michael, ed. *The Diaries of Evelyn Waugh: The Thirties Diary, 1930-39.* London: Weidenfeld and Nicholson, 1976.

The Dominion Office and Colonial Office List, 1929 and 1940. (From the Foreign and Commonwealth Office Library, London.)

Durrell, Gerald. *Three Singles to Adventure*. Hammondsworth, Middlesex: Penguin Books, 1964.

Freeth, Zahra. *Run Softly Demerara*. London: Allen and Unwin, 1960.

Gannon, Michael. *Operation Drumbeat: Germany's U-Boat Attacks Along the American Coast in World War II*. New York: Harper and Row, 1990.

German, Commander Tony. *The Sea is at our Gates: The History of the Canadian Navy*. Toronto: McClelland and Stewart, 1990.

Gibbs, Philip. *England Speaks*. London: Heinemann, 1935.

Giglioli, George, M.D. "Malaria, Filariasis and Yellow Fever in British Guiana: control by residual D.D.T. methods with special reference to progress made in eradicating A. *darlingi* and *Aedes aegypti* from the settled coastlands." *Mosquito Control Service*, Medical Department, British Guiana, 1948. [No. 21086. Foreign and Commonwealth Office Library, London]

Hingston, Major R.W.G. *A Naturalist in the Guiana Forest*. London: Edward Arnold & Co., 1932.

—. "The Oxford University Expedition to British Guiana." *The Geographical Journal* Vol. LXXVI, July 1930.

Hough, Richard. *Winston and Clementine: The Triumphs and Tragedies of the Churchills*. New York: Bantam Books, 1991.

Hudson, W.H. *Green Mansions: A Romance of the Tropical Forest*. New York: Knopf, 1916.

MacMillan, Margaret. *Women of the Raj*. London: Thames and Hudson, 1988.

Martin, Ralph G. *The Woman He Loved: the story of the Duke and Duchess of Windsor*. Scarborough, ON: The New American Library of Canada, 1975.

Mittelholzer, Edgar. *Corentyne Thunder*. London: Eyre and Spottiswoode, 1941.

—. *With a Carib Eye*. London: Secker and Warburg, 1958.

Naipaul, V.S. *The Middle Passage: Impressions of Five Societies—British, French and Dutch—in the West Indies and South America*. London: Andre Deutsch, 1962.

Nicolson, Harold. *Diaries and Letters, 1930-1939*. Edited by N. Nicolson. New York: William Collins, Sons & Co., 1966.

Orwell, George. *The Road to Wigan Pier*. Harmondsworth, Eng.: Penguin Books, 1989.

Priestley, J.B. *English Journey: Being a rambling but truthful account of what one man saw and heard and felt and thought during a journey through England during the autumn of the year 1933*. London: Heinemann, 1934.

Roth, Vincent; revised by Norman Wight. *Where Is It?: A Gazeteer of British Guiana*. Revised edition. Georgetown, British Guiana: The Daily Chronicle, 1962.

Simms, Peter. *Trouble in Guyana: An account of people, personalities and politics as they were in British Guiana*. London: Allen and Unwin, 1966.

Smith, Raymond T. *British Guiana*. London: Oxford University Press, 1962.

Swan, Michael. *British Guiana: The Land of Six Peoples*. London: Her Majesty's Stationery Office, 1957.

Waterton, Charles. *Wanderings in South America*. Edited by E. Rhys. No. 772, Everyman's Library. London: J.M. Dent and Sons, [1925].

Waugh, Alec. *The Sugar Islands*. London: Cassell & Co., 1958.

Waugh, Evelyn. *A Handful of Dust*. London: Chapman and Hall, 1934.

—. *Ninety-Two Days: A Journey in Guiana and Brazil*. London: Duckworth, 1934.

Young, Matthew French. *Guyana: The Lost El Dorado*. [Leeds]: Peepal Tree Press, 1998.

About the Author

Wendy Dathan, nee Whalley, holds an MA in Geography from McGill University in Montreal. When her two sons entered their teens in the 1970's, she began studying botany at Macdonald College in Ste.-Anne-de-Bellevue. She worked in the McGill University Herbarium, taught botany labs and non-credit courses in Edible and Medicinal Plants, and was active in the Catharine Traill Naturalists Club. Moving to New Brunswick in 1987, she was appointed Curator of the Grand Manan Museum where she worked for several years before retirement. She now has a summer art gallery on the island, does wildflower walks and talks for visitors, and is currently working on a biography of a northern botanist. Wendy says that she never did become the famous explorer that she wanted to be as a child but the large verandah on her old wooden house on Grand Manan somehow reminds her of her childhood in Guyana.